GUNJAN PORWAL, engineer 𝕭
author of the bestselling *A.*
of Dandak, which was his de

An alumnus of Indian Ins   ͻͻ, Kanpur,
Gunjan has worked in MNC: ͻ authored over 20
patents in the field of computer graphics.

Gunjan lives in Pune and enjoys reading, writing, movies
and travelling.

Visit his website at www.gunjanporwal.com.

ASHWATTHAMA'S REDEMPTION

BOOK II

THE BOW OF RAMA

GUNJAN PORWAL

Om Books International

First published in 2021 by

Om Books International

Corporate & Editorial Office
A-12, Sector 64, Noida 201 301
Uttar Pradesh, India
Phone: +91 120 477 4100
Email: editorial@ombooks.com
Website: www.ombooksinternational.com

Sales Office
107, Ansari Road, Darya Ganj,
New Delhi 110 002, India
Phone: +91 11 4000 9000
Fax: +91 11 2327 8091
Email: sales@ombooks.com
Website: www.ombooks.com

ISBN: 978-93-5376-712-9

Printed in India

10 9 8 7 6 5 4 3 2 1

For my brother, Saurabh Porwal,
the most jovial person I know.

Contents

The Story So Far

A hundred years after the Kurukshetra War (Mahabharata), an immortal but cursed and devoid-of-purpose ASHWATTHAMA, son of Dronacharya, is living the life of a recluse in a forest, far away from civilisation. VIKRAMSENA, his friend and King of Surparaka, a kingdom on the Western coast, visits him. Vikram informs him of an upcoming danger to his kingdom in the form of the resurrection of an ancient demon called DANDAK, the youngest son of Ikshvaku. Vikram tells Ashwatthama that over five thousand years ago asura Guru Shukracharya cursed Dandak to die in a mud-flood after Dandak molested the Guru's daughter but Dandak survived the curse, owing to his pact with the demon king in Rasatala, patal (sixth netherworld) inside Earth. If Dandak now resurrects, he would establish both his kingdom and the reign of the asuras, endangering Aryavarta (ancient India). Dandak has obtained a boon from Shiva—only the latter could kill the asura king with a Vaisanavastra, a weapon of Vishnu's. Vikram tells Ashwatthama that the only person who can kill Dandak is Ashwatthama himself since he is the last living incarnation of Shiva. Vikram then convinces a reluctant Ashwatthama to accompany him on a journey to recover a lost Vaisanavastra—the Kodanda, the bow of Lord Rama, hidden by his son Kush, somewhere in Himavant (The Himalayas).

Together, they ride to Avanti, where they are joined by the self-centred prince RANA PRATAP SINGH who accompanies them as the journey means personal glory for him. Avanti is also home to Guru *APASMITRA*, whose help Vikram seeks to de-crypt a verse that provides the location of the Kodanda.

Vikram, Rana and Ashwatthama set off to retrieve the bow, planning to take the route through the plains of Avanti, and then cross the Ganges. From there, they plan a halt at Hastinapur, before finally crossing the Valley of Illusions, a haunted region extending about a hundred miles, to reach the Himavant ranges where the bow is supposed to be hidden. Ashwatthama feels like an outsider during the journey and maintains an air of indifference.

During the early part of their journey, they are attacked by a huge, lion-like poisonous reptile in the plains of Avanti, then by a five-headed ancient snake in the Ganges. Both creatures are killed by Rana and Ashwatthama, respectively. They reach Hastinapur, where King *JANAMEJAYA*, grandson of Abhimanyu, welcomes all of them, including the guilt-ridden Ashwatthama, who is one of the warriors who killed Abhimanyu unethically during the Kurukshetra War. They are introduced to Janamejaya's cousin *URMILA*; Rana is immediately smitten by her. Together, they try to decipher the cryptic code, to arrive at the probable location of the bow. An adventure-seeker, Urmila insists on joining them and persuades Vikram to include her in the journey as she knows the Valley of Illusions where people confront their deepest fears.

In the Valley of Illusions Ashwatthama encounters his past, due to which he accidentally attacks Urmila, almost killing her. An enraged Rana questions Ashwatthama's ability and intentions. The next day, when they resume their journey, they are attacked by the Smoke Warriors, the ghosts of a king and his cursed soldiers. During the fight, Rana is seriously injured while saving Urmila, and the warriors leave only after Ashwatthama promises them freedom from their curse. Soon after, they get out of the valley and arrive at the base of the Himavant ranges.

Here, they must wait for Rana to recover. Ashwatthama and Urmila go in search of the route. On the way, Urmila has some queries about life for Ashwatthama. He reveals to her the truths about *the karmic cycle in the Kurukshetra War, which helps her resolve some of the doubts that had been troubling her.*

Two days later, all of them resume the journey to the top of the Himavant ranges, encountering harsh weather on their way. Exhausted, they reach the top where, after a brief interlude when they wrongly decipher the cryptic code, they find the missing bow, the Kodanda. On the way back, they are trapped in an avalanche but are saved in time by the Yetis (Bigfoot), who live in the mountains. However, Urmila goes into cold shock and becomes unconscious.

The Yetis take them to their kingdom where Ashwatthama is advised by an old Yeti to take a shorter route for their return journey. Rana is distressed over Urmila's condition and realises he loves her. They leave Urmila in the Yetis' care and head towards a lake inside the Naimisharanya Forest. They then take a route through the hidden tunnel inside the lake and reach the Matsya kingdom, emerging at the Adi-Tirth Lake.

From there, they ride swiftly across the plains evening and night. As they reach the gates of Avanti, they are challenged by one of Dandak's resurrected and trusted generals, RAKTAVIJA, who has been granted the boon of his clone being created as soon as his blood falls on the battlefield. Raktavija and his army attack the three of them but are engaged by Rana's army who appear just in time. Raktavija uses an enchanted arrow to attack Ashwatthama, who sacrifices himself and is burnt down while protecting the Kodanda.

Ashwatthama then falls into a dream-state where he meets his father, Dronacharya, who absolves him of the guilt of killing the Pandava children and other warriors unethically, in the aftermath of the Kurukshetra War. Ashwatthama finds redemption here and his dream of meeting his father again is fulfilled. He realises his life's purpose and the reason for his immortality, thereby stilling the storm in his mind.

After this Ashwatthama regains his former self, recalls his former powers and becomes the outstanding warrior that he was. He rises from his lifeless form. Lifting the bow of Rama, he finds that he is a worthy wielder of the Kodanda and kills Raktavija, thus winning that battle.

The three then ride to Avanti palace, where they are tricked and one of Dandak's generals, VIDYUT, steals the bow. A few days later, they are introduced to NYAT, King of Saurashtra, who claims that he has seen the bow as well as Dandak's resurrection in Rasatala. Nyat informs them that Dandak is not present in a physical form anymore but in the form of mud particles, which makes it extremely difficult to kill him. Ashwatthama ponders over this and sends a message to Janamejaya to join them at Nyat's palace in Saurashtra, from where they all plan to sail to the lost city of Dwarka.

They ride to Surparaka, where Janamejaya and Urmila join them. Janamejaya shows the three arrows that he has brought to Ashwatthama, who explains to everyone that they were the son of Ghatotkach, Barbarik's infallible arrows, the only things that can kill Dandak in his present particle form. They plan a covert operation to travel to Rasatala through Krishna's meditation chamber in the submerged city of Dwarka, from where Nyat had originally travelled to Rasatala.

They sail to erstwhile Dwarka together, planning to recover the bow. As they all go underwater using Guru Apasmitra's help, Vidyut and his army ambush them, and soon it becomes evident that Nyat has betrayed them. As they battle the asura army, they feel they are being overpowered, until help arrives with Guru Apasmitra bringing creatures of the deep—killer sharks, which kill most asuras, leaving the warriors to neutralise the remaining lot. Ashwatthama rushes towards Vidyut, who has stabbed Nyat. Ashwatthama and Vidyut engage in a hand-to-hand fight and Vidyut injures him but Ashwatthama manages to stab him through the heart. As Vidyut dies, he throws a protective shield around himself and destroys Lord Rama's bow. He then prepares to kill all the other warriors except Ashwatthama as he knows Ashwatthama cannot be killed. However Ashwatthama takes out Barbarik's arrows and kills Vidyut. A dying Nyat gives them the clue for their next course of action.

At an undisclosed location, a figure watches his palace being built, when a messenger informs him that Vidyut has been killed and the bow destroyed. The figure is content that his plan worked.

A week later Ashwatthama, Vikram, Janamejaya, Rana and Urmila assemble at Surparaka, Vikram's kingdom, where Vikram proposes that they get ready for the upcoming war. Ashwatthama confesses that he feels they have missed something but cannot put his finger on it. Rana and Urmila share a light romantic moment before they all disperse.

End of Part I

Map of Aryavarta (3129 BC)

यदायदाहिधर्मस्यग्लानिर्भव- तिभारत।
अभ्युत्थान- मधर्मस्यतदात्मानंसृजाम्यहम्-
परित्रणाय- साधूनांविनाशायचदुष्कृताम्-।
धर्मसंस्था- पनार्थायसम्भवामियुगेयुगे।।

जब जब भी धर्म का विनाश हुआ, अधर्म का उत्थान हुआ,
तब तब मैंने खुद का सृजन किया, साधुओं के उद्धार और बुरे कर्म करनेवालो
के संहार के लिए,
धर्म की स्थापना के प्रयोजनसे, मै हर युगमें, युग युग में जनम लेता रहूँगा।

(Whenever and wherever there is a decline in religious
practice, O descendant of Bharata, and a predominant rise
of irreligion—at that time I Myself descend.)

Bhagwad Gita, Chapter 4, Verses 7–8

1

White Magic

The tall figure waited impatiently, looking at the intricate clay model in the prince's room. The adjacent figure standing in the shadows behind the curtains prepared to attack Rana, the Prince of Indraprastha.

The pleasant evening breeze wafted through Urmila's soft hair as she walked alongside Rana in the open corridor in Ujjaini's palace which led to his rooms. Instead of returning to Indraprastha with Janamejaya, she had accompanied Rana and Ashwatthama back to Avanti to learn more about warfare.

Rana had wanted to show Urmila the terrain around Ujjaini as it would help her understand the surroundings in case there was a war. Painstakingly made over the years, the clay model of Avanti was now proving useful, even as the threat of attack from the asuras loomed large. As Rana approached his room, he was startled by a dim shadow moving around. The prince's face turned red as he hated intruders, especially his sister's friends who would go through his diary at her behest. On second thoughts though, this didn't seem to be one of them.

He paused, raising his eyebrows, and then looked at Urmila, who had her hand on the hilt of her sword, ready to pull the blade out. With the news of Ashwatthama and his group's expedition to root out and kill Dandak spreading fast, it was clear that lines would be drawn. And one never knew who in his palace might turn out to be a traitor.

Rana motioned Urmila to cover the other side of the door and slowly unsheathed his sword, the metal still smelling of the fresh blood of the asuras it had slain a week back. A sword is born for one purpose, and one purpose only—to kill. And it always yearns to fulfill its destiny. Tonight, it would taste some more asura blood.

As he cautiously pushed open the heavy ornate wooden door with the tip of his sword, Rana could sense a figure moving inside, the faint light of the torch in his hand casting the illusion of a giant.

The prince glanced at Urmila, who already had her sword drawn, and nodded. With the tip of his sword, he pushed open the wooden door slowly, wide enough for them to enter. Rana crossed the ledge and saw a tall, hooded figure standing right across the width of the room, staring at his clay model. It had a heavy club in its hand, ready to demolish the entire collection that Rana had painstakingly made over the course of several trips. The dim yellow light from the torch added to the mystery of the figure's identity as it stood with its back to Rana.

As the figure sensed the presence of another being, it turned slowly. Dressed in large black robes, with long flowing hair, the figure appeared hefty, standing almost a foot taller than Rana. It held a massive club which had patches of blood on its spikes, one that would match Rana's sword. Seemingly, the figure had made several kills to get to the room.

Rana's heart was beating fast. He thought about the route to the room, and who the figure might have slaughtered on its way. Casting a glance at his clay model, he took a deep breath and reassured himself that it had not been destroyed, yet. Raising his sword, Rana moved cautiously across the room, with Urmila shadowing him. The figure stood motionless, its eyes tracking their movements.

Rana didn't take his eyes off the hooded figure. 'Speak your name and purpose, intruder, before I slay you,' he demanded, adjusting his foot, preparing to charge.

The figure scoffed silently at the question but set the club aside. It moved its hands slowly in a circular motion, a reddish glow appearing between them.

Dark arts.

Rana was taken aback. A sword is no match for magical spells. This was beyond his abilities. The figure moved swiftly, hurling the fireball towards Rana and Urmila, who stood next to each other.

'DOWN!'

Rana ducked, taking Urmila with him, the clanking of their swords filling the room as they hit the floor. The fireball hit the wall instead, and the room lit up brightly with a red hue. Rana bounced back on his feet and dashed towards the attacker, who raised his hand. Rana was stunned as his tightly held sword was magically drawn sideways, snatched from his hand, and made to float towards the curtains. The prince looked wide-eyed towards a second attacker, who was camouflaged against the wall and held the baffled prince's sword up as a trophy.

'What...?' Rana muttered in disbelief as he drew the dagger from his belt and prepared to strike the shadow in front of him. But it disappeared in a puff of smoke. A peal of familiar laughter filled the air and a few more torches lit up the room.

The figure was gone.

Adjusting his eyes in the sudden brightness, Rana exclaimed as he took a clearer look at the second attacker, who had snatched his sword effortlessly.

'Shreya?' he asked.

'Yes, dau. How did you like my trick? I got you, didn't I?' Shreya clutched her stomach, laughing.

Rana pressed his lips together and heaved a sigh of relief. He had been worried about one of Dandak's assassins sneaking into the palace. More than himself, he was concerned about Urmila as Janamejaya had specifically asked him to be on guard for her. Holding out his hand to pull Urmila up, Rana retorted, 'This is the stupidest prank I have seen. How could you be so silly? Someone could have got hurt.'

Shreya smiled from ear to ear as she held out the sword to Rana. 'Don't be so angry, dau! My magic is a harmless illusion,' she pulled Rana's cheek as he sheathed the blade.

Rana controlled his annoyance by taking deep breaths. Had it been someone else, he might have not stayed calm at the idea of a laugh at his expense but Shreya's smiling face calmed him. Given the way things had gone in the last few weeks, he was happy to see her.

'I am sorry. I just…I thought it was someone else,' Rana waved his hands dismissively.

Shreya smiled.

Rana turned and gestured towards Urmila. 'This is Urmila, cousin of Janamejaya, King of Hastinapur. She is the Princess of Indraprastha, daughter of…uh…daughter of uh…son of…uh…grandson of…Karna. Daughter of the grandson of Karna,' Rana stressed the last few words, staring at the ceiling, oblivious of Urmila glowering.

Shreya laughed, shaking her head in disbelief. She moved forward and held Urmila in a warm embrace. 'He can't remember names. Welcome to Avanti. Delighted to have you among us.'

'It is a pleasure to meet you,' Urmila smiled, reciprocating the warm welcome.

'All right, let us proceed towards the kitchen and continue with our introductions over a meal of sweet rice and vegetable broth. My tricks have exhausted me, and I am ravenous!' quipped Shreya.

Rana was examining his clay models, looking for signs of damage.

'Don't worry. Nothing has been smashed,' Shreya giggled, 'except perhaps your ego.'

Urmila walked towards the large clay model and was immediately filled with admiration. She then turned towards Shreya, who was still grinning at having fooled her elder brother.

'How…how did you manage to do that?'

'You mean the trick?'

Urmila nodded.

Shreya looked at Rana, who had moved towards the other end of the table, and was leaning against a wall, looking at her intently. He shrugged, motioning for her to start.

'Fine. I will tell both of you. But you must keep it to yourself. Father must not know about this.'

'Don't worry about that,' Urmila assured her.

Shreya stuffed a large round black stone into the bag and paused, turning towards them.

'What you saw moments ago is a combination of two tricks, a form of the dark arts where you can create an illusion to fool someone. The technique works only in dim light…or I should say that I have been able to get it to work only in dim light.

'Magic requires years of practice. You would be interested in the second trick. It is an old technique to disarm your opponent. Quite useful in battles. But it requires time to master. This is not black magic but a milder form of sorcery. Black magic is a form of negative energy that can enter a living being and wreak havoc in his mind and soul. This energy goes from the source to the target person against the target's will.

'So, essentially, it's a mind-weapon. Dangerous, and often fatal. Prohibited in most places. Sorcerers and witches use it. Some common examples are mantras that include Uchatan—separating someone from his home, and Stambhan—paralysing someone. These can cause severe mental and physical trauma to a person.

'But not what you saw a few moments back. That is something I would call white magic. That does not harm anyone mentally or physically, if used properly. Only a handful of people can do it successfully. It needs a lot of practice to be able to do it instantaneously. Done properly, it can change the course of a war. This form of the arts has two mantras—Uran mantra—being able to fly, something only a chosen few are capable of achieving, and Hasthan mantra—taking away someone's belongings or the ability to move inanimate objects, which is relatively easier to perform.'

'So,' Urmila pointed towards Rana, 'did you use Hasthan to snatch his sword?'

'Often, I use it for fun,' Shreya chirped as she stuffed her things into her bag before tying it up.

Urmila still looked curious, eager to learn. 'Do just the mantras get the task done?'

Shreya shook her head. 'Not exactly. All magic consists of three parts—mantras, sacred objects and the rituals. If you have the knowledge of these three, you can do wonders. Also, magic is not pure. It is just something many people do not understand. It derives its energy from a source. Say, to push a rock or door, you need power, physical power. But magic means you do not need to do it physically. You can draw the power from a source. Those who are capable of magic know the technique of unlocking the source. The source defines whether your magic is black or white.

'Black magic derives its power from negative energy or the abode of demonic powers, the realm of ghosts, demons and evil. Evil entities do not work without taking a bounty in return, often resulting in disastrous consequences for the target. White magic, on the other hand, derives its force from God's universal energy, the realm of demigods, angels and cosmic energy. Practitioners of white magic cannot use it for harming others or else it transforms into black magic. Those who derive energy from negative realms are practitioners of black magic, like witches, asuras, among others. In return, they need to sacrifice their humanity, voluntarily or involuntarily.'

'But why would someone do that? Become evil voluntarily?' Urmila wondered aloud.

'Ambition. Power. Greed. Revenge. All the base vices. Consider this: a prince might want to ascend the throne of a dying king to improve the lives of the people but the inefficient king is not expected to die for the next fifty years, and he has made life miserable for the people. What do you do? Do you wait, or...' Shreya let the words hang in the air.

Urmila pursed her lips; she understood the context.

Magic corrupts the soul.

'They claim it is for the greater good but that is a relative term, isn't it?' Shreya asked pointedly.

'So, there is always this moral dilemma. Well, not always. Sometimes you want something so badly that you will do anything to get it. Like maybe a weapon, or power, for which you won't hesitate to kill anyone if that one action can propel you to greatness.'

'Where did you learn all this?' asked Rana as he looked at Shreya.

The young princess hesitated for a moment before answering.

'Uh...Pragjyotishpur, in north-east Aryavarta. It is an important centre for learning magic. There are stories that even the mighty Ghatotkacha learnt exceptional magical powers from that village.

'But the real source is Atharvangirasa or *Atharva Veda*. In ancient times, the *Rig Veda* was narrated to Agni; the *Sama Veda* to Adityas, the sons of Aditi; the *Yajur Veda* to Vayu; the *Atharva Veda* to Angira, and so its ancient name *Atharvangirasa*. The *Rig Veda* deals with knowledge, the *Yajur Veda* with karma, the *Sama Veda* with devotion. However, the most interesting is the last one, the *Atharva Veda*. This almost-forgotten text and misunderstood branch of the Vedas deals with *vigyaan* (science), spells, prayers, and m-a-g-i-c,' Shreya practically hissed the last word, drawing two semicircles in the air with her hands as if performing magic.

Rana shook his head at the drama. 'Don't lie. You cannot have gone to Pragjyotishpur...or wherever. Father gave strict instructions to you to not venture outside Kishkindha.'

Shreya narrowed her eyes in defiance and teased him. 'When I went to my cousin Radhika's palace...her maid knows many forms of the dark arts, having descended from a sorcerer's family in Pragjyotishpur. She taught me this. It's amusing.'

'And dangerous. You need to be careful. I am warning you against using it,' Rana shook his index finger at her.

Shreya stuck out her tongue at him.

'I think it was amazing,' chirped Urmila, ignoring Rana's threat.

'What else can you do?'

'Well, basic magic, like creating a power shield, though it requires a lot of concentration; moving objects around; creating hallucinations, that's pretty much it. And there is a dangerous one I know of but cannot use. It is forbidden for amateurs and is to be used only in life-threatening situations.'

Urmila smiled. 'Teach me a couple of those. Can I do them?'

'No! Don't make her a witc....' Rana left the last word incomplete, and immediately glanced away, staring blankly at the wall.

Both Urmila and Shreya glared at him.

'Not all of them. But I can show you a few simple tricks. Might get you to trick him,' Shreya laughed, pointing at Rana. 'But first, let us go and have dinner. I am starving.'

2

The Village

Raigarh, Avanti
A village bordering Dandakaranya

Emerging from the thick trees on the borders of Dandakaranya, the boy ran towards his sister.

'I got it, Neema. I got it,' he shouted.

The little girl clapped and leapt for joy, unable to control her excitement. The children had been looking for it for a long time.

'Let us show it to Ma.'

'Can I carry it, dau?'

'Of course,' the boy smiled as he handed over the white rabbit to his sister. 'Careful, or it will scurry away.'

The little girl held the furry rabbit in her arms. She could feel its heart pounding madly, probably out of fear for its life. Its eyes were dark pink, almost red; it looked scared as it tried to claw its way out of the girl's hands.

'Don't worry,' Neema held the little creature close to her cheek and stroked it gently on its head. 'We will take care of you. No one will hurt you.'

'Quick, Neema,' the boy ran ahead, motioning his sister to follow. 'Let us take it to Ma. If she approves, we will adopt it.'

The children sprinted towards their hut in the village, dodging mounds of cow-dung cakes and freshly cut bundles of crops. The sun was about to disappear among the thick trees bordering the village. The children ran barefoot, unmindful of the squawking chickens running helter-skelter for their lives.

'Ma, look what we have brought,' the children shouted in unison from outside the hut. They looked at each other and giggled.

'Raghu, I will beat you if you bring one more puppy,' thundered a voice from inside.

In a minute, when Raji came out, she found her children standing there with a white rabbit. After one look, her heart melted, and the scowl gave way to a faint smile, which she immediately concealed.

'You like it, Ma?' asked Neema.

'Can we keep it?' asked Raghu.

As the children looked at their mother with their innocent eyes, she couldn't help but feel a rush of love for them. They had been asking for a pet for months, and Raji had laid down the condition that they would have to bring one that she would like. This rabbit was *the one*. The children waited expectantly for their mother's decision.

'All right,' Raji feigned taking mercy on them. 'But you two will clean after it. Or, the next day it is out.'

'Agreed, Ma,' the children laughed happily.

'Let us build a cage for it,' chimed in Raghu, beaming at his sister.

'Yes,' said Neema, and the children ran to the wood-shed where they planned to house the rabbit. They looked for stray wooden sticks to build a cage for it.

'Be back before it gets dark!' Raji shouted, and in the same breath, sent a prayer heavenwards, thanking the gods for her children. She smiled and thought of the new clothes Neema would need for her first day at Panditji's ashram for Sanskrit lessons the following week.

As she hurried to tend to the cooking, Raji failed to notice a patrolling asura emerging from the woods, swearing and picking up a hapless chicken, before disappearing into the green cover again. She turned back on a hunch, distracted by the squeal of the chicken but didn't see anything that warranted attention.

The forest was quiet as always.

3

Yoddha

The evening sun filtered through the tinted glass, forming a pattern on the wooden table. Guru Apasmitra sifted through his scrolls, all of which lay in a heap. Ashwatthama and Rana sat at the other end, animatedly turning the pages of the dusty books in their hands. A little distance away, Urmila stood alongside Shreya, both pulling out books from shelves.

Rana shut his book forcefully, and then sneezed as the dust assailed his nostrils.

'Nothing here.'

Ashwatthama too closed his book and put it down on the table. He leaned back, folded his hands behind his head and stared at the library ceiling which was decorated with paintings of sages imparting wisdom to young students. He admired the colours of the artwork on the ceiling.

Looking at Guru Apasmitra, who was still absorbed in the scrolls, he spoke, '*Yoddha* is a vague word. Yoddha is someone who fights another warrior. There isn't any special quality associated with this word as such. There will be hundreds, if not thousands, of Yoddhas in this generation. Why would Nyat refer to a Yoddha?'

Rana looked down at his feet on the cold grey stone floor. Dust from the books which they had been sifting through since the morning, had settled on the floor.

'I am not sure Nyat would have wanted to help us in his dying moments. Why would he do that?' he asked skeptically.

Ashwatthama closed his eyes and arched his eyebrows, lost in thought. 'I believe him. A person, if he is not evil, will not wish to harm anyone in his dying moments. Moreover, his eyes spoke the truth. Nyat might have betrayed us but he was helpless. I presume any other person in that situation would have done the same if his family was in peril. He did what he could to save his family. It's likely that Vidyut revealed the truth about his family at the end, while stabbing Nyat.'

Ashwatthama re-lived those moments, when Vidyut had stabbed Nyat underwater, after defeating the asura army. Ashwatthama's reasoning was met by a shake of the head from Rana who still had a weary look on his face as if the entire exercise was a futile one.

Urmila and Shreya walked towards the table, struggling with the unwieldy pile of books in their hands. Shreya put the books on the table with a thud, even as Rana recoiled at the fresh waves of dust finding a passage up his nose. Shreya lit the oil lamps on the table and walls. The large hall lit up in shades of orange and yellow, a bright glow reflected on everyone's faces.

Guru Apasmitra looked up from the pile of scrolls. He spoke loudly, addressing the audience thus, 'All right. Consider this. According to our ancient scriptures, a Yoddha is someone who fights for a righteous cause. A Rathi is someone who can fight 5,000 Yoddhas. An Atirathi is someone who can fight 12 Rathis or 60,000 warriors at one go. A Maharathi can fight 12 Atirathis or 720,000 warriors at a go. An Atimaharathi can fight 12 Maharathis or 8,640,000 warriors at a go. A Mahamaharathi is one who can fight 24 Maharathis at a go, or...'

Guru Apasmitra looked at the ceiling with his head cocked at an angle, eyes narrowed, clearly doing calculations in his mind.

'I don't even know that much *ganit* (maths),' Rana commented, grinning at Urmila. She rolled her eyes, shaking her head in mock frustration. Shreya giggled as Guru Apasmitra looked angrily at the prince.

Rana blurted out, 'Sorry, Guruji but this gets us nowhere except for a bunch of new terms to remember.'

Ashwatthama frowned as he leaned forward, placing his elbows on the table. 'Could he be referring to some warrior who could help us? Guru Apasmitra, does any Mahamaharathi exist now?'

'None walking the earth as of now Ashwatthama,' Guru Apasmitra replied, looking into the pages again. 'Only Shakthi, the Supreme Goddess and Mother of all Creation, Shiva, Vishnu, Kartikeya, Ganesh and Hanuman have been Mahamaharathis in the cosmos, so far.

'An Atimaharathi has weapons of the Trinity and is invincible as long as he holds them. Among Atimaharathis, Parashurama is the only known one still roaming around.'

'So, that makes you a Maharathi?' Rana asked, looking at Ashwatthama.

Ashwatthama remained silent, still absorbed in his thoughts.

Guru Apasmitra continued, 'Many warriors of the Kurukshetra War—Karna, Arjuna, Bhishma, Dronacharya, among others—were Maharathis.'

Ashwatthama shook his head. 'This does not get us anywhere, unless...'

'Unless what?' Shreya asked.

'Guruji mentioned that an Atimaharathi possesses the three weapons belonging to the Trinity. What if...' Ashwatthama pursed his lips as he stood up, unsure if he wanted to finish the sentence.

Rana let out an exasperated breath. 'Please don't kill us with suspense now.'

Ashwatthama remained silent for another moment as he got up and paced around the table. All eyes followed him.

'What if Dandak wanted to become one...he has the Brahmastra from Brahma, the Agneyastra from Shiva and the Kodanda from Vishnu.'

The group fell silent. What Ashwatthama said made perfect sense. If that were true, then Dandak would be invincible.

Urmila broke the stunned silence, looking at Ashwatthama. 'But that is if he still has the Kodanda. It was broken; Vidyut broke it.'

'True,' Ashwatthama nodded uncertainly. 'The weapon that is supposed to kill him is also the one that would make him invincible.'

'Great!' Rana muttered, shaking his head, drumming his fingers on the table in frustration.

'Should we assume that Dandak will now strive to attain a weapon of Vishnu?' Ashwatthama wondered aloud.

'Are there more weapons that we need to know of?' Shreya asked, worried, looking at each member in the room.

Guru Apasmitra shrugged. 'None that we know of. Parashurama has his axe but I doubt anyone can reach him. And God help those who do! Krishna returned the

Sudarshan Chakra to Vishnu before he shed his mortal form. The Kodanda was the last one as far as I know.

'So, I think we have to consider what is more important to Dandak: destroying a weapon that is capable of killing him or keeping it, so he remains invincible. The only threat he faces on Aryavarta and beyond is from Ashwatthama, so he has to remove one factor. Either Ashwatthama or the weapon.'

'And Ashwatthama cannot die, no matter what Dandak and his army do. So, he went with the easier option—that of destroying the Kodanda,' Rana leaned back even as he continued drumming the table with his fingers.

Ashwatthama settled back in his chair.

Urmila frowned. She placed the book in her hands on the table.

'Remember, Guru Dronacharya was killed when he put down his weapons after news of...uh... Then, Karna was killed when he put the Vijaya bow down while taking out his chariot from the mire; his boon was that he could not be defeated as long as the bow was in his hands.'

Ashwatthama recalled the conversation he had had with her on Himavant during their journey to retrieve the bow. Urmila, conscious of the first reference she had made, avoided looking at him.

Ashwatthama nodded. 'Right. Then again, two of these three weapons are astras, invisible weapons that can be recalled only by the warrior. Only the Kodanda was a shastra, one which he has to physically hold. If Dandak has obtained that, along with the other two weapons he already has, he can wage war even on the Gods, and no one can defeat him.'

'Is there a way he can hide the weapons?' Rana asked, looking at Ashwatthama who shrugged. They glanced at Shreya.

The Avanti princess was taken aback by the sudden focus on her. 'Uh...yes...but only if Dandak knows the art of Alakshyan,' she said. 'It is an ancient technique to enable a warrior to hide the shastra and recall it when he wants to use it. Not many in the present age know it but then Dandak is not from the present age.'

'Agreed, some warriors in the Kurukshetra War could do that. I wouldn't be surprised if Dandak knows this art, since he is from before the time of Lord Rama,' Ashwatthama said. And then as if on cue, he added, 'But it seems we have digressed from the main topic—Yoddha.'

Guru Apasmitra, who was once again looking at the scrolls, spoke without lifting his gaze, 'We have not been able to figure out the meaning of what Nyat said. I am sure it holds a link to Dandak. We have gone through the entire library for a reference to what Nyat might have meant but it has eluded us so far.'

Ashwatthama leaned back, shaking his head slightly. 'All right. Let us give it time, and look again tomorrow. We have been on this since morning.'

'I agree,' Guru Apasmitra said, putting down his scroll and wiping his forehead with his *shela* (robe). The heat from the lamps made him want to run outside for some fresh air.

'What is the plan, apart from our massive research of the word Yoddha?' Rana asked, miffed with the indecision.

'Let us not underestimate Nyat's clue,' Ashwatthama said calmly.

Rana shook his head as he raised his voice, thumping the table lightly. 'I agree with that. But we cannot just sit idle. Why do we feel things are beyond our control? We have spent the last one week trying to figure out one damn word a dying man said. Instead, let's make the right choices, take action and events will be under our control.'

Ashwatthama replied calmly, 'It's not so simple, Rana. Sometimes, things are not in our hands yet we have to try and do our best. Not everything always happens with effort. Sometimes you need to back off and restart, for a fresh perspective. We need some clue, some direction on how to counter this enemy.

'Anyway, here is some other news. Vikram is sending messages to potential allies. A few might turn out to be helpful, mostly from western and southern Aryavarta, kingdoms which did not participate in the Kurukshetra War and so did not lose their armies. After Vidyut's death, all has been quiet in Dandakaranya. But Dandak is not one to remain quiet for too long. That worries me.'

'Maybe he has lost interest in us because the bow is broken...ouch, it hurts...he doesn't love us anymore,' Rana quipped.

Urmila frowned and nudged him with her elbow.

Ashwatthama spoke in a dejected tone, 'I should have protected that bow. Something so divine and unique. The last weapon of Lord Rama.'

'It's not your fault,' Rana said gently. He recalled the underwater battle at Dwarka, and how Ashwatthama had tried his best to save the bow.

'Lord Rama's bow, marvellous!' Shreya exclaimed. 'I wish I could have seen that. I've always had a desire to visit Ayodhya and see Lord Rama's palace, though I have heard it is in ruins now. The kingdom was devastated after the Kurukshetra War, wasn't it?'

Something in what Shreya said struck Ashwatthama. He remained silent for a moment, thinking. Then he banged his hands on the table, disturbing the dust. Rana eyed the rising dust and jerked his head back. Everyone was startled by the sudden thump on the table.

'That's it. It's not Yoddha,' Ashwatthama said.

'What? What is it, then?' Guru Apasmitra looked up with wide eyes, his curiosity roused for the first time during the meeting.

'Ayodhya,' Ashwatthama exclaimed, looking around, 'Nyat wanted us to go to Ayodhya.'

Guru Apasmitra was silent. He pondered for a while. It was indeed possible that Nyat's voice had been muffled underwater before he died, and that they had misinterpreted his speech.

'I have spent last week going through everything in this library, discussing the matter with my peers and consulting every source possible,' the Guru said. 'The word "Yoddha" simply does not fit anywhere. But if what you say is true and Nyat meant Ayodhya, then it might be a lead.'

Rana was silent, thinking hard, still drumming the table lightly with his fingers. He stared at Urmila, who seemed to be absorbed in contemplation. She had been going through the books in the library with Shreya since the morning. The past week, they had just focused on this single word, each of them trying to figure out what clue it held for the fight against Dandak.

'But what will you find in Ayodhya?' Rana asked. 'It's in ruins.'

Ashwatthama looked absent-mindedly at the table with its pile of scrolls, and stroked his chin. 'We have to begin somewhere. There has been absolute silence from the enemy. We do not have any clue about Dandak's plans. After the news of the bow's destruction reached him, there has been no movement from his side. Right now, we don't know where the war is headed and what his next move will entail. But we do need to take steps and make our position stronger. It won't be long before the enemy tries to challenge us again.'

'I agree,' Guru Apasmitra said. 'We had high hopes regarding Barbarik's arrows but they have all been used.'

'Can't they be recalled?' Shreya asked.

Ashwatthama shook his head. 'Barbarik's arrows were supposed to be used only once. Unfortunately, the arrows disappeared after being used on Vidyut. Each arrow, like its wielder, seeks its destiny. A warrior gives this destiny to the arrow. I gave the matter much thought, why the arrows disappeared after I used them when they were supposed to be employed multiple times. I think they were gifted to Barbarik by Lord Shiva for a reason. Some weapons are given for a one-time use, to avoid misuse by the receiver. Barbarik did not use the arrows for any purpose as such. They were just used once, before I used them on Vidyut, when Krishna tested them. And that does not qualify as actual use.'

'All right,' Rana concurred. 'Do we go ahead on a hunch then?'

'As of now, this is the only approach that makes sense. We have been working on it continuously for a week; nothing seems more appropriate. The journey began with Lord Rama's bow. It is possible that we will find something relevant in his kingdom,' Guru Apasmitra replied.

Rana waved his hands dismissively. 'All right. I will go with it. At least, this allows us to move ahead.'

Guru Apasmitra looked up. 'We do not have much information about Dandak's activities but news has been floating around that after Vidyut's death, he has appointed a new asura, Kaalnemi as his general and commander of armies. Kaalnemi is rumoured to come from Rasatala but little more is known about him. Then again, he is said to be as ferocious, if not more, than the others.'

'Anyway, we don't expect them to be the shy and docile,' muttered Rana.

Guru Apasmitra frowned at him, then replied, 'As I said, not much is known about Kaalnemi. I tried researching his origins but we have scant information on Rasatala itself. If he has emerged from the depths of Rasatala, it means Dandak will be summoning the armies of the netherworld to march on earth.'

'How many are we talking about?' Ashwatthama asked.

'Over a hundred thousand, I am afraid.'

'A hundred thousand?' Urmila gasped.

'How did we get this number?' Rana frowned.

'A conservative estimate,' Guru Apasmitra answered. 'This was the number documented as the army of the rakshasa king in Rasatala. Since the original army of asuras is gone, it is this army that is likely to take over.'

Rana shook his head. 'And we have less than thirty thousand soldiers.'

'What about their weapons?' Shreya asked.

'Not much is known about them. But villagers on the outskirts of the forest have reported the large-scale migration of birds and animals, in droves of thousands. Wild animals have started crossing village borders.'

'Are trees being felled?' Shreya asked.

'Yes.'

'Arrows, swords, clubs and spears then, mostly.'

Guru Apasmitra looked at Shreya. 'That won't be all. They will be bringing a large number of weapons from Rasatala, some of which have not been seen in any battle on earth so far. These would be weapons that were used in the olden days, in the war against the Gods. Prepare for some surprises.

'Actually, I think all of you should know this. There is a rumour afloat about Dandak having a secret weapon, one he has obtained from Rasatala. The weapon is reputed to be a battle-winner. It could change the course of the war in a single stroke.'

'Any idea what it might be? Even a faint one?' Urmila asked.

'None at all. There is hardly any way to get our spies into Dandakaranya. The asuras have set up a closed perimeter around the forest. So whatever information we have, is coming from sources who have overheard the asuras or bribed them with meat for information.'

'Could it be that this news is deliberately being spread by them?' Ashwatthama questioned.

'I would not know, I am just stating the facts. All I have heard is that the secret weapon is said to be able to defeat any army of Aryavarta and beyond.'

'Well, if we don't have a clue now, we will see it on the battleground. We should expect that it might not be a weapon of this age. But no use worrying now,' Ashwatthama stated.

Guru Apasmitra nodded. 'You must proceed to Ayodhya. I will send a message to the Panchrishis. We have information about three of them but one is yet to be located. Rana and Shreya, together with our new army commander, Abhayajeet, you must make sure that our armies are on standby. We cannot afford to be lax. Dandak is likely to have spies inside the kingdom.'

As Rana glanced at a visibly excited Shreya, he shuddered. He had seen the same excitement on Urmila's face, just before they had set off for Himavant through the Valley of Illusions. A memory of Urmila's injured, limp body at Himavant flashed before his eyes.

War. It was never fun and always more dangerous than it seemed.

4

No Allies

Surparaka

Vikram threw the scroll with a message on the table behind him; it landed among many other scrolls.

'Another one?' Manvita asked.

'This one's from Trigarta, the kingdom in eastern Aryavarta. They say they have already pledged allegiance to Dandak, in return for no harm done to their kingdom, and for trade treaties.'

'But don't they already have trade treaties with Avanti?'

'No one wants to go against Dandak. Despite my reassurance that Ashwatthama is with us, they are distrustful and suspicious. Many have responded saying that the bow was broken and there is no way Dandak can be killed now, so why should they sacrifice their lives for no purpose.' Vikram paced around the room restlessly, his hands smoothing his wavy locks.

'So, Dandak is sending peace treaties to everyone except us?' Manvita asked.

'Avanti, Surparaka and Hastinapur. And the Yeti Kingdom. Saurashtra is kingless after Nyat's death and will not put up any resistance. He has singled out kingdoms which were against his resurrection. It clearly is vengeance.'

'Will there be war?' Manvita asked, her voice trembling a little.

'Probably,' Vikram slowed his pace, expounding aloud. 'Hastinapur is still the biggest kingdom in the country, with the mightiest army, followed by Avanti. We stand nowhere, we are just one city. If Dandak can crush us and the Yetis, there is no stopping him. He knows that he will have a hard time fighting against the combined might of the kingdoms. If he offers a fake peace treaty now, he would face singular armies, rather than alliances, like in the Kurukshetra War.'

Manvita's eyes narrowed as she drew a deep breath. She said glumly, 'I don't believe this; three months ago, my worry was only how to get Shrutika to eat her vegetables.'

Vikram smiled wryly. 'One never knows how one's life might change. Sometimes, the events of our lives are decided by factors outside our control. What we can control, though, is our response to the events in our lives, and we should focus on that. Life is extremely unpredictable, Manvita, probably the most unpredictable of everything in the entire universe. One never knows what will happen even a moment later. That is the blessing and the curse with which we all have to live. Our lives, our destinies, are altered by the smallest of events.

'You might have made a hundred plans but the fluttering of a butterfly can lay all those plans to waste. Contrarily, the same fluttering could transform your misfortunes to fortunes, too. This unpredictability is what makes our lives interesting and scary at the same time. We must never try to control our lives but rather, make the best of what we have.

'And do remember, hope is a powerful thing, Manvita. We must always believe in hope. It brings courage. In the darkest of times, that's the one thing that takes one across the winning line. It's easy to give up but fifty years from now, we can look back and say, 'Yes, it was hard but I did not give up!' Everyone dies but not everyone fights. We must strive to be fighters.'

Manvita nodded, looking into Vikram's eyes. In the past few months, events had moved so fast that the two of them had hardly managed to share a moment together. She missed the old days. She walked up to her husband and caressed his face. 'I know you and have never doubted you, my love. No matter where this path goes, I am with you in all your decisions.'

Vikram nodded in acknowledgement. He held her hand and they ventured out onto the balcony that overlooked the city. 'Events are becoming hazier,' he sighed. 'We seem to have lost our sense of direction. There is no united front and that worries me. I am afraid that on our own, we are not strong enough.'

'So why are these allies not fighting? Is it not true that some of them come from families famed for their brave acts in war?'

Vikram grimaced. 'The fools do not realise that this treaty with the asuras is a ploy, or they know it and are hoping someone else will solve the problem for them. Once Dandak is done with Hastinapur and Avanti, he will go for the smaller kingdoms, one by one. He will not stop until the whole of Aryavarta is an asura kingdom. These kings are squandering their chances of survival for a temporary truce.'

Manvita thought for a moment and asked, 'It seems Dandak is afraid the humans will wage war with him. What if the asuras want peace, the way they did in Lanka?'

A sudden silence fell as Manvita realised the absurdity of her question.

Vikram, however, replied calmly, 'I didn't think of it that way, ever. We can argue over that but asuras are known to be backstabbers. If their intention was peace, they would not have ambushed us at Dwarka. Remember that they attacked first. Do not underestimate their trickery. It has ruined many kingdoms in the past.

'Since time immemorial, it has been established that humans and asuras cannot live together. Asuras live by the law of the jungle. The males are promiscuous and treat their women disgracefully, oppress them, do not allow them a voice of their own. Their trials are always by weapons. Their philosophy has violence at its core. They want to dominate, by any means. Their's is not a society fit for humans.

'Sooner or later, a conflict will arise and the asuras will wipe out humans, with all ferocity. Their powers grow at night, and humans are not nocturnal beings. Dandak, during his earlier reign, started annexing all the northern kingdoms and he had reached the Yeti kingdom. It was sheer luck that he was not able to exert his full power owing to the curse.'

Manvita nodded, having understood Dandak's ulterior motive. She looked at Vikram in anticipation and hope. 'What are you going to do if the kingdoms are not agreeable to fighting together?' she asked.

'I have to try harder, Manvita. The Mandara Kingdom is still undecided. They have a huge army, enough to counter thousands of asuras. The Kimpurushas that reside in the forest will follow Chief Druma into any battle. Those half-human, half-horse beings know how to fight. Blessed with superhuman strength, extremely long life and impenetrable skin, they are one of the fiercest warriors in all of Aryavarta.

'Unfortunately, they are hunted by humans, who kill them as soon as they enter civilisation. The humans are afraid of them and the Kimpurushas in turn, hate the humans and see them as slaughterers. They have not been heard of after

Janamejaya's coronation, which was attended by Druma. They do not move freely among the humans. I know Chief Druma. He is sensible but so far, he has not responded to my offer to join us.'

'Do not worry too much,' Manvita smiled. 'The Gods are on our side. We must believe in Ashwatthama. He will lead us to victory.'

Vikram nodded. 'I know. He is the best hope we have. I trust him completely, though it seems that he too is conflicted in his own way. I feel I must help him in whatever way I can.'

The Surparaka King looked at Manvita and asked, 'Are you afraid?'

Manvita shook her head. 'Not as long as you are with me.'

Vikram smiled but a chill ran down his spine. Having seen the asuras in action, he knew that after each battle, he had his lucky stars to thank for staying alive. Sometimes, it is not death that frightens you. It is the thought of the grief of the loved ones left behind that is scary.

5

The Lanka Pact

The guard struggled to keep his eyes open in the warm night. The lack of a breeze and the high humidity in the air made him restless. He was hardly getting any sleep nowadays with a newborn at home and night duty at the palace. He had applied for a transfer of shift but so far, had heard nothing back. At the moment, he felt like slumping down at the main palace entrance and falling asleep. Sometimes he felt that death was preferable to the bouts of headache and weary eyes he suffered from all day long. His tired eyes discerned a blurred form approaching but he couldn't get his eyelids to open fully.

'Wake up, fool,' a familiar voice told him but he couldn't comprehend anything clearly. Sleep was taking him into its fold as quietly as fog blankets a cold morning.

It was not until the last moment that he realised a sharp object was about to slice his neck. Adrenaline then kicked in and his eyes were wide open. It was too late. He saw a heavily-built figure, dressed in black robes, with a flowing red-black fiery cape, swinging a black sword towards his neck. And then he felt terrible pain. He felt as if he was in free-fall but it was just his head falling from his body.

A human head can survive for about five seconds after being cut off. The last scene that the hapless sentry saw was the sword that had decapitated him merging into his attacker's hands. He was not sure if it was an illusion. But he didn't have to care anymore. Pain took over as he saw his newborn's face flashing before his eyes, and then everything went dark.

~

'You killed a guard of mine, for no reason,' Ajeeth said, pouring himself a drink from the golden pitcher. He poured another one and handed over the goblet to his guest, who was wiping blood off his hands.

Dandak took the drink and settled on a nearby chair. He sipped the aromatic wine.

Ajeeth eyed Dandak suspiciously. He was not sure he liked the asura king. Lanka had been peaceful for centuries and the rakshasa king intended to keep it that way. His rakshasa community had grown large, after being almost annihilated by Lord Rama. Ajeeth had worked hard to revive the community and make them more civilised. Vibhishana had followed a good path and shown the way of righteousness to the rakshasas in Lanka. In time, they had become humane. So Dandak's visit was not a welcome one.

'You come here at short notice,' Ajeeth said. 'What brings the asura king to me?'

Dandak sipped his drink, taking the measure of his peer. 'I have a proposition for you,' he said, smiling wryly. 'Let me keep it simple. We are going to wage war against the humans and conquer Aryavarta.'

Ajeeth coughed and almost spilt his drink. He put it back on the table, trying to make sense of Dandak's words.

He could not immediately determine what unsettled him more, the absurdity or the shock value of what Dandak had just said. He wiped his mouth, then spoke, 'You have been dead for over five thousand years, or so I have heard. Do I have to remind you that one of my ancestors tried the same stunt, ages ago? A mere mortal and an army of monkeys trounced him.'

Dandak scoffed. 'I know all about Rama and his valour, if you call it that. But this is not Tretayuga. It is not Dwaparayuga, either. There are no more living Gods. No man and a monkey are going to get the better of me. At this point, I can even wage war against the Gods and not blink.'

Ajeeth shifted uncomfortably at Dandak's proclamation. 'War against the Gods?' he asked, wide-eyed. 'What weapons do you have?'

'Let us stick to talking about our proposal here.'

'And what about Ashwatthama? Word is that he is your arch-nemesis.'

'Ashwat-thama.' Dandak jeered as he took another sip of the maroon drink, the wine and sweet smell of grapefruit intoxicating him mildly. 'He is a coward living in his guilt-ridden world. Before he can utter Shiva's name, I will cut off his head. Then we will see how immortal the Immortal is.'

Ajeeth quailed. He was feeling queasy as he anticipated Dandak's proposal. He decided to warn Dandak once again.

'Even Ravana said similar things about Rama,' he said. 'When Ravana went to Mareecha to ask for help in abducting Sita, Mareecha warned him repeatedly about not going after her as Rama would strike back. Mareecha had experienced the wrath of Rama, back in the forest of Tadaka, when Rama had killed Tadaka and the other demons who were disturbing the sacrificial fire of Sage Vishwamitra. The force of Rama's arrows had flung Mareecha hundreds of miles away. Mareecha dreaded facing Rama again, for the third time but Ravana decided not to listen to him.'

'The third time?'

'Once, while Rama was in exile, he was killing rakshasas by the thousands. An enraged Mareecha assumed the shape of a large, two-horned bull and rushed towards Rama to kill him. Two other demons were with him in this foolhardy attempt. On seeing them charge, Rama shot three arrows towards them. Mareecha turned his back and fled. The arrow spared him since Rama did not attack anyone from behind. No avatar of Vishnu strikes an enemy on the back. The other two demons, however, were not so wise or lucky.'

Dandak waved his hand in dismissal of the veiled warning.

'What is the problem with your kingdom, Dandakaranya? It's quite large, I have heard,' Ajeeth said.

'Too small. Even if I raise troops in my kingdom, the humans will conspire and attack. They will not allow the asura community to flourish. It is not a question of annexation but survival.'

'But we have flourished,' Ajeeth interrupted. 'We are living peacefully, side-by-side with the humans.'

Dandak glared at Ajeeth with bloodshot eyes, which looked as if the wine had seeped into them. He snarled, 'The day the bridge between Lanka and Aryavarta appears again, your illusion will vanish. Do you think humans have not attacked you because they have made peace with you? Look around.

'In the Kurukshetra War, they slaughtered all the rakshasas. Not one survived. You are alive because your ancestor Vibhishana decided not to participate in the war. Except for the five Pandavas, the three Kauravas and Krishna, nobody else survived the Kurukshetra War. Vibhishana knew the outcome of the war beforehand. Where is he, anyway?'

Ajeeth shook his head. 'No idea, meditating somewhere, probably.'

Dandak pointed at the Lanka King and sneered. 'You are protected because of the sea surrounding this island. The moment the humans get a chance to attack Lanka, you and your rakshasa army will stand no chance before them. Look at their weapons and strength. You have, what—a ten-thousand strong army? How will it stand against the combined armies of Aryavarta?'

'We have the…' Ajeeth stopped abruptly as he suddenly realised the reason for Dandak's visit. He leaned back restlessly. It was true that whenever some rakshasas ventured into Aryavarta, they never returned. The humans were hostile to both, the rakshasa and asura race. In fact, the humans had been hostile to every race other than their own in Kaliyuga. They saw them as threats to their supremacy. If it ever came to war, there were no doubts. The rakshasas did not have any soldiers or weapons in their arsenal that could match what the humans had.

Except one.

'What do you want? And what's in it for us?'

Dandak stood up and strolled around, looking at the entrance where a couple of rakshasas were cleaning the blood of the dead guard. 'First, let me tell you what you will gain,' he said. 'We will conquer Aryavarta, from Himavant to the southern seas. You will have complete control of the Aryavarta region south of Kishkindha. In a way, think of it as retribution by your arch-nemesis, Hanuman.'

Ajeeth was not amused. He knew what Hanuman had done to Lanka in just one night.

Dandak continued. 'As for your first question, you might have guessed the answer by now. We want your giants and your ships.'

Ajeeth sighed and shook his head. 'It's too heavy a price to pay. And why do you need them when you said you can wage war even against the Gods?'

'I know they are your last line of defence,' Dandak said. 'I would not have asked if I did not need them. I hate wasting time in trivial battles. But trivial battles too need to be won. Your giants will win my war. And then, you can have your share of the prize. I am not asking you to participate in this war. Whatever or whoever remains at the end of the war will be returned to you.'

Ajeeth had creases on his forehead now. The two lamps on both sides of the room threw gigantic shadows of Dandak on the walls.

'What will you do with the ships?' he asked. 'The entire fight is going to be inland, anyway.'

'I want only your answer,' Dandak glowered at him.

Ajeeth felt his stomach churn as he put the glass of wine down. 'I am not too worried about my ships; we can build more,' he said. 'But we have less than twenty giants left.'

'Seventeen to be precise,' Dandak corrected him.

'And they are not breeding anymore. These are all male giants. You know how useful they are. Very long lives, hundreds of years. High agility. Bodies impenetrable by normal weapons. They cannot be easily downed, and one giant can kill thousands single-handedly in a day.'

'I know all about them. Your answer?'

'What if I say no?'

Dandak's nostrils flared. He breathed hard and clenched his fists. 'There is no middle ground here. Choose your answer carefully, rakshasa king. Do not test my patience.'

Ajeeth sighed. The humans were dangerous but not aggressive. Dandak was both. After the humans were finished with, Dandak would come for his remaining enemies. Either way, the giants were doomed. The least Ajeeth could do was save his people.

'All right. You can have them. But I will need the deal in writing.'

Dandak took a deep breath.

One giant each had created unimaginable havoc in the Lanka and Kurukshetra Wars. Now he had seventeen.

6

The Attack on Surparaka

The sea was furious again, throwing up large waves as if trying to break free from the clutches of the full moon. It was well past midnight when the guard at the lighthouse saw the first of the ships. In the dark, often nothing was visible on the western seas, except for the occasional trade ships. The ships brought a kind of comfort to him, the dim deck lights moving slowly and then disappearing over the horizon as smoothly as a snake disappears in the sand. This was the best part of his job, and he would spend long moments looking at a ship as it slowly melted into the horizon. The sea always made him comfortable and he was happy to be in the patrol team, rather than with the attack division which had to go to war. Being a lighthouse guard was safer than being a soldier.

Today, however, things seemed different. Instead of one, he had seen many lights. He wondered aloud as he saw the lights moving in sync, 'Are these trade ships?' He wanted to rush to the signal room and ring the bell but decided he needed to be sure rather than raise a false alarm. His sleeping mates would not take kindly to it and he would have to clean vessels for a week.

In wars, it is often safer to go with one's first instinct. This was what the poor guard realised too late. In the next minute, as his eyes focused on the black sea, he could make out over a hundred boats rowing under the cover of darkness, swarming towards the shore. The intruders had left the decoy trade ships.

Attack! It was an attack!

As he ran towards the signal room, something whizzed through him. He looked down and saw an arrow sticking out of his chest. The next moment, he collapsed. As he fell, he caught a glimpse of hundreds of black-clad men wielding swords, shields, bows and scimitars, jumping out of the boats and entering the kingdom stealthily.

~

Vikram was startled by a grinding noise. He wondered if he was dreaming but looking around, he saw no movement. He checked for his sword by the bedside and closed his eyes.

Whirrr...

This time the sound was more pronounced.

Vikram sat up, alert. He looked across to the balcony and thought someone was sawing off the metal railings. But then, a slight glow from the side of the room attracted his attention. A red-hot blade had entered through the crevice of the door and was smoothly cutting through the metal of the latch. Alarmed, Vikram shook Manvita awake and pulled the sword by the bedside towards himself, unsheathing it.

'What is it?' Manvita asked, sitting up and rubbing her eyes. Vikram motioned towards the side of the room.

'Something's wrong. Take Shrutika, get inside the chamber. Follow our escape protocol.'

Manvita looked at the door as she grasped the situation. She jumped out of bed, ran to the adjoining room and picked up the sleeping Shrutika. Holding the little girl, she sprinted to the side of the room, keeping an eye on the blade cutting through the last latch. As she pressed four bricks in sequence, a sliding door appeared in the wall, at waist height. Placing Shrutika inside quickly, Manvita entered and pulled the lever from behind the door. The door slid shut, camouflaged itself into the side wall, and the bricks went back to their original positions. There was no way anyone could know there was an escape chamber inside the king's room. Many kings got such chambers built in their bedrooms for added protection from assassins.

Vikram moved slowly towards the door, sword and shield in hand. He cast a glance at the chamber door sliding shut and aligned himself with the wall adjoining the entry door of the bedroom. As the attacker's blade went through the last latch, many intruders, dressed in black from head to toe, walked in swiftly, stealthily. The attackers surrounded the bed where Vikram had hurriedly put the pillows below the sheets. In a single motion, the intruders raised their swords and brought them down on the bed.

Vikram drew a deep breath, clutching his sword tighter.

Ten mercenaries, trained to kill.

He darted forward, slashed the heads of two leftmost attackers and then slashed the torso of the third. The remaining attackers rushed towards Vikram, making him lose his balance. As he fell, three intruders jumped on him. Vikram blocked the attack using his shield. With a swift move of the other hand, he wielded his sword and the blade went through the legs of three attackers, all of whom hollered as their legs were separated from their bodies. Vikram then rose and looked at the last four attackers around him.

As the four men moved into position, coordinating their movements to attack at once, Vikram raised his shield and sword, getting ready to defend himself. The men moved swiftly, intending to kill but were frozen in place by a shower of arrows. The attackers fell dead on the floor, all at once. Surparaka soldiers entered the room and continued to rain arrows on the enemy.

'Maharaja, are you all right?'

Vikram recognised the voice of Kaustubha, his army general.

'Maharaja,' Kaustubha gasped as he paused to catch his breath. 'Mercenaries. Attack from the sea. Hundreds of boats. Came in trade ships.'

Vikram breathed hard as he surveyed the attackers in case any of them was alive, then, sheathed his sword. He could feel the blood pulsing in his head. He picked up an extra sword hanging above the bedstead. Turning around, he instructed, 'Let's get them.'

'No, Maharaja,' Kaustubha halted Vikram in a loud voice, stopping him in his tracks. 'Over. It's over.'

Taken aback, Vikram turned to look at Kaustubha. 'What's over? What do you mean?'

'The city has fallen, Maharaja. They have come in the thousands. The army was taken by surprise. No one was ready. Going out now is suicide. There is no way we can win. They have set fire to the armoury and the garrison. The fleet...the entire fleet is gone.'

Vikram rushed forward, not fully absorbing what Kaustubha had just said. 'No. We have to save the city. I cannot abandon my people,' he cried.

The army general pulled him back. 'This is not your city anymore, Maharaja. Please listen to me. They will kill you before you even reach the street. For once, listen to me and save your family. The only consolation is that these are paid mercenaries and not asuras, otherwise, they would have massacred the civilians. Right now, the city is under their control. If you live today, you can fight tomorrow to reclaim what is yours. They have come prepared. And they want you. They are here to kill you. Don't let them succeed. If that happens, they win. For now, please think of the Maharani and the little one. You must go.'

Vikram felt dizzy. Never in his life had he run away from a fight. But Kaustubha was not wrong. There is a thin line between foolishness and bravado, and many have perished when they failed to recognise that difference. Logic must always prevail over emotion in war.

This was war. Sometimes losing a battle was necessary to win the war.

Vikram sighed, looking at the dead in the room. His general had given him the right advice. He nodded grimly.

The relieved general gestured to his fellow soldier and the latter brought out a cloth bundle. 'Maharaja, this contains food for about a week, and a few gold coins to help you get to the nearest kingdom. Right now, the safest place for you would be...' Kaustubha scratched his scruffy beard, looking at the ground as Vikram prepared to leave.

'...The Mandara Forests,' Kaustubha continued.

'Wait, why Mandara? Why should I not ride to Avanti? It is about the same distance.'

'We have word that the road to Avanti is packed with asuras. If one of them spots you and word gets out, you won't make it to Avanti. This was a planned attack, Maharaja. You should head towards the Mandara Forests, north of Matsya. In five days, you should be there. Chief Druma is a sensible person and he will be able to guide you further. We have placed horses and ten soldiers at the end of the tunnel. The Maharani and you should not face any mercenary attack along the way.'

Vikram shook his head in disbelief at what was happening. 'I never thought it would happen so soon. I thought we had more time.'

Kaustubha looked at him and swore, 'You will always be our king. Find a way to come back and save the city, Maharaja. For now, though, you must go.'

Vikram hurried towards the chamber, pushing at the bricks in order to open it. As the chamber door opened, he found a sweaty Manvita, almost in tears, cupping her hands over her daughter's ears as the little girl slept on her lap. Vikram nodded in farewell at Kaustubha and entered the tunnel. He then pulled the lever from the inside, and the tunnel door slid shut.

Vikram hugged Manvita warmly, and she felt life seeping back into her. He lit the torches stored inside the pitch-dark tunnel. Handing one to Manvita, Vikram took Shrutika in his arms, and they strode towards the other end, almost a mile away.

7

The Living Nightmare

Raghu and Neema lay on their cotton mattresses, their sleepy eyes watching every movement of the rabbit as it nibbled on the stem of a vegetable.

'Sleep,' Raji commanded as she cut up vegetables for their meal the next day. 'Tomorrow your new school lessons start, Neema. You need to sleep well.'

'Yes, Mother,' replied Neema, before closing her eyes, lying in the same position. The children were happier than ever with the little rabbit. Raji looked at them, smiled and raised her eyes to heaven in a quick, silent prayer.

The next moment, the roof exploded. Raghu and Neema yelled as they saw a big burning log falling on the rabbit's cage, destroying it and setting the animal on fire. The poor creature squealed for a few seconds, running madly around in its wrecked cage, before falling, kicking its legs violently, and then going still.

'No!' Raghu and Neema both screamed. Two hands lifted them up, and they found themselves being taken out of the hut.

As Raji stepped outside the burning hut, the scene sent a chill through her bones. Asuras were attacking the village. They were hurling torches on the roof of huts, forcing people out. The asuras brandished swords, axes, spiked clubs and spears. They were setting the hay on fire and slaughtering the cattle. The soil was slowly becoming damp with the blood of humans and cattle alike, and the smell was nauseating.

Raji desperately looked for a place to escape but the asuras were everywhere. Her heart was beating faster than ever and her legs trembled, heavy as if they had suddenly turned to metal. The noise around dulled her hearing. She saw the asuras attacking men, left and right. The men were stabbed, hit with clubs and hacked by axes. Young children were picked up and thrown into the burning huts. A few asuras were tearing the clothes off women and violating them. If there was a hell on earth, it would have to be this. Raji went numb and dropped the children on the ground. Her mind stopped working. Staring at the raging fire that was her hut, she stood motionless.

'Ma!' cried the children, tugging at her clothes.

'Huh!' Raji came to her senses, and picked Neema up with her left arm and took Raghu's hand in her right. She made it past the burning huts and piles of crops, which now sent large yellow-orange flames towards the sky. The piteous cries of men, women and children permeated the air. As she passed a hut, she saw two asuras violently raping her neighbour, while another cut down the woman's husband.

She stumbled, falling headlong over a body, which she recognised as Neema's friend's. The girl used to visit their hut to play with Neema. Raji hardly had any strength left in her legs but knew that she had to hide before the asuras spotted her. Raghu and Neema were crying loudly, and she couldn't blame them. No one could expect a seven and a five year old to stay calm when grown-ups were breaking down.

Nestling Neema against her hip, Raji dragged a crying Raghu along. The trees bordering the Dandakaranya Forest were hardly fifty steps away. If she could make it, she could probably hide there, to survive—just survive. As Raji sprinted the last few steps, an asura saw her. He ran after her, shrieking with insane lust. Raji ran into the forest, and kept going until she was so exhausted that she could not run any further, and collapsed. The voices from the village were now distant and the raging flames were just a candle-flicker in the distance. Raghu and Neema were silent now, their cries having turned to sobs. The little ones were traumatised by what they had seen.

As Raji picked herself up, she pulled both children into a tight embrace. For children, the greatest protection in the world is their parents, and Raji made a promise to herself that she wouldn't let any harm come to them as long as she lived. As she consoled the children and wiped their tears, Raji heard the rustling of leaves. She knew an asura had seen her but was not too sure he had followed them this deep into the forest. Putting her finger on her lips, Raji gestured at the children to remain silent and hid them all behind the trees. Her eyes were adjusting to the darkness, the dim moonlight aiding her vision. Her hearing was enhanced in the darkness and she strained her ears to pick up a sound—any sound.

It was then that she remembered something. She had shoved the vegetable knife into her sari when the attack had started. She hoped the knife had not fallen down. Moving her hand in the darkness, she felt for the knife and sent up silent thanks when she found it. Taking it out, she kept it ready in her hands for the attack.

What monsters were these? Where had they come from?

A hundred questions haunted her. Their life, she knew, was destroyed. Her husband, Samba, the woodcutter, had gone to Ujjaini to bring back supplies. He was supposed to return late at night. Raji shuddered, sweat flowing freely down her forehead and her heartbeat spiking. They would kill Samba even before he entered the village. Should she take the outer route to intercept and warn him? It was a huge risk. The children would be in danger.

But that could only happen if she survived the asura hunting them. The leaves rustled again, this time closer. Raji listened hard. She heard the asura's loud breathing, not more than two trees away. Turning her head slowly to one side, she could see him. He had a spiked club in his hand, blood trickling from it. The asuras seemed to have a good sense of smell. Raji moved around the tree, motioning for the children to do the same, to avoid being in the asura's direct line-of-sight. As the children moved with her, one of them stepped on a twig.

CRACK!

The asura turned. He saw Raghu's shirt jutting out from the side of the tree. Growling furiously, he sprinted towards the tree and in an instant, picked up his club and smashed it above the shirt, where the child's face should have been. But instead of feeling the satisfaction of killing the child, the asura felt a blinding pain at the back of his neck. He turned around, only to see a defiant Raji, Neema, and a shirtless Raghu. Before he could move his club again, he fell, gasping for breath, with the knife stuck in the nape of his neck.

Raji pulled the knife out and along with the children, fled towards the heart of the jungle, where she hoped to survive the night.

8

Kimpurushas

After crossing the desert near the Matsya kingdom, Vikram and his companions arrived at the outskirts of the Mandara Forest, late one morning. The green forest was soothing to their eyes, after having ridden for days in the hot sandy plains. The cool breeze from the trees provided a respite for their dry and dusty faces.

Vikram slowed his horse to bring it in line with Manvita's mount. 'What is it? Are you intimidated by the forest?' he asked.

Manvita shook her head. 'It's been years since I entered a forest. I've never seen so many trees growing so close together. Although this forest does appear dense, I feel relieved.'

Vikram offered his hand and Manvita took it. With a deep breath, they entered the forest and signalled to the others to follow. He warned everyone not to make a sudden movement if they saw any Kimpurushas, for the latter were aggressive by nature and could attack without warning if they felt threatened. Also, Kimpurushas were not known to harbour amicable feelings towards humans.

Moving deep into the forest, they realised this was a region that had been left untouched by kings, soldiers and tribes. There were flowers as large as pumpkins growing here, and small forest creatures roamed about freely. They could see rabbits, deer and even a couple of tigers, who lay lazily in the distance. The forest floor ran riot with little white, yellow and purple chickweed which adorned the green grass. The air was surprisingly cold and pure. The calls of sparrows, cuckoos and insects created a unique melody, pleasant to the ears. Manvita was surprised that such a place existed in Aryavarta. In all the kingdoms she had visited, the cities had taken over the green areas and there was hardly any sanctuary for animals and birds. But here, it seemed like nature had preserved a home for its mute children. The horses happily ate mouthfuls of grass as they moved along.

'How far inside do we need to travel?' Manvita asked Vikram.

Vikram shook his head, worry lines on his forehead, looking around cautiously, even as Manvita gazed at him in surprise.

'How are we going to reach them? It's been almost half a day of riding through the forest...'

Vikram raised his hand and gestured for her to be quiet. He motioned for everyone to stop moving, even as the rustling of leaves indicated the presence of another being. As they waited with bated breath in the silence broken only by the chirping of birds, an arrow whizzed past, zooming right in between them, almost missing a soldier's head. The riders froze as a group of Kimpurushas emerged from between the trees, surrounding them on all sides.

The Kimpurushas were a sight to behold: the upper half of their body was human, while the lower half resembled a horse's, complete with tail. They had pointed ears and elongated faces, with their hair tied up in a ponytail at the back of their heads. Their features were sharp, and they wore similar brown jackets with a bow each on their shoulders, a quiver of arrows on their back and a sword at their waist. Manvita could not help but notice that of the group of about twenty Kimpurushas, five looked female, with long hair and beautiful feminine faces, though they carried the same weapons and seemed as fierce as their male counterparts.

One Kimpurusha came forward, his bow and arrow held in position. He asked, 'What business? Who comes here?'

Vikram raised his hands to dismiss any indication of hostility. 'It is Vikramsena, King of Surparaka, a friend of the Mandara Kingdom. We seek to meet Chief Druma.'

The Kimpurusha looked at the other soldiers in the group and then at Manvita. Noticing Shrutika sitting with her, he lowered his bow. He spoke to Vikram again, 'No weapons.'

Vikram nodded and signalled for his riders to comply with the orders. The soldiers dropped their weapons on the ground, which were collected by one of the Kimpurushas. Vikram handed over his sword, dagger, bow and arrows. Manvita followed suit, handing over her sword.

'Follow,' the leading Kimpurusha said and galloped as the riders followed him.

~

Manvita was wide-eyed as she took in the settlement of the Kimpurushas. Thousands of huts, built in an orderly fashion and scores of Kimpurushas moving around, gave the place an otherworldly feeling. She had never seen any other tribe except humans, before this.

'The Kimpurushas are among the last of the ancient tribes,' Vikram whispered to a wonderstruck Manvita, who was glancing keenly all around her. 'Like the Yetis, they strive to protect their civilisation and keep it pure.'

'I can see that,' Manvita nudged Shrutika, pointing at the various wonderful designs of the settlement.

'How do you know about them? I mean, how did you make their acquaintance? I never heard a word about the Kimpurushas until you told me a few days ago,' Manvita said.

'Janamejaya introduced me to them, during his coronation. They are extremely reserved by nature, never venturing outside the Mandara Forests as humans have killed many of their kind. They are skilled warriors, extremely agile and strong but they do not fight without a cause. Their arrows and blades are dipped in the poison of the most venomous plants, which can bring the mightiest of beasts down. They did not participate in the Kurukshetra War, fearing total annihilation of their tribe. The world knows next to nothing about them.'

The riders arrived at the centre of the settlement in front of a wood and bamboo hut that was larger than the others.

'Wait,' the leading Kimpurusha said, raising his hand and entering the hut.

'Father, can I sit on one of those?' Shrutika asked, pointing towards a baby Kimpurusha almost her size, who went galloping by.

'I don't think that would be a good idea, Shrutika! These are not horses but people like us,' Vikram replied as a large Kimpurusha emerged from the hut. His skin was dark brown and he wore a necklace of large, teal beads.

'Vikramsena. Long time. What brings you here, friend?' the large Kimpurusha asked in a hoarse voice.

Vikram got off his horse and bowed. The others followed suit.

'Chief Druma, my family and I seek refuge among your tribe for a few days. My city has been attacked by mercenaries and asuras, led by Dandak.'

Druma narrowed his eyes. 'Asuras. Dandak. Bad,' the Kimpurusha leader said.

'It's a long story, and I will narrate all that has happened to us. For now, we wish to know if you can provide refuge to us for a few days.'

Druma smiled as he held Vikram by the shoulders. 'Guest welcome. Feel home, friend.'

The Chief Kimpurusha then called out to his son Shifa. A younger Kimpurusha appeared; he looked like a warrior, with his sharp eyes and athletic torso.

'Shifa, our friends and guests,' the Chief said. 'Take them to visitors' hut. Take rest, Vikramsena. You look tired. We talk at dinner.'

~

Vikram couldn't fall sleep, unlike his wife and daughter. They were catching up on their sleep but Vikram felt his stomach churning.

A king must stand and fall along with his people. A king who flees in times of adversity does not deserve to be king.

He woke up, his restless mind not letting sleep overcome him. His body was drenched in sweat and he struggled to concentrate. He had failed his people in not being able to detect and deflect the attack. Nobody had had any inkling that there would be an attack from the sea. All the soldiers had been stationed on the forest side, from where the asura attack was expected. Hardly any coastal kingdom spent much of their budget on ships; wars happened on land in Aryavarta. Still, Surparaka was one of the few kingdoms that had a strong navy. As Kaustubha had mentioned, the navy ships had been destroyed by the mercenaries and they had exclusively targetted the army, ensuring that no fight-back was possible. It had to be someone driven with a specific purpose: sabotage the palace, and the rest of the kingdom would come down.

This threat seemed to have come from outside Aryavarta but no doubt orchestrated by Dandak. Someone had loaned the ships to the asura king. The good news was that his citizens were not massacred. The mercenaries were different from asuras in their philosophy, and driven only by money; they uprooted kingdoms, assassinated kings and looted treasures. They rarely killed civilians as this was against their code of conduct. Their target was Vikram, his family and the soldiers of Surparaka. The kingdom was in the control of the mercenaries now and by extension, in Dandak's control. Once the main war was over, he would not think twice about plundering it. Right now, diverting forces to Surparaka was not something the asura king would be planning as it wouldn't serve any purpose. So, Vikram had some time, albeit a tiny window. It all came down to one war. The war for existence. Between the humans and the asuras.

Vikram sighed as he sat on the edge of his cot. It is easy to talk of courage when things are going in the right direction but it takes the strongest of hearts to tackle adversities head-on. It was time to take the next step. Vikram rubbed his head, feeling relieved that his headache had gone. He stood up and walked out of his hut.

The whole settlement was glowing with an orange hue, cast by the lights from covered lanterns and torches tied to trees and tall posts. Some Kimpurushas moved around, looking curiously at Vikram as he walked across the row of huts towards Druma's residence. Vikram informed the sentry of his identity and was led inside.

Chief Kimpurusha came forward and greeted Vikram. 'Come Vikramsena, King of Surparaka.'

'Not anymore,' said Vikram wryly.

Druma pressed his lips together and said in a low voice, 'Sorry about Surparaka attack.'

'You do not have to be sorry, Chief Druma. It is I who have failed my people.'

Druma turned and motioned to Vikram to sit on a block of wood. He poured a green liquid from a pot into a clay cup and handed it to Vikram. Vikram described the entire chain of events to Druma, starting from the inclusion of Ashwatthama in the journey to Himavant to the death of Nyat at the submerged city of Dwarka. The Chief listened attentively.

'Drink. What you plan next?' Druma asked, gulping the juice down.

Vikram shook his head. 'I am a bit clueless. I was not expecting this sudden attack. I have been looking for allies to counter Dandak. You received my message, Druma but have you made a decision?'

Druma looked into Vikram's eyes and waved. 'Look after the safety of my own. Cannot let the tribe in danger. Sorry. No war for Kimpurushas. Not fight Kurukshetra, not fight Dandak.'

Vikram looked at the tall Chief, who towered a good two feet above him.'You can help us, Druma,' he said. 'Kimpurushas are great fighters. With your strength alongside, we will have the upper hand over the asuras. Dandak is no fool to grant the Kimpurushas security. He has long dreamt of a united Aryavarta under his rule. Once the war with the humans is over, he will go after other tribes.'

Druma shook his head. 'I take that chance. No pact with Dandak. Kimpurushas not afraid of anyone. No asura enter this forest. You rest, Vikram. Stay for a few days. Be guest.'

Vikram lowered his head and nodded. He took a deep breath and gulped down the drink, which tasted like wheatgrass. Bowing to Druma, he walked out of the hut. He still felt uneasy, though. Having the Kimpurushas on their side would have given them a massive advantage.

However, the Kimpurushas would not fight. It was upto the Hastinapur army now.

9

No Mercy

The mother and children moved further and further away from the lights. The pitiful cries of the villagers seemed like a distant nightmare now. They halted at what looked like a safe place, by the side of a large tree. Raji gazed at Raghu and Neema; their shock had worn off and the dirt on their faces was streaked by tears. She hugged them, trying to suppress her own shock.

'It's all right. We are safe now. Nothing will happen to you.'

Both children hugged their mother tightly and embraced each other. The biggest succour in tragedies is the company of our loved ones.

'Ma, water!' a parched Neema said.

Raji had worried that this would come up. Where would she find water in this jungle?

She observed the surroundings, trying to find a fruit tree that could provide temporary relief to the children. She had to make sure the children would be okay till morning. The asuras would be gone by then or she could take the passage around the village.

Luckily, a patch of bamboo trees, whose stems are rich with drinkable sap, stood nearby. Raji seated the children by the bamboo patch and in the dim light of the crescent moon, pulled up a low-lying stem towards her. She took out the knife from her waist, cleaned it and cut the stem of the tree. As water started dripping, she beckoned to the children, made them stand below the stem and got them to drink a sufficient quantity of the water. Finally, after taking a few sips herself, she let go of the bamboo stem.

The children, though hungry, were very sleepy too. Raji let them both lie down on her lap and patted them until they fell asleep. Exhausted, she too closed her eyes, and within moments, drifted into sleep.

~

Sometime past midnight, a loud crash shook Raji awake. She opened her eyes, wondering if the sound was real. She had dreamt of asuras, the kind she had seen the previous evening. She tried to listen again but couldn't hear a rustle. Then she heard it again, at a distance. It seemed some trees were being felled. She could make out the sawing of metal on wood and loud voices.

Her heart sank. The asuras seemed to be coming back. She struggled to see in the dark. How long had it been? Could she pass through the village? She looked at the sleeping children and started crying softly. If only there was a way she could take them to safety; she would give anything for that chance. She said a prayer to her Gods, imploring them to help her. Gathering the last ounce of strength and courage she had left, Raji got up. She had to do something. She hated to wake the children but she couldn't carry them both. She shook Raghu awake; his eyelids were still damp with tears. He opened them with difficulty and drifted into sleep again.

'Raghu. Wake up! We need to go,' Raji whispered.

She shook him hard again.

This time, Raghu realised that he was not in the comfort of their home. He sat up weary-eyed, and looked at Neema, who was still sleeping.

'Where will we go, Ma?'

'Follow me,' Raji said as she picked up Neema and hurried through the forest, hoping not to cross paths with the asuras again.

It's only this night. Only this night.

As she walked, she felt better. The voices seemed to be fading away. She was not worried about wild animals as she knew most of them did not make unprovoked attacks. There were no man-eaters in the region, so that too, was not a worry. Suddenly, Raji bumped into someone big, with such force that she almost fell down. As she struggled to keep steady, a hand caught her, and pulled her up, preventing her from falling.

She turned to look at him. He was a tall man, with brooding black eyes and wavy hair. His face was not clearly visible in the dim moonlight. Nevertheless, it was a better sight than the terrible asuras.

'Help us, please, the asuras have raided our village. They are killing everyone, even children. I managed to escape with my children with great difficulty.'

The stranger stared at the trio for a while. 'Where are you from?' he asked.

The soothing voice made Raji relax. She pointed towards the forest border. 'Raigarh, just by the forest border.'

The stranger smiled. It was then Raji noticed the sigil on his armour. The silhouette of a dragon breathing fire, in shades of blue and red. The sigil was the same as the one she had spotted on the asura flags. Panicking, she took a few steps backwards. The next moment, the stranger moved, so fast she couldn't see him. He was next to her, face to face.

'Do you know who I am?'

Raji shivered with fear. She felt her legs quivering—she would collapse any moment. Her heart had never beaten faster, and there was only one thought in her mind.

My children. Please, not my children.

The muscular asura jerked a sleeping Neema from Raji's hands and he picked up Raghu by the latter's neck. Raji cried helplessly, joining her hands in entreaty, mutely pleading with the stranger to spare her children. Neema started crying, half asleep, while Raghu struggled to free his neck from the bulky asura's clutches, his small fingers trying to pry open the huge hands. In a quick movement, the asura stretched his arms, holding both children as if they were props on display. Then, in a swift move, he moved them back and dashed the heads of the children together.

Raji collapsed on her knees, howling hysterically, doubling over.

The asura threw the bodies of the children aside casually. He moved forward, grabbing Raji by the hair until she looked into his eyes. She saw a menacing redness in his eyes that chilled her to the bone. Strange black smoke seemed to be engulfing the asura.

'Your children await you, woman,' he hissed.

Slowly, he moved behind her as Raji wailed inconsolably, on her knees. Gripping her whole head with his left hand, the asura twisted her neck sideways, thoroughly. He continued twisting it beyond the point of bearable pain, so slowly that Raji could feel her bones cracking. Her wailing gave way to a long cry of pain. The mighty asura heard the bones of her neck crack, and pulled back his hand.

Raji's lifeless body swung and fell on the forest floor, next to her bloodied children. Her pain was over.

Kaalnemi had made his first kill.

10

The King's Arrogance

The footsteps in the hall, followed by other hurried steps behind them, indicated the arrival of Janak Singh. As Janak Singh entered, he cast a glance at Rana and acknowledged him with a movement. Bowing down to Guru Apasmitra, he took the central chair in the meeting chamber. He then looked at the girls, Urmila and Shreya, and then at Rana.

'How deep are they in it?' he asked.

'Top to bottom,' Rana quipped.

Shreya couldn't control her laughter and made a snorting sound as she tried to muffle it. Janak Singh gave her an angry glance. He then turned to Abhayajeet, the new commander of Avanti's army, the man who had succeeded Valari.

'What news do we have, Abhayajeet? Why call a meeting at this hour, in the middle of the night?'

'Apologies, my king. The news is urgent, and so I had to disturb everyone's sleep. There has been a sighting of asuras, in large formation, heading towards Ujjaini.'

Rana took a deep breath, flinging an I-told-you-so glance at Janak Singh. If only they had some more time. He wondered what Ashwatthama would find in Ayodhya, though it was doubtful he would be back before an attack.

Janak Singh did not seem perturbed. 'So?' he asked.

Abhayajeet was startled. 'Maharaja, we need to prepare our army. If the asuras attack the fort, the palace is in danger.'

'How many of them?'

'Over ten thousand, Maharaja.'

'Why should we worry then?' Janak Singh said curtly. 'We have a thirty-thousand strong army, the second largest in Aryavarta, ready to take on any enemy. Our weapons are sharp, and the will of our men is strong. What makes you afraid?'

Abhayajeet was quiet. He knew it was pointless arguing with the king.

Rana interrupted. 'My king, if the fort falls, the whole city of Ujjaini will be in danger.'

Janak Singh looked at Rana. He walked up to a small bookshelf and pulled out a map, putting it down with a thump on the table for everyone to see.

'The fort and palace are built on high ground, above sea level. It is much higher than the entire city of Ujjaini, which sprawls down the hill from the other side. As you know, any army that has to attack the fort will have to climb in full view, almost a mile from the front. To enter Ujjaini, the attackers would have to conquer the fort first. Anyone with basic knowledge of battle plans would know it is suicide to do so. Our archers and flame-throwers will take down the enemy in no time. For ten thousand of them, even five thousand soldiers of ours are enough. The enemy won't dare to cross the fort on either side, since the same fate will greet them on both sides. So, tell me now—what worries you?'

Janak Singh straightened up and looked squarely at everyone, crossing his arms.

'That they know this, and have planned for this already,' Urmila said calmly, focusing her gaze on the table.

Janak Singh looked at her for a moment, before registering what she said. He ran his fingers through his salt-and-pepper beard, looking at the map.

'If they already know what we'll do, why are they walking into the line of fire?' he challenged Urmila's opinion.

'Because that's not their plan,' Guru Apasmitra interrupted, looking into the king's eyes.

Janak Singh sat quietly with his hands folded and stared into space.

Rana leaned forward, placed both his hands on the table and looked at the king.

'My king, all we are saying is that we must not take this lightly. The asuras would not have planned this attack unless they had a strategy in place. Dandak is no fool to waste a tenth of his army on an attack he knows he cannot win.'

'I don't get it,' Janak Singh looked at Rana. 'Guru Apasmitra, Urmila and you have fought the asuras. They do not seem invincible. Why send them?'

Rana shook his head. 'I don't know, maybe they have a secret.'

'We are not going to be threatened by a bunch of amateur asuras,' Janak Singh announced. He paused, framing his next words. 'Umm…nevertheless, wars are often lost by carelessness. Abhayajeet, send scouts to find out their plan.'

'We already have, Maharaja. There was nothing we could find that could cause panic as of now. But that is precisely what worries me.'

Janak Singh thought for a few moments before speaking. 'I think then they are testing our mettle. They want to see our full strength and our weapons. Let them come. Abhayajeet, lay the traps on the road to the fort. Warn the civilians not to venture outside the fort area. Ask them to store essentials. Ensure there is no panic or rioting. And keep the archers and flame-throwers ready. Not a single asura should go back alive.'

'Yes, my king,' Abhayajeet bowed and prepared to leave.

'That's all for now. Hail Vishnu,' Janak Singh dismissed the meeting and went out of the room.

Abhayajeet followed him.

Rana looked at Guru Apasmitra. 'What do you think, Guruji?'

Guru Apasmitra frowned and shook his head. 'It's a decoy for sure but for what purpose?'

Rana looked at Urmila, who returned his expression with a matching one.

Unless they figured out what the asuras were planning, Avanti was doomed.

11

Fire and Death

Vikram sat up with a jerk as he heard a loud commotion outside. He had barely slipped into sleep when the voices became too loud to ignore. The night was still young but he could make out the flickering fire outside through the gaps in the door. The noise bordered on panicky shouts and cries, and was disturbing.

Shaking Manvita awake, Vikram leapt out of bed. He opened the door and scanned the surroundings. A horrifying scene was on display—many of the huts were on fire, and there were a bunch of riders on horseback, who were slaughtering the unprepared Kimpurushas with their arrows and swords. A few attackers were throwing torches on the thatched roofs and others were setting fire to the trees that hedged the settlement. The dark night sky was alight and sparks flew all around like millions of fireflies lighting up a forest.

Two riders spotted Vikram and pointed at him. He instinctively put his hand over his waist but his sword was missing. Fortunately, the two asuras were not within striking distance.

'Here,' Manvita picked up the blade from the headrest and tossed it to him.

Next moment, the asuras crashed into the hut, their horses breaking down the wall. They swung their weapon for the kill but Vikram ducked and plunged his sword into the nearest attacker, bringing him down. The second asura raised his sword and came dangerously close to Shrutika, hesitating a moment, then decided to bring the weapon down on her. Manvita shrieked and leapt over Shrutika, shielding her. Vikram dived towards the attacker, pulling him down from his horse. Manvita took Shrutika in her arms and huddled in a corner of the room.

Vikram punched the asura hard on his face, making him spit blood. He looked angrily at Vikram and punched back, his metal glove connecting squarely with Vikram's jaw. Vikram felt a couple of his teeth going down his throat, mixed with blood. He felt dizzy from the punch that had shattered his jaw.

The asura towered over him, raising his sword for the final blow. Vikram felt helpless, his head hurting from the heavy blow of the metallic glove. He raised his hands to block the attack but knew that it was useless. From a distance, he could hear Manvita's cries for help.

The next instant, Vikram felt a splash of blood on his face. He looked down at his torso—there was no wound. Raising his eyes, he saw that a sword had gone through the asura's stomach, felling him. A Kimpurusha stood right beside him, lifting the writhing asura in the air like a piece of meat on a stick, and tossing him aside. As Vikram spat out the blood in his mouth, a familiar face extended his hand to lift him up. Chief Druma's son, Shifa, covered in blood and grime, helped the Surparaka king up. He handed a cloth to Vikram to wipe his face.

'You hurt bad?'

Vikram shook his head, looking at Manvita, who was tightly hugging Shrutika and sobbing silently. Vikram felt the gap in his lower jaw with his tongue. Two of his lower side teeth had taken the blow. Ignoring the pain, he picked up his sword and walked out of his hut.

Several houses were on fire and numerous bodies of slain and injured Kimpurushas lay on the ground. Many of them had been grievously injured, with their legs cut off. The element of surprise had given the upper hand to the asuras. Some members of the warrior tribe were dousing the fire with water, while others were busy tending to the injured. The lifeless bodies of several asuras lay among the Kimpurushas. Vikram tried to count them, stopping after fifty. He saw the Chief instructing others to tend to the injured Kimpurushas.

Vikram rushed towards the nearest burning hut and started searching for survivors. Unable to escape, most of the inmates inside had burnt to death in their sleep. This was not a war but a massacre.

Hours later, as exhaustion set in, Vikram felt his stomach churn. Many Kimpurushas continued their wailing over the dead and the injured. After Surparaka, this was the second location where the asuras had targeted him and there had been massive damage. Death seemed to have latched on to him like an inseparable shadow. He felt miserable and walked back to his broken hut.

Manvita was standing by the entrance, looking equally exhausted. She had helped to clean many huts and erect temporary tents for the survivors. Tears streamed from her eyes as she saw some mothers wailing beside their children's bodies. The couple looked into each other's eyes, finding themselves at a loss for words.

Vikram walked wearily towards the hut and sat down, holding his head. Manvita sat by his side, her arm around him.

Vikram shook his head despairingly. 'So many dead. What do I do, Manvita? I will happily give up my life if they stop the killings.'

Manvita took a deep breath and brought her face close to his. 'They won't stop there. I can tell you that. The more power one has, the more one wants; there are no limits. Just look at the audacity of this attack. We have no option but to fight back. Our personal priorities have to take a backseat, Vikram.'

'I didn't think you would be telling me this,' Vikram said, surprised.

Manvita nodded as her teary eyes stared into the darkness.

'All this while, I had been afraid of losing Shrutika and you. But I see that all these soldiers who fight for us, their families are no different than ours. Why must I be selfish to prevent you from going to war? And I will come with you to the battlefield, no matter what the cost.'

Vikram's eyes widened. 'I hope it does not come to this as long as I am...'

He was interrupted by a tall Kimpurusha who entered the hut, with a few others following him.

Druma snorted, his expression a mix of anger and sorrow. 'Why, King Vikram? You bring death with you—so many dead. So many injured. Fire and blood all over.'

Vikram looked at the Chief in anguish. The Kimpurushas were innocent and he had dragged them to the brink of war.

'I am sorry, Chief Druma,' he said. 'I never intended for this to happen. I don't know how the asuras got wind of this location.'

Druma stared at Vikram, taking long, laboured breaths. He paused for a few moments as if waiting to arrive at a decision.

'I save my people, Vikramsena. Cannot put danger on them. Stay the night. Morning, you go.'

Vikram looked at Druma and then at Manvita, who nodded.

'I will, Chief,' he accepted wearily.

Druma nodded and turned to leave, instructing Shifa to arrange for a new hut for the guests for what remained of the night.

Vikram walked out of the hut and looked up at the sky. This night had been the darkest one of his life, and it did not seem to be over. Dawn still felt like a distant dream. And then their journey would continue.

When would this madness end?

12

Ayodhya

A sweating Ashwatthama alighted from his Yeti horse at the entrance of the broken palace gates of Ayodhya. The strong afternoon sun had not been kind to either the horse or the rider. He was not expecting any kind of welcome but he was taken aback by the derelict condition of the Ayodhya palace. A silent miasma hung over the place and the air smelt acrid as if it had hung there for years. The palace gate, where Lord Rama's grace had once allowed anyone to enter unhindered, today stood cold and forbidding.

Holding the reins of his horse, Ashwatthama pushed open the iron-gate, which creaked and gave way to the rare visitor. The palace complex was much larger than he had imagined. Once the epitome of the best reign in all of the country, Ayodhya had been magnificent in its days of glory. The name of Lord Rama had been enough to bring in scores of settlers. After their father's time, Luv and Kush had gone their separate ways, establishing their own kingdoms. Through the ages, the kingdom of Ayodhya had gone through massive changes under different kings, though none could bring back the glory of Lord Rama's reign.

The walk from the gate to the main palace building was a good quarter of a mile. Although tempted to remount his horse in the blazing sun, Ashwatthama wanted to walk through the vast compound. As he moved nearer to the main building, he could discern the outlines of the different areas.

The ruins were massive, redolent with decades of dust and decay. Spread over a colossal area, the palace exuded grandness despite being abandoned. Rumoured to be the largest palace ever built in Aryavarta, the fall of Ayodhya had been significant. Luv and Kush had established their own kingdoms. Luv had set up Sharavati in the Kosala region and Kush had created Kushavati in the Dakshin Kosala region. Kush was said to have returned later to Ayodhya, to defeat the Naga king Kumud and marry his sister Kumudvati. Their union had resulted in a son, Atithi. The lineage continued, and the last known descendant of the Ikshvaku dynasty, and the twenty-fifth generation scion of the lineage of Lord Rama, was Brihadbalam, who was killed by Abhimanyu during the Kurukshetra War. After Brihadbalam, Ayodhya had fallen into disrepair without a ruler, like many other kingdoms which had participated in the War.

The events that followed Sita's banishment by Lord Rama made it look like Ayodhya was cursed, never to rise to its former glory again. The locals called it Sita's curse, harking back to when the innocent queen was forced to prove her chastity. Despite coming out of the fire unscathed, her character was questioned by the citizens. Even a lone washerman questioning the queen's character was enough for Sita to be banished to the forest. The washerman's own wife had stayed outside his home for one night and he had refused to take her back. In a condemning tone, he had shouted, 'I am not Rama that I will take Sita back even after she spent ten months in Ravana's palace.'

This event had marked the downfall of Ayodhya's society. Ideally, the washerman should have been ostracised for daring to question the queen's character and for throwing his wife out of his house on a mere suspicion. Instead, nobody spoke against the washerman, and people watched on shamelessly as the drama unfolded. They stood mutely, watching the royal family crumble before their eyes. Nobody protested, in stark contrast to the time when they had vehemently objected to the decision Lord Rama took—to leave Ayodhya on exile. This time, they seemed to support the washerman with their silence.

It is tragic but people want to see their heroes fall. It makes them feel more human. They are better able to relate to their hero, knowing that he too is not infallible. And thus it happened in Ayodhya. Ultimately, to uphold the law of the land, Lord Rama banished Sita and stayed unhappy without her, for the rest of his life. Any city that treated the pure at heart so badly was fated to meet its doom. Ayodhya's doom began the day Lakshmana was sent to abandon Sita in the forest, without apprising the ill-fated queen of her fate. Ayodhya never saw happy days again. At one point, Lord Rama had even banished laughter in the kingdom, so unhappy had he become. Eventually and inevitably, Ayodhya had ended up a ghost town.

Ashwatthama looked around him and could make out the faint outline of the palace in the afternoon light. The sun was like a child, playing hide and seek with the clouds. There were large statues of warriors and damsels that shone in the golden gleam, some of them vandalised by miscreants, while others had fallen victim to the vagaries of the weather. The statues, each over a hundred-feet tall, adorned the sides of the palace walls, which were over twenty-feet high and had multiple entry and exit gates. In the middle of the complex, there was a large stretch dedicated to trees and plants, that now was derelict and bereft of the gurgling fountain and pool that had stood there.

Once, birds had freely sung here and the heady fragrance of flowers and fruits had scented the air. But all that was long gone. Now, dead trees stood on both sides of the stretch and the water had dried up long ago. Ashwatthama noticed the brown vines that had made their home on the outer periphery of the palace building. A few creatures scurried for cover as he walked on the grass that rose above his ankles, and he had to exert caution so as not to step on a sleeping reptile.

The palace was massive, built in white stone, some of which still retained its shine, despite its antiquity. The main door of the palace was a high wooden one reinforced with metal, one that would require some effort to open. The steps leading up to the door were partially broken but climbable. Ashwatthama decided against taking the horse inside the palace and left it to graze at the bottom of the steps.

'Rest here, Arya, while I go inside,' Ashwatthama said, patting his horse, before taking out the bag of grams and hay and some water. 'Here, have some of this. Holler if you need me. I think we both need some rest.'

The horse was happy to get some rest after travelling for more than a week. It gobbled up the food and then lay down; its Yeti masters had taught it to get its share of well-deserved sleep and preserve its strength. Weariness and extreme exhaustion could kill a horse, and it could drop dead instantly.

Ashwatthama had to exert himself to push the wooden dust-laden doors, which made a creaking sound as they opened slowly. He felt the cold whiff of stale air inside the courtyard. The pillars and walls were abundant with cobwebs, the spiders having a free run of the place. A thick layer of dust had settled on everything. The roof had been stripped of its gold by robbers or perhaps members of the royal household before they deserted the palace.

The hall was large, and the evening light filtered through the broken part of the roof, gilding the golden throne with a bright glow. Using a stick to remove the cobwebs out of the way, Ashwatthama walked through the long court with its broken pillars and idols on either side. He visualised the coronation of Lord Rama, after his victory over Ravana. This was the place where it had all happened—Lord Rama's birth, his exile by King Dasaratha and Queen Kaikeyi, Bharata's rebellion, Lord Rama's welcome after his return from exile, the grand coronation, Sita's banishment to the forest and Lord Rama's last days. These events were lost in the mists of time, similar to the history of the Pandavas and the Kauravas. Tretayuga had been no less eventful than Dwaparayuga. The warriors of those ages had become legends, a part of Aryavarta's history, those who had been instrumental in shaping the future of the mighty nation.

Ashwatthama sighed. He moved towards the golden throne, his sandals clinking on the broken stone floor. The throne was huge, with chairs for ministers near it. Surprisingly, the gold in the throne were still intact. There were marks on the edges of the throne's legs, which indicated that failed attempts had been made to break them for the gold. There were scratches on the armrests and the seat too but it seemed that the gold had been fused with a process that made it impossible to remove. Ashwatthama moved his hands over the throne, marking the patina of dust with his fingers. He recalled the time when they had found the bow at Kanjiroba peak, after crossing the ice bridge. It had only been possible due to the invocation of Lord Rama's

name. Ashwatthama wished he had known more about this
valiant son of Dasharatha. Only the sages in Dwaparayuga
knew the complete story of Lord Rama and they were gone,
all except Sage Markandeya.

The sage had related Lord Rama's story to Yudhisthira,
during the Pandavas' initial days in exile. It had happened
on an eventful day when Draupadi was resting in the forest
and the Pandavas had been out hunting. Jayadratha had
kidnapped Draupadi when the latter rebutted his advances.
The harried Pandavas had chased down and defeated
Jayadratha, sparing his life only because he was the husband
of the sole Kaurava daughter, Dusshala. Bheema had spared
Jayadratha but only after tonsuring half his head and blacking
his face, a humiliation Jayadratha did not forget. He later
avenged it by having Abhimanyu killed.

After the incident, Yudhisthira had lamented his fate to
Sage Markandeya, ruing that he was the unluckiest warrior
ever. It was at this time that the sage had narrated Lord
Rama's story, motivating him to face the tough phase of his
life as Lord Rama had done. Ashwatthama recalled how
Dronacharya had asked him to learn as much about the
Vedas as about weapons but all he had wanted to learn was
to be one of the most powerful warriors in the land. He
regretted that now, wishing he had spent more time learning
about the previous avatars of Vishnu, wishing there was
someone who could have told him why the name of Lord
Rama was so powerful that it could make even a stone glow.

Ashwatthama moved around the hall, mesmerised by the
faded grandeur, almost forgetting the purpose of his visit.
He walked slowly, feeling the throne and the massive pillars,
once again imagining the coronation of Lord Rama. It must
have been a magnificent sight, seeing thousands of vanaras
and even the Gods, bearing witness to the grand ceremony.

He wondered if there would ever be a greater archer than Lord Rama. The seventh avatar of Vishnu was the model for how a man should be in this worldly life, putting all else above his interest. For some reason, Ashwatthama was obsessed by Lord Rama and overcome with eagerness to know more about him. For now, he had forgotten all about his original purpose in coming to Ayodhya.

Subconsciously reminded of that moment on Himavant when he had accidentally discovered the ice bridge after uttering Lord Rama's name, Ashwatthama whispered, 'Rama.'

And then, suddenly, a punch on his gut threw him on the concrete wall, almost halfway up towards the roof. The wall, already in shambles, immediately lost a few more bricks. The last rays of sunlight poured in through the newly created fissure in the wall, and lit Ashwatthama's back as he fell hard on the ground, to the sound of his bones cracking.

No ordinary human could have landed such a punch.

13

Kaalnemi

The dim light from the torches effectively lit up the small room. The makeshift wooden chamber smelt of fresh bamboo. It was an upgrade from cloth tents, and the figure sitting inside stared intently out of the window, at the construction activity in the distance. A group of asuras was busy slashing down trees at an incredible speed and large elephants were dutifully moving them to a site close by, where the foundations of what seemed like a large palace were being laid.

Madhumanta, the lost capital city of Dandakaranya, was being rebuilt.

A large area had been earmarked for the palace and raw material was piled up in one corner. The figure in the room had his makeshift chamber built three floors above the ground but the raw material seemed to tower above that. Moments later, another figure, almost identical in build to the one inside, appeared at the door.

'And how may I serve the asura king, Dandak?' the visitor said, bowing.

'Kaalnemi,' Dandak turned and gestured to the visitor to enter.

Kaalnemi seated himself comfortably with all the assurance of being an asura king himself. In the dim light, it was hard to figure out the difference between the two asuras.

Dandak sat opposite Kaalnemi, staring at him for a while, before speaking.

'As you know, the humans are putting up fierce resistance to asura supremacy over the land. Their greed for rule is not allowing us to co-exist with them. They see us as the lower race, despicable, hateful and uncivilised,' Dandak said.

His voice grew louder as he continued, waving his hands about angrily. 'What they do not know is that we are the rightful owners of this land. The devas had tricked us, otherwise asuras would be the dominant race on earth.'

Kaalnemi nodded.

Dandak continued, 'The bad news is that there is a celestial among them—Ashwatthama.'

Kaalnemi nodded again, no expression on his face. Nothing seemed too big a challenge for him.

'He finished off both Raktavija and Vidyut. He and I are destined to perhaps meet. But before that, I want you to crush his soul,' Dandak said.

'And how do you propose I do that?'

Dandak got up from his seat. He walked towards the ledge.

'He has made a few friends after he lost everything in the Great War, over a hundred years ago,' Dandak said. 'His curse seems to have been revoked by the Gods…or his dead father, perhaps. Kill his friends and their families. Surparaka is conquered. Now, take an army and rout Avanti. After that, we will march towards Hastinapur.'

'Yes, my Lord.'

'Kill anyone who comes in the way. I will finish Ashwatthama myself.'

Kaalnemi nodded.

'Where would you be going next?'

'You know where, Kaalnemi. The place where no mortal can ever go. The last place I went to before Shukracharya's curse hit us.'

14

The Other Immortal

The impact of the punch rattled Ashwatthama. No mortal could have survived that blow. For a few moments, he lay on the ground writhing in pain, without even being able to see his attacker. His hands and back hurt from the fall, and he felt as if he would keel over from the pain in his abdomen. Minutes later, he moved, thinking it wise to see who his tormentor was and to dodge the next attack if it was on the way, although it would have happened by now if it had to. He used his hands to prop himself up on his knees and looked up at his attacker.

A tall monkey stood before him.

'Hanuman?' Ashwatthama arched his eyebrows in disbelief.

The majestic figure stood expressionless, looking intently at him.

'Why...why are you here?' Ashwatthama asked, wincing as he spoke.

'You expressed an intense desire to know about Lord Rama. To me, there cannot be greater joy than narrating his stories. Anyway, a visit to this place was long overdue and so I decided to come,' Hanuman said calmly, walking around, surveying the dilapidated condition of the palace interior.

'What...' Ashwatthama lowered his face, still trying to absorb the pain of the punch. His torso had turned red, clearly showing the effect of his broken ribs.

'Why did you punch me?' he asked.

'Because you lost the Kodanda,' Hanuman replied calmly.

Hanuman came closer and Ashwatthama stared at him, still gasping for breath, each inhalation causing intense pain as his broken ribs moved. It seemed for a moment that the messenger was ready to land another blow on Ashwatthama but instead, Hanuman offered his hand for support. Ashwatthama held it and got back on his feet. Hanuman towered over him and Hanuman's face shone with an immaculate radiance. Dronacharya's son bowed in reverence to him.

Hanuman looked around the courtyard. This had been his home once. It was here that he had been blessed by Lord Rama to be close to the Lord forever; here, Devi Sita had given him the necklace that Lord Rama had once gifted her and asked her to give it to her favourite person. This was the place where he had served his God.

Now it lay in ruins, bereft of the presence of Lord Rama, and Hanuman felt a hollowness in his chest as so many memories surfaced. He had been avoiding paying a visit to this place for this precise reason—to steer clear of these memories. Hanuman composed himself and looked at Ashwatthama, who was clearly in pain. He gestured at Ashwatthama to head outside. Ashwatthama's abdomen hurt badly but he didn't utter a word.

'How did you know I was here?' Ashwatthama asked in a muffled voice as he wobbled along, with Hanuman lending him his shoulder to lean on.

'I am a messenger, Ashwatthama. I am present wherever my Lord's name is taken with devotion. You too are Shiva incarnate and I am obliged to help you. True Shiva devotees are hard to come by. I wanted to see you in person.'

Ashwatthama was stumped but equally curious. Why would Hanuman personally visit him to narrate Lord Rama's story? Something did not add up.

As they walked past the palace door, Ashwatthama could see Arya resting peacefully on the grass. The sun had taken leave for the day and moonlight bathed the palace compound; the stone warriors and damsels along the route to the palace gate glittered silver. Beyond that, it was pitch dark, not a soul in sight.

Hanuman motioned for Ashwatthama to sit by his side on the stairs outside the palace door but the latter asked him to wait for a moment. He went down the steps to find his bundle, which he had left next to Arya. He brought up some fruits and water for Hanuman, who graciously accepted them. Ashwatthama then poured some water over himself to clean himself of all the sweat and dirt, and then, he washed Hanuman's feet. He wiped the stairs free of dust and stones, gesturing at Hanuman to sit down. After this, Ashwatthama took a seat a step below Hanuman.

They sat silently for a few moments, Hanuman still lost in his memories and Ashwatthama trying to contain his pain. After he had heard about both Arjuna and Bheema meeting Hanuman in the forest during their exile, he had had an intense desire to meet the dutiful devotee of Rama. But it had not come to pass. Until now.

'You should not have taken Lord Rama's bow, Ashwatthama. It was not meant to be lost to the asuras,' Hanuman said, looking at the dark horizon.

Ashwatthama remained quiet. He felt his ears go red in embarrassment and shame. Vikram had persuaded him to go along on the journey and while on the path, it had seemed that events were moving according to providence, even the loss of the bow. However, Hanuman's words jolted him back to reality. What was it that he had not understood?

'I...I never meant to disrespect Lord Rama,' he said.

Hanuman sighed and shook his head. 'Lord Rama cannot be disrespected by anyone, Ashwatthama. Mortals think that they can love or hate God, or respect or disrespect Him. But the Gods are beyond all that. You talk profoundly of karma and yet do not seem to rise beyond it.'

A confused Ashwatthama looked blankly at Hanuman. The heat of summer had given way to the cold breeze of early evening, which ruffled Hanuman's fur-like hair.

Now it was Ashwatthama who spoke calmly, 'It was Lord Rama's name that led us to the bow. I have never heard much of him, except that his name removes all miseries. Is that true?'

Hanuman nodded as if he had been waiting for that question. He loved singing the praises of his Lord. 'Listen to the origin of Lord Rama's name, Ashwatthama. But as you listen, make sure all your questions are answered, for I will not repeat anything. So ask questions if you are curious.'

Ashwatthama nodded, ready to take in the divine knowledge.

'Rama's name is the purest in the world. Sage Vasishtha, who was invited by King Dasharatha to Ayodhya to name the king's four children born, suggested it. The wise sage decided to name the eldest son Rama.

'Sage Vashistha said:

रमन्तेसर्वेजनाःगुणैःअस्मिन्इतिरामः

(In whom all people take delight for his virtuousness, thus he is Rama.)

'The name Rama is a combination of two words: Ra, which is the seed in Om Namo Narayana, and Ma, which is the seed in Om Namaha Shivaya. The combination of these two seeds form the word Rama. And so, taking the name of Rama is equivalent to invoking the name of Vishnu and Shiva, the Preserver and the Destroyer. It is also the reason why Lord Rama is so dear to Lord Shiva; gaining the devotion of one is not possible without gaining the devotion of the other.'

Ashwatthama queried, 'But I thought Rama was an incarnation of Vishnu, and Sita an incarnation of Lakshmi.'

Hanuman nodded as he continued, 'Rama was the living avatar of Vishnu. When Vishnu decided to appear as Rama in the human avatar, Lakshmi wanted to accompany him. And so, Devi Sita was found at the edge of the golden plough, the daughter of the earth in King Janak's backyard, when the latter was ploughing his garden during a terrible famine. Sita means the one found in a furrow. In each avatar of Vishnu, Lakshmi accompanies him, unable to bear the separation. Even in his ferocious Narasimha avatar, Lakshmi appears as a tribal woman to bring him back to his original form.

अहंनारायनीनामसासत्तावैष्णवीपरा

(I am indeed Narayani, Lakshmi, the Supreme Essence of Vishnu.)

'Do not ever consider Lakshmi to be any less than Vishnu. She is as powerful, and represents the female form of Vishnu. Without Lakshmi, Vishnu cannot exist and without Vishnu, Lakshmi cannot exist. They are bound together by their souls. If Lakshmi is lost, Vishnu will search the entire universe for her.

'And so, Lakshmi took birth in the form of Sita, representing *prakriti* or nature itself. She was the combination of the primary elements of nature: *prithvi, jal, agni, vaayu* and *aakaasha* (earth, water, fire, wind, sky). Her purpose on earth was to appear for the elimination of Ravana. Sita was pure Brahman, the highest singular representation of all that is divine. Or else, she would not have made it out of the pyre alive after Ravana was killed and Lord Rama put her through an *agni-pariksha* (trial by fire).

'The reason Sita was found in that field, inside the furrow as a baby, was due to an earlier vow of Lakshmi's. In a previous incarnation, Lakshmi was born as Vedavati, the daughter of Sage Kusadhvaj. The sage wanted to give Vedavati in marriage to Vishnu but this remained an unfulfilled desire. So, Vedavati started a rigorous penance to fulfill her father's wish. As her penance neared its culmination, tragedy struck. Ravana, who was passing by in the sky above, saw Vedavati and was filled with lust. As he had done with many women before, he swooped down and molested her.

'Filled with rage, Vedavati cursed Ravana that she would be reincarnated and become the cause of his destruction. She also declared that if Ravana ever touched a woman against the latter's wishes again, his head would explode. With that, Vedavati created a yogic fire and immolated herself. This curse, given by an earlier incarnation of Lakshmi, was a device to save herself from Ravana's lust in another birth when she would be born as the venerable Sita.'

Ashwatthama felt the strings of his heart being tugged at. Never had he paid such rapt attention to something with such reverence. Hanuman's voice wove magic as the Lord's principal devotee narrated the story of one of the greatest avatars of Vishnu. There had been tales of how even rocks melted when Hanuman narrated stories of Lord Rama's glory. Even Arya looked intently at the stranger whose voice mesmerised the noble beast.

Hanuman continued, 'Janak fostered her as his soul-born daughter and as she reached marriageable age, Mithila's king ordained that courage would be the only virtue for her husband. At that time, the bridegroom's family would give property, money or bounty to the bride's family in exchange for a worthy bride. Janak wanted only valour for Sita. Hence, he kept the condition that anyone who would be able to lift and string the Pinaka, the bow of Shiva, would be worthy of Sita at the swayamvar.'

Ashwatthama interrupted, wishing to know more about the bow. His journey too, had begun with a bow.

'But why did King Janaka choose the Pinaka and not some other weapon?' he asked.

Hanuman nodded, thinking back wistfully. 'The Pinaka was no ordinary bow. It was the bow created by the mighty architect Vishwakarma, the same one that Shiva used to fire his mightiest arrow Pashupatastra, to destroy the iron, silver and gold fort city of Tripura.

'Hear the story about this magnificent weapon, Ashwatthama. Once, Lord Brahma offered a boon to three demon brothers, Vidyunmali, Tarakaksha and Viryavana, who wanted immortality. That would have gone against the laws of nature, so Brahma granted that the three brothers would have three forts made of iron, silver and gold on earth, in the sky and in heaven, respectively. These three forts were floating cities in themselves, and constantly moving. The demons also asked that anyone who wanted to kill them would have to destroy the forts at one go with a single arrow. Brahma agreed. However, he twisted the boon so that once in every thousand years, the forts would be aligned in a single line for a split second.

'Once the demons knew that they were almost invincible, their atrocities increased. Consequently, Shiva was approached to kill the demons. With the mighty Pinaka, Shiva used the Pashupatastra and fired the arrow at the three forts in the very fraction of the second they were aligned in a single line. So, the Pinaka was no ordinary bow, Ashwatthama. A bow of the Gods, transported on a wheeled casket-cart with eight wheels, and drawn by hundreds of bulls and robust people.

'Coming to your question about why Janak chose the bow, it had more to do with an incident in Devi Sita's childhood. Once, when Devi Sita was a child, she was playing with a few other girls, and their flower ball rolled under a cart. None of the other girls dared to touch the cart since it was a revered one but Devi Sita pushed it with her left hand as easily as pushing a baby's cradle, and retrieved the ball. It was no ordinary feat as the Pinaka was so heavy that not even ten men with all their strength could move it an inch.

'Many opine that Lord Rama had to exert some effort in stringing the bow. But that is not true. The weapons in that era listened to their bearers. As soon as he picked up the bow, it became soft as a stick and bent however he wished it to. Moreover, Lord Rama was ambidextrous, and with the training given by Vishwamitra, his dexterity had multiplied. One must know that the bow broke at the handgrip, which would tell you how hard Lord Rama must have held it while stringing it. At the very instant the divine bow broke in two, a deafening "Om" rattled the palace, equivalent to the sound of a thousand thunderbolts rumbling at one go.'

Ashwatthama listened with rapt attention to Hanuman's story of the swayamvar. Not many knew the detailed story of Lord Rama's life.

He looked up at Hanuman and asked, 'And that act of valour sealed the union of Lord Rama and Devi Sita?'

'Yes, and so the marriage of the four princes of King Dasaratha was solemnised with four princesses at the same time. Rama and Lakshmana married two daughters of Janak, Devi Sita and Urmila, respectively. Bharata and Shatrughana married Maandavi and Shrutakiirti, the two daughters of Janak's brother Kushadhvaja, King of Sankashya. If Lord Rama was an incarnation of Vishnu, Lakshmana was an incarnation of Sheshnaag and Bharata and Shatrughana were incarnations of the conch shell and disc that Vishnu holds in the two upper hands. The four brothers were inseparable and had immense love for one another.'

Hanuman then told him about the wedding of Rama and Sita in detail, and how the Gods had blessed the divine couple.

He continued the narration in his magical voice, 'After the marriage, when the party was returning to Ayodhya, Parashurama appeared, keen to duel with Lord Rama in retaliation for breaking the divine Pinaka.'

Ashwatthama did not understand the connection between Parashurama and the bow. Looking up at Hanuman, whose face shone in the moonlight, he asked, 'Why was the bow so important to Parashurama?'

Hanuman spoke slowly, as if he could see the incidents before his eyes, 'Ashwatthama, this is the story of the origin of the Pinaka bow. No greater powers than Brahma and Vishwakarma had created the bow. It is not made of any ordinary metal but from Sage Dadichi's bones, and is unbreakable by any weapon in war.

'Once, a Brahmin named Vritra turned to violence and adharma, defeating and killing even the demigods. Known as Vritrasur, he threw Indra out of heaven as he possessed a boon that he could not be killed by any weapon created up until that time, and that no weapon made of wood or metal could harm him. Indra went to Lord Vishnu for help, and Lord Vishnu said that only a weapon made of the bones of a pious sage, who had given it out of his free will, would work.

'Indra, along with other demigods, went to Naimisharanya to Sage Dadichi's ashram. Sage Dadichi willingly agreed to sacrifice his bones but he wanted to make a pilgrimage to all the holy rivers before giving up his mortal body. To save on the time that the sage would take to visit all the holy places, Indra brought together the waters of all the holy rivers and thirty-five million water bodies on earth to Naimisharanya, and Sage Dadichi's desire was fulfilled. After this, the sage gave up his body. Indra took the sage's bones to Brahma, where the latter, along with Vishwakarma, forged powerful weapons such as Vajrayuddha, Indra's thunderbolt, and three exceptional bows, the Saranga, Pinaka and Gandiva.

'Says Parashurama:

श्रुत्वातुधनुषोभेदम्ततोअहम्द्रुतमूआगतः ।।
ततूएवम्वैष्णवम्रामपितृपैतामहम्महत् ।
क्षत्रधर्मम्पुरस्कृत्यगृह्णीष्वधनुरुत्तमम् ।।

(Then, after hearing about the breakage of Shiva's longbow, I have promptly come here. O, Rama! Wield this supernatural and superlative longbow of Vishnu, which is passed on to me from my forefathers and my father. Keep your fealty to Kshatriyahood in mind, and wield this as you have wielded Shiva's longbow.)

'Sage Agastya, too, praised the glory of Pinaka:

इदम्दिव्यम्महत्वाचापम्हेमवज्रविभूषितम् ।
वैष्णवम्पुरुषव्याघ्रनिर्मितम्विश्वकर्मणा

अनेनधनुषारामहत्वासंख्येमहासुरान् ।
आजहारश्रियम्दीप्ताम्पुराविष्णुर्दिवओकसाम्

(This sacred bow that is decorated with gold and diamonds is crafted by the divine architect Vishvakarma and pertains to Vishnu. By this bow, O Rama, once Vishnu eliminated horrible demons in war and brought back radiant prosperity to the celestials.)

'The bow of Lord Rama, with which he killed Ravana, was the Saranga bow of Lord Vishnu. Lord Vishnu gave it to Sage Richika, who passed it on to his son Jamadagni. The latter, before he died, gave the bow to his valorous son, Parashurama. It was this bow that Lord Parashurama passed on to Lord Rama. Its possessor is invincible, and it is more powerful than the Pinaka. Like the Pinaka, this bow too is indestructible by any weapon or mortal.'

Ashwatthama listened carefully as Hanuman continued relating the story of the bow. He did not know why Lord Rama used the Kodanda when he had the more powerful Saranga bow, the most indestructible one. He wanted to ask Hanuman but decided not to interrupt him.

Hanuman continued the story of the Saranga bow.

'Parashurama gifted this bow to Lord Rama when the latter was returning to Ayodhya along with his family, shortly after the marriage ceremony. At that time, Parashurama had realised the divinity of Lord Rama. But you must not take the gifting of this longbow by Parashurama to Lord Rama as the mere transfer of a divine weapon. It was, in fact, the moment that Vishnu transferred his aura, his divinity, from his sixth avatar to his seventh.

'And so, in that visit to Mithila, Lord Rama received the two elements that became the source of Ravana's doom. King Janaka gave Sita, the ultimate cause of Ravana's destruction, and Parashurama gave the tool with which to kill Ravana—the indestructible Saranga bow.'

'But I thought the Lord had used the Kodanda to kill Ravana? And...I lost it and it was broken,' Ashwatthama confessed, lowering his gaze.

Hanuman took a deep breath as a cold breeze blew over them. 'Ashwatthama, you do not grasp what I am trying to convey. The indestructible Saranga is also known as the Kodanda.'

15

March of the Asuras

'They are just forty miles away! Accurate information from two different sources,' a messenger told Abhayajeet breathlessly.

'How many?'

'Over ten thousand. They are rampaging and looting all the villages along the way, leaving no man or child alive. The women they are…they are…'

'What?' Abhayajeet snapped.

'They are raping them and hanging them on the trees thereafter.'

Abhayajeet went silent. He had known the way of asuras, having heard stories from his ancestors. So much for those who had any doubts about what Dandak's reign would foster!

'Go now, and send word to the soldiers to prepare for battle. Recall any soldier who might have gone on leave. Send word to start preparing the flame-throwers and placing the weapons at the fort's edge. Sound the emergency bugle for the soldiers.'

'Yes, Senapati.'

'Wake up Bhrideshwar. Tell him I have summoned him immediately.'

~

A little later, a tall bearded man entered the room and stood towering over Abhayajeet.

'You called, Senapati. Are we going to war finally?' Bhrideshwar chuckled, rubbing his hands and yawning at the same time. He looked around for something to drink but found nothing.

'There is no need to get excited about this, I have to go and update the king immediately. Before that, I want you to head to the armoury to oversee preparations,' Abhayajeet said, pulling out a map of the fort and laying it on the table for both of them to peruse. 'The enemy is about forty miles away. That way, they will be here within three days. The messenger reported a count of ten thousand and over.'

'That's a big number to be coming in one go,' Bhrideshwar yawned again, his hands folded.

'Yes,' Abhayajeet answered. 'But, that's not unusual. Asuras are known to attack in large numbers. The detail we need to pay close attention to is whether they have any special weapons or armour that will make it hard to kill them. Otherwise, our archers and flame-throwers should be able to handle almost everything.'

'They will be attacking from a mile out in the open, that too at night. How do they expect to win?' Bhrideshwar scratched his head, frowning.

'I don't know. Asuras are brutal but not stupid. That's why I am concerned if they are bringing something that will give them an edge.'

'As long as the fort wall is safe, nothing can harm the city. Not a single asura can enter through the fort walls. What is worrying you, Senapati?'

'You are speaking like our king, and that's what is worrisome. Do not take the enemy for granted. Think, why would an army of ten thousand attack an army of thirty thousand, that too from a disadvantageous position?'

'Maybe they are stupid?' Bhrideshwar replied casually.

Abhayajeet glared at him and said, 'Asuras are brutal and short-sighted but their commanders have shown themselves to be strategists. Look at Ravana, how skillfully he fought the war with Rama, even though he lost. He exhausted all other options before appearing on the battlefield. Also, there is word about Kaalnemi leading this attack.'

Bhrideshwar shifted uncomfortably, 'I have heard of him. He is being groomed by Dandak directly. Unfortunately, we know so little about Rasatala that we are in the dark about Kaalnemi.'

'Now go and get everyone ready for battle. It's early morning. We should get all the equipment and weaponry to the fort by tomorrow evening.' Abhayajeet busied himself with his map again.

Bhrideshwar bowed and exited the room, feeling more nervous than he had been when he entered. This, of course, was due to the talk about Kaalnemi he had just heard.

~

The soldiers lined up on the fort wall, over a hundred feet above the ground. The fort had three levels of defence; the lowest level was the drawbridge, the entrance gate over the twenty-feet-wide moat, and the front wall which comprised multiple bastions. It was where the cavalry was stationed. The middle level was about a hundred feet above the ground, designed primarily for the reserve army and flame-throwers. There were large reserves of barrels kept at this level, along with stoves used to heat the barrels which contained a gelatinous tar.

The tar was a black, sticky substance, prepared by covering burning wood with dry soil to completely cut off air. This lack of air prevented the tar from burning completely and melted it; it was then drained through a small opening and collected in large barrels. Heated and poured over the enemy, it was the worst way to kill them.

The top level of the fort was the archer's zone, the best vantage point with a good range for the arrows. This was where the king stood and oversaw the battle. The view below was breathtaking, had it not been a presage for the horror that was to follow. Thousands of asura soldiers carrying torches, swords, maces and spears, had lined up and were shouting menacingly. Their armour emitted a diffused golden light, although that could be the reflection from the torches.

Abhayajeet stood next to Janak Singh and Rana, looking through a view-glass. He turned it around to scan the horizons on either side.

'Is it me or can someone else see their armour glowing?' he commented, handing over the view-glass to Rana.

'I can see that; how strange!' Rana muttered.

Shreya replied, 'It's asura armour, designed way back during the Tretayuga. It is stronger at night, drawing its power from darkness. It becomes weaker by day. However, at night, it can withstand strong attacks from arrows, spears and maces. No one today possesses the skill to design such armour.'

Rana gazed at her with raised brows and narrowed his eyes. 'How do you know...uh, forget it. Can it be pierced?'

'This is not traditional armour. It will keep becoming stronger as the night progresses. Aim for their heads, necks and legs, wherever they are uncovered. That would be the best approach,' Shreya said, handing over her view-glass to Urmila.

'Heads, necks and legs it is, then,' Rana repeated. 'Spread the word through the army, Abhayajeet; the soldiers must know.'

Abhayajeet summoned a few soldiers standing near him and dispatched them to different areas in the fort with the news.

'I don't see any mammoths or weapons worth mentioning that should be a cause of worry,' Urmila said as she looked at the asura army.

'And that worries me,' Shreya admitted. 'It's easy to fight when you know what you are up against.'

Clad in metallic armour, the women looked as feisty as a pride of hungry lionesses. Rana had persuaded Janak Singh to let Shreya be in charge of the Kshatriyanis, a group of five hundred women soldiers selected and trained by Valari, the first of its kind in all of Aryavarta. Had Valari been alive, he would have led the women into battle. But today, Shreya had a big task on her hand. Not just to lead the Kshatriyanis but also to ensure their safety. This made her nervous.

Nearby, Janak Singh gauged the Avanti army and his chest swelled with pride. 'The fort is impenetrable. Let them try as much as they want. Kill them. Leave no survivors,' he ordered haughtily.

Close to them, a few soldiers were rolling metal barrels of half-burnt wooden logs to the fire pits set up at designated spots along the edges of the fort. The barrels were hoisted on a wooden mount, where they were heated to melt the tar which would then be poured over the enemy below.

'Brutal!' Urmila shuddered, looking at the barrels.

'Wars always are, child!' Janak Singh replied curtly.

'I don't see their leader. Why is that?' Shreya wondered aloud.

Abhayajeet scanned the enemy camp.

'We had word that Kaalnemi was coming here for this attack. But he has not revealed himself yet,' he said.

'Maybe he has changed his mind,' Janak Singh said, arrogantly.

Rana chose to not speak, instead focusing his thoughts on how to inflict maximum damage on the enemy troops. He had witnessed the ambush near the Charmanvati River. He had seen it again, underwater at Dwarka. Both times, it had been foiled because of Ashwatthama's presence. But today, Dronacharya's son was far away from Avanti, looking for answers. Rana realised that Ashwatthama had been the game-changer in both battles. He recalled Vikram's words that this demon was no ordinary one; they were facing a supernatural being. And to counter that, they needed a divine entity.

Rana pulled out his sword from the sheath as the asuras drew closer to the fort. He wondered if Ashwatthama had got hold of something that would help them.

16

Providence

Ashwatthama was stunned. He couldn't put the pieces of the puzzle together. What had happened at Dwarka underwater, then? How could Vidyut destroy a celestial bow? Did he even have the power to do so? Was it all some trickery by Dandak?

Ashwatthama hurriedly rummaged through his bundle and took out a piece of the broken bow, which he had picked up after Vidyut had broken it. He had been carrying it with him, wrapped in his clothes, and now he held it out to Hanuman who picked it up curiously, then, threw it on the grass. Ashwatthama gasped.

The Kodanda was still out there.

Hanuman did not keep anything in which he did not see his Lord Rama. A surge of excitement went through Ashwatthama. If the bow was unbroken, it meant there was a chance of recovering it. He decided to hold on to the thought and focus on Lord Rama's story still being narrated by Hanuman as he knew that he would never get this kind of opportunity again.

Hanuman continued with the story of Lord Rama, Sita and Lakshmana, describing their exile and how they had reached Chitrakoot, from where Ravana had kidnapped Sita after the Surpanakha episode. And then, Hanuman told him the story of his meeting Lord Rama.

'After Lord Rama, Lakshmana and I got to know each other; we rejoiced in our bond. I took them to Sugriva, who asked for Lord Rama's help to kill Bali.'

'But you could have killed Bali, couldn't you? Why did it need to be done by Lord Rama?' Ashwatthama asked curiously, the questions coming to him as fast as Hanuman was telling the tale.

Hanuman nodded in agreement. 'My powers were indeed greater than Bali's. But at that time, I had no recollection of them. For being mischievous during my childhood, I was cursed by a sage to forget them. Jambavana the Immortal, the King of Rikshas, made me realise that during the search for Sita. The curse could only have been revoked by my being of service to Lord Rama.'

Ashwatthama sat in a state of reverence for Hanuman, appreciating the revelations coming his way. Like a devoted student, he asked, 'If Vishnu was so powerful, why did he make the task so tough for Lord Rama? Why could he not have made Lord Rama all-knowing, and lead him directly to Lanka?'

'Ashwatthama, there is a cosmic order for things to happen. If the Lord himself does everything, what would his devotees do? On the path to killing Ravana, the Lord gave many devotees the chance to serve and redeem themselves. The karmic cycle leaves many of us in the trap of sin, and God lays down the path for us to achieve salvation. It helps the world become a better place.

'Remember Ashwatthama, there are two powerful forces in the cosmos—good and evil. Evil is as powerful as good. The Gods support the good and the demons support the evil. The latter draw their power from the higher evil realms, which have similar power to the Gods. This constant fight between good and evil is not simple, and both plant their soldiers on every path of life. So, God has to plan his moves, so that when his task is executed, it creates widespread goodness and destroys evil.

'And so, Lord Rama had to make the arduous journey to find Sita. Along the way, he eliminated innumerable rakshasas, demons and evil forces. If he had eliminated Ravana straight away, those evil ones would still have existed, and many innocents would have suffered. So the task of Lord Rama and Lord Krishna was to ensure that they could root out maximum evil from earth in their human avatars.

'Consider this: even Bali said this to Lord Rama after he was wounded by a fatal arrow fired by Lord Rama—Bali could have single-handedly brought Sita to Rama. But that was a misconception on Bali's part. If Bali had fought with Ravana, despite his boon of absorbing half the strength of his opponent, due to the power of the pendant given to him by his father Indra, it is not clear what the result would have been, since Bali would have had to fight Indrajit and Kumbhkarna in an all-out celestial war. If Bali had indeed defeated Ravana and brought Devi Sita to Lord Rama, it would have been a blot on Lord Rama's name. On the other hand, if Ravana had offered a truce to Bali and taken him as an ally, then decided to attack Lord Rama, Lakshmana and Sugreeva, the entire monkey army would have joined hands with Ravana's army, thereby making rescuing Devi Sita a far more difficult task. Moreover, Lord Rama had given his word to Sugreeva that he would rescue the latter's wife Ruma from Bali.

'The Prince of Ayodhya could not have gone back on his word. Bali had committed an injustice by forcibly taking Sugreeva's wife, and trying to kill Sugreeva. He had been following Sugreeva, trying to kill him wherever the latter went. Ultimately, Sugreeva had to take refuge in the Rishyamukha Mountain, which was the only place that Bali could not reach, because of a curse by Sage Matanga—Bali would turn to stone if he ever stepped on Rishyamukha. However, before the Vanara king died, Lord Rama granted a boon to Bali—as he had been killed by Lord Rama, he would achieve salvation.'

Ashwatthama asked, 'How did the Gods bring this to a conclusion? Ravana was thousands of miles away from Ayodhya.'

'Ashwatthama, look at the beauty of the Lord's creation. Starting from the birth of Lord Rama to his time in exile, everything was preordained to get him to kill Ravana. Lord Rama was an avatar, the one sent to do something no one else could do. Ravana, the Rakshasa king, had become so immensely powerful that even the Gods could not kill him. He was merciless towards the sages and killed them all. Ravana's misdeeds are too many to be recounted briefly.

'Lord Rama's banishment was a ploy to get him to go towards Ravana. If you trace the path of Lord Rama's journey, it took him from Ayodhya to Chitrakoot. Lord Rama could have stayed right outside Ayodhya and served out his exile. But providence pushed him towards Ravana. Each sage he went to charted him a path, which took him one step closer to Lanka.

'The path of Lord Rama, starting from Sage Bhardwaj in Prayag to Sage Atri and Devi Anusuya at Chitrakoot to Sage Sharbhanga's ashram in the Dandakaranya Forest, were all steps closer to moving towards southern Aryavarta. Sage Sharbhanga guided them to Sage Suteekshna, who guided them to Sage Agastya near the southern Vindhyachal range—Ramtek—in the Dandakaranya Forest. The last sage

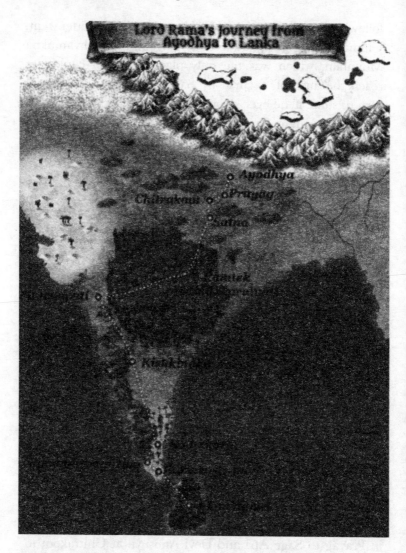

gave many weapons to Lord Rama and Lakshmana, and sent the banished princes and Devi Sita to Panchavati, the home of the demons, Khara and Dushana.

It was at Panchavati where Surpanakha attempted to attack Devi Sita but her nose and ears were cut off by

Lakshmana. It was all done by the Gods to move the trio towards Ravana's territory. That is how the latter's end would be plotted. Finally, they reached Janasthana, where the first encounter with Ravana's demons started. After Ravana kidnapped Devi Sita, Lord Rama and Lakshmana met the cursed Gandharva-turned-rakshasa Kabandha, who was mortally injured by the warriors in a fight. Kabandha requested the duo to burn his body, promising to reveal a secret that would lead them to Devi Sita. As his Gandharva avatar rose from the funeral pyre, just before his salvation, Kabandha instructed Lord Rama to befriend Sugreeva at Rishyamukha Mountain, near Kishkindha.

'The latter would disclose that he had seen Devi Sita while she was being kidnapped. From Jatayu's last words, it was clear that Ravana had kidnapped Devi Sita but nobody knew the location of Ravana's kingdom. It could have been in any part of the world, in the netherworld below or the heavens above. Lord Rama could have spent years trying to find his beloved wife and yet find nothing. All the hundreds of thousands of vanaras sent to different parts of the world returned empty-handed. Only Sampati's words, which completed the second half of the verse Jatayu was about to say, gave us the exact answer to the location of Devi Sita. Before dying, Jatayu spoke thus:

पुत्रेविश्रवसःसाक्षात्भ्रातावैश्रवणस्यच ।...

'He only mentioned that the demon was the son of Vishravasa, and the brother of Kuber. But this information was incomplete. Jatayu was badly injured and could not complete the verse before he left his mortal body in Lord Rama's arms. The puzzle was solved after Sampati, whom we met at the southern coast of Aryavarta, told us the following:

पुत्रेविश्रवसःसाक्षात्भ्रातावैश्रवणस्यच ।
अध्यास्तेनगरीम्लंकाम्रावणोनामराक्षसः ।।

This information was sufficient for us to deduce that it was Ravana who had kidnapped Devi Sita and taken her to Lanka. The verse mentioned that Lanka was beyond the sea, so it needed to be searched for. It was our last hope.'

Ashwatthama listened with interest to Hanuman's retelling of his visit to Lanka, followed by his tale of finding Devi Sita at Ashok Vatika, his subsequent capture by Indrajit, and the burning of Lanka. Hanuman also recounted how the entire army had first tried to cross the sea at Kodikkarai but had found it difficult to build a bridge to Lanka. Thereafter, they proceeded to Dhanushkodi (Rameswaram)—where the bridge was then built.'

'Did Lord Rama know that he was an avatar of Vishnu and that his sole purpose was to kill Ravana?'

Hanuman replied calmly, 'Do we all know that we have Gods inside us? Yes, and even then, we do not feel it most of the time. We do not act like it. Do all humans act in the best way, despite knowing this? Do we know what our specific purpose in this birth is? What is the one path we must choose? The web of this world is an intricate one. Everyone acts in their own interest, and that is the ultimate truth. We may think that we love another person more than ourselves but the truth is that a person does not love anyone more than himself or herself. That is the harsh truth.'

Ashwatthama nodded, the words resonating with him.

Hanuman went on, 'To answer your question Ashwatthama, Lord Rama didn't know that he had been sent to kill Ravana. For Lord Rama, his own identity was that of an exiled prince who wanted to fulfill his father's orders, provide all comforts to his wife, protect his brother and take care of his subjects. He never wanted to cause hurt to anyone without reason. All he knew was that he had to follow the right path, come what may, even if it meant making personal sacrifices. Lord Rama was that rare example of a person who loved others more than he loved himself. He was the epitome of humanity. Never has a person more idealistic in values and behaviour walked on this earth. Lord Rama laid down the principles of how a man must live his life.

'Once, when Lord Rama was in the forest, he went to meet Sage Sarbhanga. However, at that moment, Indra was visiting the sages. When he saw Lord Rama coming, Indra got up and requested the sages not to tell Lord Rama about his visit. Vishnu had strictly instructed all His devotees not to meet Lord Rama or tell him about the purpose of his incarnation. If Lord Rama's identity as the avatar of Vishnu was revealed, his status would have been elevated, and Ravana would have survived, since the latter had the boon that neither Gods nor demigods nor any animal would have the power to kill him. Ravana had always despised humans and considered them weak and inferior, and so did not think of seeking protection from humans. Ravana had to see Lord Rama as a human throughout the conflict.

'Now Ravana was no ordinary rakshasa. He was a staunch devotee of Shiva. He did not get his ten heads by birth; Shiva gifted them to him. Once, during penance, Ravana sacrificed his head in devotion to Shiva. However, his head grew back each time he sacrificed it. It happened ten times in a row. Lord Shiva, pleased with his devotion, granted him all the ten heads. Those heads signified the six shastras and four Vedas that Ravana had mastered.

'So, it was never going to be easy to kill Ravana. It was Mareecha who made it possible. When Lord Rama killed Mareecha, it is widely thought that the latter had wanted the welfare of Ravana but it was the other way around. Twice, Mareecha had dissuaded Ravana from kidnapping Devi Sita but Ravana had threatened to kill Mareecha if the latter did not support the asura king in his endeavour. So, when Rama shot the arrow, Mareecha knew he was going to die but he wanted the destruction of the one who caused his death—Ravana. The only way for this to happen was to set up a confrontation between Lord Rama and Ravana. Hence, Mareecha called Lakshmana, set things in motion so that eventually, Ravana would bring about his own destruction by kidnapping Sita. Mareecha's soul then merged with Lord Rama's.'

'…Bringing about Ravana's end,' Ashwatthama added. 'However, I do not understand what made Ravana think he could win the biggest of battles. What weapons did he possess that made him so confident of his victories that he even challenged the Gods?'

Hanuman went on, answering Ashwatthama's queries calmly.

'Ashwatthama, the biggest enemy of a person is his ego. It is the ego that leads to all the vices—anger, lust, jealousy, envy, greed among others. It was Ravana's ego that killed him. He was one of the most powerful rakshasas, a master of the mystic arts. But he also had indestructible faith in his son Meghnaad, who was almost invincible. His chariot was pulled by four sabre-toothed tigers, all of them as swift as Garuda, the eagle who was the vehicle of Vishnu. He could remain invisible on the battlefield. He killed thousands of vanaras on the battlefield with his Brahmastra. He could easily destroy any enemy. And he almost did, when he bound both Lord Rama and Lakshmana using the Naga Pasha, the Naga weapon which can bind its target in an unbreakable coil of living venomous snakes. Eventually, the Gods had to intervene and Garuda came to kill the Nagas who held the two brothers in their fierce grip.'

Ashwatthama nodded. 'But how could Indrajit have suffered defeat at the hands of Lakshmana, when Indrajit was an Atimaharathi, the wielder of the weapons of Brahma, Vishnu and Shiva?'

'Indeed. Indrajit suffered defeat because of a specific condition to a boon, that he chose to ignore. Brahma had granted a boon to Indrajit—no one would be able to defeat him on the battlefield, no one other than a person who has had not slept for fourteen years. It is impossible for an ordinary mortal to go without sleep for fourteen days, let alone months or years, and it is the same for the devtas. None of them could stay awake for fourteen years.

'It so happened that on the first night of the exile, when sleep started overcoming Lakshmana, he requested it to spare him for fourteen years as he had to protect Lord Rama and Devi Sita; he told sleep to instead go and overcome his wife in Ayodhya. So, Urmila, Lakshmana's wife, slept almost for sixteen hours a day, for the next fourteen years. Thus, there emerged a man who had not slept for fourteen years—Lakshmana.

'Just like Ravana, Indrajit too, despised humans. Once, when Ravana waged war on the devas, he was defeated and captured by Indra and the demigods. Meghnaad (as Indrajit was also known), marched and defeated Indra and the other demigods, and rescued Ravana. It was for this act that he came to be known as Indrajit. Father and son captured Indra and brought him to Lanka, where they wanted to kill him. But Brahma intervened for the life of Indra and offered Meghnaad a boon instead. Meghnaad wanted immortality but Brahma reminded him that it would be against the laws of nature.

'Instead, Brahma granted him a boon—after completing a yagna of his native Goddess Prathyangira at a sanctuary named Nikumbhila, he would get a celestial chariot in which he would be invincible. He would become invisible even to the Gods, making his defeat impossible. However, Brahma cautioned him that whoever disrupted the yagna would be the cause of his death. There was another boon granted by Brahma in which he mentioned that only a person who did not sleep for fourteen years would be able to kill Indrajit, and Indrajit immediately assumed such a person did not exist. Both these conditions were fulfilled on the eleventh night of the war when Lakshmana disrupted the yagna.

'After Indrajit died, Ravana was inconsolable and devastated but also furious. He sent such a large number of asuras to the battlefield that it seemed the vanaras would be decimated without a fight. Then, Lord Rama used the Gandharvastra. The weapon helped the Lord to move at the speed of light and annihilate multiple targets at once. It also allowed him to appear at several places at once. In a few moments, the Lord had destroyed most of Ravana's armies.'

Hanuman then continued with the tale of how Lord Rama showed extreme valour in killing Ravana, using the Brahmastra. He concluded the story with the end of Ravana.

'After Ravana's death, Lord Shiva came to earth, along with the spirit of the princes' father, Dasaratha, who hugged both his sons. Many other Gods visited and blessed the warrior duo. Indra told Lord Rama to ask for a boon and the latter asked that all the vanaras and bears who had lost their lives in the battle, may come back to life. The vanaras were not simple monkeys but divine beings who were demigods in reality and had taken birth at the behest of Brahma to assist Lord Rama in killing the asuras.'

Ashwatthama sat silently for a while, taking in all that Hanuman had said, his curiosity about the story of Lord Rama at last satiated. It was the first time Ashwatthama had heard Lord Rama's story in detail. From the conversation, it was evident that the Kodanda was still out there. However Ashwatthama was not sure how he could take it back from Dandak. And even if he took it back, nothing short of a Brahmastra would kill Dandak.

But Ashwatthama could not conjure one now, having used it once according to the restriction put by Dronacharya.

'You can tell me all about weapons, right? I need to know how to invoke a Brahmastra, the Ishiika. I knew it in the last yuga but I could do it only once,' he said.

Hanuman looked into Ashwatthama's eyes as the moonlight swept over both of them. 'Each divine weapon is presided over by a deity. The Vajra's presiding deity is Indra. Or the Pashupatastra, whose presiding deity is Shiva. So, when these weapons are given as a boon to warriors, the presiding deity binds them to these weapons. When the warrior intends to use these weapons, the Gods appear in those weapons and cause the destruction or the healing, depending on the nature of the weapon. They are bound by the boon they have given to fulfill the weapon's purpose. Thus, each divyastra is unique and takes on the characteristics of its deity.'

'I had the Brahmastra in the last yuga,' Ashwatthama murmured, 'Is it possible to recall it?'

'You cannot have it, Ashwatthama,' Hanuman replied evenly. 'Not unless someone grants it to you. Lord Brahma grants the Brahmastra and along with the weapon, the carrier is given the knowledge to use it. But I believe you already know that.'

'I cannot use it again. I squandered that chance,' Ashwatthama confessed.

'You are responsible for your actions; you used it when you wanted to. You had the most powerful of all Brahmastras—the Ishiika, the one with the four heads of Brahma. In contrast, an ordinary Brahmastra carries the power of only one head of Brahma and so is much less powerful. You have lost the Ishiika. You are still missing a part of the puzzle, Ashwatthama,' Hanuman said after a quiet moment.

Ashwatthama looked at Hanuman's face. The mighty God never lied. It seemed that he, Ashwatthama, would not get the Brahmastra to kill Dandak. Even if Ashwatthama managed to snatch the Kodanda from the asura king, Drona's son had no matching arrow that could destroy Dandak. Mildly powerful weapons such as the Indrastra, Suryastra or Garudastra might be able to weaken or injure Dandak but were unlikely to finish him off completely.

'I have lost all my knowledge of divyastras. I can invoke simple astras but the higher divine astras like the Brahmastra or Nagastra are still beyond my reach.'

'That is because you are still incomplete, Ashwatthama. The power of invoking the Brahmastra or for that matter, many divyastras, is generated through our internal devotion.

'Even Arjuna forgot the knowledge of all his astras after Krishna left earth. That was the reason he was not able to save Krishna's wives, after the latter had left, when bandits attacked the women. He forgot all the mantras. And it was then he realised his time on earth was over.

'Astras work only if the presiding God is present in the warrior's body. If the presiding God leaves, the astra is useless, just like in the case of Arjuna, when Krishna, the presiding God of many of Arjuna's weapons, left his body. The same thing happens if the warrior forgets the mantras.'

Ashwatthama listened carefully as Hanuman continued.

'For using astras, you need to invoke the Gayatri Mantra in a particular way. There are two kinds of sounds—Anahata Nada and Nahata Nada. The Anahata Nada is the Gayatri Mantra invoked in reverse to reach the celestial realm. The Anahata Nada is inaudible to humans, unlike the Nahata Nada which is used for normal weapons. Remember that only by invoking the Gayatri Mantra in Anahata Nada will you be able to invoke your divyastras.'

Ashwatthama was confounded. The day had been a long one. He could faintly remember chanting the Anahata Nada on the fatal night when he had been cursed. To invoke celestial weapons, one had to say prayers that reached the celestial realms. Only then would the Gods descend to preside over the weapons.

'But how can I invoke hymns that will carry over to the celestial realms? Even though my body seems restored, I still do not have the powers to invoke divine weapons.'

'You were able to do it then; you will be able to do it again. Some events are meant to happen at the right time. You will know when these happen, Ashwatthama.'

Ashwatthama sighed. There was nothing drastically different in him. He tried to remember. And then he felt it... the burning sensation on his forehead. He felt the wound.

The gemstone!

But that was not all. Ashwatthama felt a strange uneasiness that refused to budge. There was something else that bothered him but he could not put his finger on it.

Hanuman looked at Ashwatthama.

'What do you seek?'

Ashwatthama looked at the darkness in front of him. The path was not visible to him. He didn't know what was causing the uneasiness in his mind.

'My mind is still not at rest.'

The moon shone on both Hanuman and Ashwatthama, who felt lighter after having had this conversation. Hanuman smiled as he looked at the son of Dronacharya.

'You worry unnecessarily about events that are beyond your control,' Hanuman said. 'You focus on the past which you cannot change. You are concerned about the future which has yet to arrive. Have faith, for it will carry you through the darkest of times.'

Ashwatthama nodded in agreement as he looked gratefully at Hanuman. 'Thank you for fulfilling my desire to hear Lord Rama's story.'

Hanuman gave a hint of a smile, and rose to leave. The son of Vayu looked back at the palace with wistful eyes and spoke, 'I should thank you, Ashwatthama. You brought me here, a place I had been apprehensive about visiting for ages. It has all the memories of the best period of my life. It brought me happiness to recall those times today. May you too find what you seek.'

With that, Hanuman touched Ashwatthama's abdomen. Instantly, the pain that was lingering from Hanuman's blow disappeared. Ashwatthama bowed to Hanuman.

Hanuman raised his hand in blessing, 'Jai Shri Rama.'

By the time Ashwatthama raised his head, Hanuman was gone.

17

The Battle of Avanti

A lone arrow, travelling the distance between the plains and the fort, hit the fort wall.

'Prepare to fire,' Janak Singh commanded. Abhayajeet nodded and ran through the ranks of his soldiers, shouting his war cry. Both Urmila and Shreya looked on with awe, having never witnessed a war before.

The archers raised their bows, lighting the tips with fire from the smouldering wood kept in vessels in front of them. The arrows lit up the night sky as they zoomed towards the asuras. Soon, the cries of the asuras filled the air. The archers reloaded and let loose a second wave, which led to more cries. The asuras started throwing spears and arrows and they ran forward, bellowing loudly but most of their weapons did not even reach half way to the fort.

The front row of asuras was massacred each time the archers let loose a wave of arrows. They fell in hordes but this did not stop their march. Even with the casualties, they stomped within close range of the Avanti soldiers and a few of their arrows started to hit their targets. Some asuras carried slings and shot stones at the top of the fort. A few Avanti soldiers started falling to their death. As the asuras came closer, Avanti soldiers rolled the wooden barrels containing hot tar. These were fitted on specially designed slings that dispatched the barrels high in the air.

One soldier fired an arrow with an explosive tip at the barrel, which was in motion mid-air. The barrel exploded, spraying burning hot tar on the asuras, scalding them in droves. Loud cries filled the air as they burned. The higher the barrel exploded, the more asuras were hit with the burning tar. Soon, a burning smell filled the air and smoke started spreading across the battleground, making it difficult for people to breathe. All eyes burned from the acrid smoke rising from burning flesh.

However, the asuras did not stop. They seemed driven to attack, irrespective of their fate. They started hitting the fort wall with their maces even as hot tar poured over them. They kept attacking in large numbers, prepared to kill or die. Any other army would have retreated but not the asuras; they were relentless.

An hour passed, and the asuras had not made any inroads.

Janak Singh chuckled. 'Huh, fools. Trying to break a ten-foot thick wall with their clubs.'

Rana gripped his sword hard; he had an uneasy feeling in his gut. It could not be this easy. Something was wrong. And then he realised that no one was leading the army. The asuras had assembled in front of the fort in a disorderly fashion and attacked randomly. There was no order to their formation. They had had an order in the attack near Charmanvati, when Raktavija was leading it. They had also maintained order during the underwater fight at Dwarka with Vidyut at the helm. How could this attack be different?

'Something's wrong, father,' Rana shifted uneasily. 'This does not seem to be the main attack.'

'What do you mean?' Janak Singh asked testily. 'Look at them, falling like pins. What more do you expect from these uncivilised brutes?'

'What do you mean, this is not the final attack?' Urmila looked worried.

'Look at them. They are just meant to be here. They have no order or purpose. They only want to exhaust our soldiers and resources.'

'But where is the main attack then?' Shreya asked anxiously.

They did not have to wait long for an answer. Moments later, the ground rumbled as if mammoths were running all over it. The vibrations made them feel like an earthquake was in progress. All of them held on to something or the other to avoid falling. At that moment, it was clear why the asuras had come without any leader. A row of almost twenty-foot high, iron-clad Giants came thundering down the plains, with heavy metal clubs and hooks in their hands.

'Giants,' Rana shouted at the top of his voice, sprinting through the line of soldiers. 'Change to spears.'

The soldiers promptly obeyed and picked up spears.

'Aim at their eyes,' Rana shouted. Throwing the weapons anywhere else would be futile. The four Giants were completely covered from head to toe in customised metallic armour. The soldiers aimed their spears and threw them at the oncoming beasts but most of their attack was futile. It was hard to aim accurately from a distance. Moreover, the Giants wore metallic armour that dulled most of the attack. Arrows were useless on them as were the hot tar-filled barrels which the Giants caught mid-air and flung back at the soldiers, with disastrous results. Janak Singh took a deep breath as he considered the situation nervously. He realised that Rana's apprehensions had not been without merit. The asuras did have a surprise up their sleeves. They had planned this thoroughly. The Giants were game-changers in most wars.

And then Urmila saw him.

Seated atop a massive horse, with chains attached from a large metallic neckband on the beast in the place of reins, a figure slowly moved towards the fort. Clad in grey metallic armour from top to bottom, the figure held the reins of the chains in one hand and a large metal rod in the other. The rod had a spiked mace at its end. A large hammer and a rectangular shield were tied to his back. The warrior's hands were covered with metallic gloves; his face was shielded by metallic headgear, leaving only the eyes visible. His armour shone brightly in the light from the asuras' torches.

Urmila looked through the view-glass and shuddered. She had never seen anyone so heavily armour-clad before.

How could one asura carry this much weight?

She strode towards Rana, who was busy monitoring the Giants. She asked, 'Do you see him?'

'Who?'

'Him,' Urmila pointed towards the farthest area of the plains where she had seen the warrior approaching, handing over the view-glass to Rana. He eyed the location Urmila was pointing at.

'Dandak?' Urmila arched her brows.

Rana shook his head as he lowered the view-glass.

'It's Kaalnemi.'

~

The Giants, meanwhile, were wreaking havoc on the Avanti army. They carried huge slings and put large boulders inside them, swinging them wildly at the fort. The boulders caused more destruction than any other weapon, with their speed and massive size. Cracks started slowly appearing on the fort wall.

Janak Singh felt uneasy. All his talk about the Avanti fort being impenetrable was about to be proved wrong. The fall of the fort meant the fall of the city. There was no way they could defend the city from the asuras, not with the Giants backing the former. Even an army of ten thousand men would not be sufficient to stop the Giants on a rampage.

'Bring the aml,' Janak Singh ordered, loudly.

The aml was the last resort Avanti had. It was a solution developed by the weapons researchers that could melt most metals. But it had never been used. The delivery technique had not yet been perfected and only glass could hold the liquid without melting.

Rana cautioned Janak Singh, 'Father, the liquid is far too dangerous. It will endanger our soldiers.'

'There will be no soldiers left, son, not if those Giants are standing,' Janak Singh replied, pointing at the relentless beasts, even as he oversaw the soldiers bringing large cauldrons of the dangerous fluid. The cauldrons were connected with thick tubes to large glass dispensers.

Janak Singh supervised the dispensers being filled with aml as the Giants approached the fort again, battling spears and flames from the harried soldiers with ease. He had never thought that they would need to use the aml.

As the Giants strode forward, oblivious to what lay in store for them, the Avanti soldiers moved the large glass containers to the edge of the fort walls. Rana watched anxiously. He had a premonition that this was not going to end well. It was akin to playing with fire. Ducking the arrows and spears flying all over the place, he ran towards the other side of the fort where Guru Apasmitra was busy repelling the asuras with his water waves.

'Wait!' Janak Singh ordered the soldiers to hold back as the Giants moved forward for another strike at the fort wall, which already had wide cracks in them. The cracks were being mended speedily on the spot by blacksmiths and carpenters. As the Giants raised their maces again to strike at the fort walls, Janak Singh thundered: 'NOW!'

The soldiers pushed the handle of the container and wide streams of aml flew towards the Giants, hitting them right in their faces. There were ear-splitting shrieks as the aml burned through the masks of the Giants, blinding them immediately. Blinded and mad with pain, they dropped their weapons and thrashed about violently, trampling asuras and running back towards the forest, howling loudly.

Janak Singh heaved a sense of relief. The biggest threat seemed to have been dealt with, and the tide had to turn in Avanti's favour now. One Giant, partially blinded and raging at the Avanti soldiers, raised his mace and, instead of striking the fort wall, decided to punish those who had blinded him. He ploughed his mace right at the top edge of the fort wall and ran directly through the length of the wall. Pieces of flesh, stone and glass flew all over as the mace connected with the soldiers and their weapons. Unfortunately, the mace also struck the glass cauldrons containing the aml.

There was a huge eruption as the cauldrons exploded, splattering aml all over. Huge volumes of aml landed on the Avanti soldiers, some of whom melted on the spot. Others ran as the liquid fell on their skin and bones, burning the body parts it came in contact with.

Only a miracle could save Avanti now.

18

The Girl in the Forest

Soothed by the cold breeze, Ashwatthama sat on the palace steps for a while after Hanuman had left. Arya was up and awake, refreshed after the rest. He looked at his master in anticipation of another ride. Ashwatthama went over to the Yeti horse, patted its neck and placed some more food and water in front of it. Arya moved freely inside the palace compound. The Yeti horses were known to be loyal and to stick with their masters even when let loose.

Ashwatthama lit a torch and went into the palace. He walked towards the dark throne, unsure of his next move. Although Hanuman had not indicated what needed to be done next, the message was clear.

The Kodanda was out there.

Ashwatthama doubted they would ever figure out what Nyat had meant or if they had misinterpreted it. Maybe Nyat had meant something entirely different. He tried to think about the possible meanings but was overcome with fatigue. As he looked around, Ashwatthama realised that it would be tough to search for anything with the limited visibility in there. He had had very little rest during the week-long journey and his body yearned for a night's sleep at the very least.

He decided to resume the search at dawn and keep looking till the afternoon, before heading to Avanti. Guru Apasmitra might have had some new findings by then. They would need a new plan.

He cleaned up the small patio in front of the throne, laid the thin bedding he carried with him and lay down, resting his head on his arms. Looking at the starry sky through the broken roof, he tried to pinpoint the uneasiness which had lurked in his mind ever since he had killed Raktavija. Something inside him was crying for attention. He knew that the Kodanda was unbroken and that was a relief. He had realised on Vikram's palace terrace that Vidyut had used some deception but there had been no way to be sure until now. The search for a divine arrow that could kill Dandak was still on... Moments later, he fell asleep.

~

A hand reached out and Ashwatthama held it. He felt much younger and lighter of heart. Soon, he found himself running through the meadows of a village. A face appeared, beautiful, unmatched in grace and innocence. There was love there, love that made him feel like spending every moment of eternity with her. She smiled.

And then the smile faded. She was being pulled away by invisible forces. The image changed to that of a large arena. The entire scene was lit in hues of red and orange. The heat was terrible, drenching him in sweat. All around, there were pits of lava and monstrous creatures roamed everywhere, growling and attacking all. Scores of men and women were being punished for their misdeeds, some of them thrown into the fire, others tortured with different types of metallic weapons. The scene was too harrowing for Ashwatthama. He ran around, looking for her in the unbearable heat and stench, mad with grief. He couldn't explain why he was in hell but this was clearly hell, and he knew what he had to do.

*The punishment being meted out to sinners was heart-wrenching.
The roads were littered with blood and a small piece of flesh stuck
to his foot. Ashwatthama vomitted, bile gushing over his hands. As he
wiped his mouth, he saw her face again. She was tied to a mast with
chains, hanging over the roaring fire, her feet scalded by the intense
heat from below. She was being assaulted repeatedly with a spiked
chain. The skin on her back was peeling off and blood oozed from
all over her body. She opened her bloodied eyes and looked straight at
Ashwatthama, mutely appealing for help. Her soundless appeal tore
apart his heart. He ran towards her, trying to reach her and pull her
out but the faster he ran, the further she seemed to recede, until she
seemed to vanish into the darkness. He cried out in horror as he felt
his helplessness.*

'No!' shouted Ashwatthama, waking up with a jerk. His
voice reverberated in the dark courtyard, like an echo in a
haunted valley. He was sweating profusely, the clothes and
bedding wet with his sweat. Ashwatthama looked around.
It had been a nightmare. He panted heavily, reflecting on
his nightmare. He knew the cause of his uneasiness now.

Because Ashwatthama knew the face.

Rati.

19

A Betrayal

'Fall back,' Rana shouted as he ran. But the warning came too late.

The Giant's mace was crashing into the glass cauldrons, smashing them and spilling aml all over the Avanti soldiers. Loud cries rent the air but this time it came from the humans. Innumerable Avanti soldiers had been burned by the splashing aml, the liquid burning their flesh to the bone, and the smell fouled the air.

Rana ran on the archers' level, yelling at the soldiers to retreat. He shouted for the medics to rush to the second level. Guru Apasmitra was busy at the end of the fort wall, repelling the attack from the corners where they were most vulnerable. The panchrishi had been provided with numerous cauldrons of water to repel the attack.

'Guruji,' Rana pointed his sword at the lower level as he ran shouting towards the sage, 'The aml!'

Guru Apasmitra had caught sight of the exploding cauldrons and instantly pushed the water wave towards the lower level of the floor, where scores of Avanti soldiers were being lethally scalded by the aml. The water wave contained the hissing liquid and prevented further casualties, bringing succour to a few injured soldiers. Guru Apasmitra then drained the diluted solution down the fort where it fell on the unsuspecting asuras, scorching them, forcing them to retreat.

The half-blind Giant was still running through the edge of the wall but as the aml kept splashing, it burnt through his metallic armour and mace, which were eventually reduced to mangled wrecks. Finally, his strength gave in and as the last splash of aml fell over his helmet, melting through to his head, the Giant quivered like a leaf.

Rana looked on in dread as the Giant stood confounded for a moment, next to the crack one of the other Giants had made in the thick stone wall. The prince muttered a silent prayer: *not there.*

The Giant stumbled and fell lifeless on the wall, right on to the crack. The asuras were awaiting this moment, for the wall to crumble. But the wall stood fast against the weight of the Giant. The Avanti soldiers heaved a sigh of relief. Rana looked at his father who seemed content with the defeat of the Giants. A hush had fallen over the asuras as all the Giants had been either maimed or killed. There was no way they could deal with the Avanti army as long as the fort wall stood, and the humans held the higher ground.

And then, in a delayed reaction, the wall gave in under the weight of the fallen Giant. With a boom, the fort wall crumbled, throwing up clouds of dust and fragments of stone. Some Avanti soldiers fell into the gap with cries and a few ran atop the fort to save their lives as the wall started caving in. The asuras cheered at this sudden turn of fortune. The breach had provided a direct passage for them, right in the middle of the fort. There was loud cheer as they ran in unison towards the fallen wall, not caring about the shower of arrows aimed at them. The asuras swarmed inside in wild fury.

Rana shouted to the king's guards to form a protective ring around a shocked Janak Singh, who stared in disbelief. The asuras had penetrated the fort and the rows of soldiers defending the fort were now the last line of defense. They succeeded in repelling the first wave of the enemy but the second wave was beyond their capacity. Slowly, the defending soldiers fell before the asuras.

'They are everywhere,' cried Rana as he joined Urmila and Shreya. They watched helplessly as the first swarm of asuras started arriving at the topmost level of the fort to take down the king.

The attackers butchered the Avanti soldiers as they marched on fearlessly, their battle cry echoing in the air. Their fierce and wild appearance sparked fear in the hearts of the Avanti soldiers who were not too experienced in warfare, never having fought a war themselves. At a moment when calm was required the most, their nervousness showed. Their every move was wrought with fear of the might of the asuras. Consequently, the unearthly brutes had a free run, chopping down the humans all around.

It was not the strength of the asuras that led to the fall of Avanti but the fear of the unknown; the fear of asura strength and their menacing appearance broke the soldiers' spirit. Fighting a battle for the first time, they failed to realise that one must conquer the fear inside or else the battle was lost. Rana, Urmila and Shreya rushed forward to tackle the asuras, who were wildly swinging their swords in all directions, thus making it easy for the trained fighters to dodge their attacks and slay them. A furious Janak Singh too joined them.

But then the attack doubled. An injured Giant returned, spraying bricks and stones all over, killing many soldiers and asuras as well in the process. Behind him, a larger wave of asuras infiltrated the fort. It looked like it was all over for the Avanti soldiers.

'Take cover. Retreat!' Janak Singh shouted as he realised that the fort had fallen. All he could hope was to regroup the soldiers to increase their courage, and then fight again. For now, it seemed that his soldiers had given up. They all moved back as the Giant ploughed through. Rana took a spear and flung it at the Giant but to no avail. The furious Giant then did something unpredictable; it brought down its mace heavily, right where the group stood. They jumped sideways to avoid the blow but Rana tripped and a large piece of stone fell over his leg. Another stone broke the fall and prevented his leg from being reduced to a pulp but the limb was pinned between the stone and floor.

The asuras moved closer to the royal warriors, one of them getting behind Janak Singh in attack position. Rana shouted but his voice was drowned by the clank of metal, roars and cries. Janak Singh was busy fighting the asuras in front of him. Rana frantically tried to pry his leg free from the rubble but in vain. His eyes tried to find Shreya but there was no sign of her. Close by, he spotted Urmila who was busy slaying as many asuras as she could.

~

In another unfortunate twist for the Avantis, the large asura in heavy metallic armour emerged from the broken wall. He looked at the exhausted king, sneered and galloped towards the corner of the fort where Guru Apasmitra was deftly repelling the attack, killing scores of asuras with the weapons he was conjuring up out of the water. Kaalnemi rode on his horse towards Guru Apasmitra, who eyed him from afar.

Watching the asura leader getting closer, Guru Apasmitra formed a wall of water and hurled it with massive force. An ordinary asura would have been blown away by the impact of the water wall. But Kaalnemi dismounted and sprinted towards Guru Apasmitra, gripping his sword with both hands and holding it in front of him.

Guru Apasmitra looked in disbelief as the asura chief kept running towards him, cutting through the water barrier. The sage created a huge sphere of water and engulfed Kaalnemi inside it, dislodging him. The sphere carried Kaalnemi over the fort, and the asura chief hung helplessly in the air. Kaalnemi gasped for breath inside the sphere, whereas any mortal would have drowned within moments. The asuras and humans momentarily stopped fighting to watch the battle between the supreme sage and the asura chief.

Guru Apasmitra held his hands in front of him, applying absolute power to contain Kaalnemi inside the massive water sphere he had created. The panchrishi twirled his fingers, which moved the water inside the sphere frantically. Initially, Kaalnemi was thrown around haphazardly inside the sphere but in a few moments, he stopped struggling, regained his posture and stood still, staying calm, despite the massive turbulence the water produced. To everyone's surprise, he slowly started moving out of the sphere, in the same standing posture.

Guru Apasmitra gasped.

Impossible!

And then, in one swift movement, Kaalnemi pulled a spear from his back, and hurled it towards Guru Apasmitra. The old sage immediately formed a large water wall, which looked strong enough to stop a speeding chariot. The spear seemingly broke on impact with the wall, shattering into hundreds of pieces but immediately reformed on the other side as if it had smoothly passed through the wall. It struck the sage on his chest and went through, pinning him to the ground. The sage gave one last look of horror at his nemesis and his body went limp, impaled on the spear that had gone ahead and penetrated the stone.

~

'No!' Rana shouted as he writhed in helplessness. He saw Kaalnemi moving towards Guru Apasmitra's body to make sure he was dead. Rana looked around helplessly. Defeat stared them in the face. The asura soldiers were swarming around like bees, filling every crevice of the fort. He tried to move the stone that pinned down his leg but could not exert enough strength in the position he was trapped in. He kept warding off the asura soldiers who moved towards him, intent on killing him, although he knew that his defense could not last long. Ultimately, a few of them would attack in tandem and then it would be over for him. He looked at his father, who was valiantly fighting the enemy off. Despite his advanced age, the king managed to prevent the asuras from getting past him.

And then, Rana saw Urmila standing in a corner, firing arrows at the asuras coming through the fort wall. But only a few asuras were focused on her. Their direct instructions were to kill the king and take over the fort. In what seemed like an eternity, Rana saw what was about to happen. A large asura, with a string of fingers strung around his neck, black paint smeared across his face and body, and swishing a large blade—a cross between a sword and an axe—moved menacingly towards Janak Singh. Rana frantically looked around but Abhayajeet was far away. At that very moment, his eyes met Urmila's. She looked confused. The asura behind Janak Singh moved within striking distance, the king unaware of the impending attack on him.

'Take him out, Urmila, quick!' Rana shouted hoarsely.

Urmila moved her hands to pull out arrows but her quiver was empty. She threw the bow away and drew her sword, moving her gaze from Rana to the king. She considered attacking the asura—it would be easy for her to mount a surprise attack from behind and injure him before he could kill the king, though at great risk to herself— but her eyes moved sideways, and the Indraprastha princess took a moment to decide before she ran towards the other part of the fort.

'Urmila, no!' yelled Rana, looking helplessly as the large asura moved closer to Janak Singh. Taking position carefully, the asura stabbed the Avanti king on his back. Janak Singh doubled over in pain, dropping his sword. The asura took out his sword, and attacked again, this time, targeting the king's neck. The king didn't survive the second blow and his body fell on the floor with a thud.

'No,' Rana cried, 'Father!'

As Janak Singh fell, the asuras erupted in cries of celebratory joy. Immediately, loud bugles sounded in the asura camp, conveying the news of the king's death. The asuras then circled Rana, who was still on the ground with his leg pinned under the debris. He lifted his sword up in defense but it was kicked aside by an asura. Rana looked at the merciless faces of the attackers. More than helplessness, he felt anger at his inability to help his father.

And at Urmila's betrayal.

The asuras raised their swords and clubs, ready to strike him. Rana looked into their eyes—the darkest shade of black, echoing the darkness in their hearts. All of a sudden, Abhayajeet appeared out of nowhere, surprising the attackers.

In a fleeting stroke, he slew all the five asuras circling Rana. The large asura moved towards Abhayajeet but he was no match for the general's agility. The Avanti general dodged his attack swiftly and swung his sword, beheading the beast who had killed Avanti's king.

Moving towards Rana, Abhayajeet quickly lifted the heavy stone pinning down the prince's feet and pulled him out. He checked Rana's foot for injuries but the latter dismissed it. Abhayajeet walked to the edge to take a look at the battle below. He looked sideways and found Kaalnemi taking out his spear, gloating over his significant kill. It wouldn't take long for the asura chief to reach this part of the fort. He rushed back to Rana.

'The soldiers have almost given up. You won't believe the carnage the asuras are wreaking. New Giants are marching towards the fort. We must leave.'

'Stop, Abhayajeet. Father?' Rana looked sadly at his father, hobbling towards the latter's motionless body. He went down on his knees. Placing the king's head in his lap, Rana embraced his dead father. A wave of pain and regret washed over him. It had happened so suddenly, and Rana realised he never had a chance to express his love for his father. Despite Rana resenting him, Janak Singh had loved him deeply, something he did not show overtly, though deep in his heart, Rana had known about this love. However, a bit disgruntled by the king's behaviour, Rana had made it a point to show his resentment. And now, all this became meaningless as he held his father's body. The pain of not showing love towards his father would haunt him forever. A man leaves the world in peace if he knows there are people who will miss him when he's gone. That was what made one's life worth living. No amount of material possessions could replace the love of one's kin. Rana hugged his father and kissed him on the forehead, his tears falling on the old man's lifeless face. He prayed silently for his father's soul to be at peace.

Abhayajeet looked nervously from the top of the fort as the events unfolded. From his vantage point, he could see massive figures approaching them; they were still about half a mile away. These were not the same Giants who had attacked before. He turned and ran towards the prince.

'Rana, we must leave,' Abhayajeet put a hand on Rana's shoulder. 'Or it will be too late.'

Rana understood. There was no time for sorrow. He took a last glance at Janak Singh as he placed the body carefully on the floor, placing the king's sword in the latter's folded hands. He sighed deeply. Casting a final glance, he moved ahead with Abhayajeet, slashing the asuras who came their way. The headed towards the palace, where they hoped to find Urmila and Shreya. Everywhere they looked, they could see asuras slaughtering Avanti soldiers.

Another bugle sounded, and as Rana and Abhayajeet glanced towards the source, they saw the kingdom's flag being torn down from the fort and a black flag with the symbol of the asuras—a dragon breathing fire—being hoisted onto the flagpole.

Avanti, the second most powerful kingdom in Aryavarta, had fallen to the asuras.

20

A Narrow Escape

The Giants had done the job for the asuras. Eight new Giants now entered the fort and killed every soldier in their path. Avanti was terribly underprepared for such an attack. Until now, Janak Singh had only factored in an attack by a human army but the Giants were different. One Giant was enough to tilt the battle in favour of the army it was fighting, and seventeen Giants were a another game altogether. The war which would have raged for days, was finished in no time. Before the Avanti soldiers could even decide which weapons to use, the Giants had destroyed the entire armoury. It was a massacre.

The asuras fanned out through the city of Ujjaini. Widespread chaos ensued; men, women and children were slaughtered. There were cries everywhere and blood flowed freely on the streets. The asuras ran amok, burning down houses, landmark buildings and public areas.

Rana, Urmila and Shreya had managed to evade the asuras with Abhayajeet's help. He led them out of the city before the asuras could track them. Shreya had been stabbed and needed urgent stitches on her wound. A worried Urmila was carrying Shreya on her horse, holding the reins with one hand and balancing Shreya with the other, applying mild pressure on her abdomen to ensure she did not lose much blood.

Rana's head was bursting with grief and madness. He felt responsible for the fate of his city but there was nothing he could do. The death of his father had shattered him. And finally, he no longer felt any love for Urmila, and this hurt him even more. He had been sure that Urmila was the one he could spend his whole life with but with her betrayal on the battlefield, he could not bring himself to forgive her. Ironically, he was the one who had persuaded her to join the battle and so, he could not blame her for choosing to look after herself.

Abhayajeet took them further north of the Charmanvati River, to a distant village. They dismounted near an abandoned hut, a little distant from other huts in the same area. Abhayajeet went in and lit a torch. Rana helped Urmila to bring Shreya inside. The Indraprastha princess arranged a pile of clothes and helped Shreya lie down on it. Urmila took out neem leaves as well as the cloves and lavender flowers that she had asked Abhayajeet to pick along the way. She crushed all three and made a paste, which she applied around the injury. She then sterilised a needle and thread that she had managed to borrow from a household en route, and stitched up Shreya's wound. The paste had numbed the area around the injury, which helped to reduce the pain of the impromptu surgery and contain the infection. Shreya's bleeding stopped with the stitches but the wound looked like it needed time to heal.

Abhayajeet took a careful look around before entering the hut to see if any curious villager was observing them. After tying the horses to the rear of the hut, he also surveyed the nearby areas to ensure there was no chance of an ambush. The enemy had not yet figured out their location.

'We can catch our breath here for a bit, it is safe for now. The asuras won't bother as they have the city. We could reinforce our supplies tomorrow and then ride north.'

'We must go to Hastinapur,' Urmila suggested, looking at Rana. She felt something was wrong but was certain it was the death of the king and the siege of the kingdom by the asuras that had upset the prince. She was scared and uncomfortable but for now, her priority was to save Shreya. Rana's coldness was disheartening but she did not push him. She desperately longed for a friendly shoulder. Wars were brutal—it had not taken her long to realise that simple fact. As she took a break after checking on Shreya, she closed her eyes and, at that moment, realised why Ashwatthama had been reluctant to be part of the group initially—death, destruction, loneliness, fear and loss. Wars begin with a bang and then take away everything one holds dear.

'We will ride to Surparaka,' Rana told her coldly, checking on Shreya's wounds. He leaned against the hut's wall, sitting cross-legged on the floor.

'We should not,' Abhayajeet said. 'The whole eastern passage might be surveilled by the asuras, and who knows, they might already be in Surparaka. We should keep moving north to be safer. That way, we will be ahead of the asuras. Urmila has correctly suggested that we should head towards Hastinapur. They are the only allies we can reach safely, and the ones we can trust right now. We do not have an army of our own any longer. At Hastinapur, we will get more time and resources to prepare our counter-attack. Dandak's army will take over every region as they move along. Our best bet now would be to move northwards. That way, we can keep on putting some distance between them and us.'

'How did this happen, Abhayajeet?' Rana asked ruefully, massaging his injured leg. 'Why did we have no information about the Giants?'

'No one knew, Rana. Giants are not found in Aryavarta anymore. The last few are in Lanka.'

'Which means Dandak has appropriated them from Lanka,' Urmila leaned against the wall, exhausted, closing her eyes.

Abhayajeet nodded, glancing outside the window for any sign of movement. Rana pushed himself along the floor towards the hut's wall, sitting diametrically opposite Urmila.

'Then we are outmatched—eight fully armoured Giants. I am not sure what will happen if they get to Hastinapur. A larger army will not make much of a difference.'

'Not *if, when*. But at least now we know what we are up against. We can come up with a defense if we have some time,' Abhayajeet replied.

'I am concerned about Kaalnemi. He is mightier than we assumed. Anyone who could kill Guru Apasmitra could not be an ordinary asura by any means,' Urmila said worriedly.

Abhayajeet lay back and closed his eyes. Urmila also tried to sleep.

Rana, exhausted as he was, looked at her and wished earnestly that he had not seen her running from the battlefield. He felt sorry for her and even sorrier for himself. Some moments make one wish they had never happened, for they go against the fundamental principles a person holds dear and they also demand a decision, a choice that is heartbreaking both ways.

He could never love a coward.

21

The Rise of the Asuras

The asuras celebrated their victory by wildly careening around the palace, drinking and feasting. The Giants too celebrated but they sat around lazily, doing nothing more than devouring livestock. Kaalnemi arrived at the gates of the palace. He went up the stairs to where the palace door had once stood. As far as the eye could see, there was rubble. The palace had been razed to the ground, converted into the grave of those who were trapped in there and couldn't escape.

Kaalnemi turned around and clapped his hands loudly. The jubilant asuras fell silent and looked towards their leader, whose strategy had led them to victory.

'Asuras,' Kaalnemi thundered.

The asuras scuttled and assembled around the wall.

'This is our moment. The time for humans is over. We, the asuras of Rasatala, are the true inheritors of the earth. Long ago, we were tricked by the devas, who sent us to die in the depths of hell.'

Kaalnemi raised his voice as he strode aggressively. 'No more. Now we take back what is rightfully ours.'

The asuras cheered every sentence Kaalnemi uttered, with excited shouts. He continued, his voice drowning out everything else.

'Avanti is just the first step. Do not feel victorious here, for there are many more kingdoms to be conquered, many more humans to be killed. We will wipe out humans from the face of Aryavarta and establish our reign here. A new age will be ushered in. The Age of Asuras, the Age of Kaalnemi.'

A deathly silence suddenly fell over the asuras. They looked at each other in dismay. One bold asura, who might have been raised by his parents to ask inquisitive questions, spoke in a harsh voice.

'What about Dandak?'

Kaalnemi looked for the source of the question but all the asuras looked similarly ugly to him. He answered in a loud voice, 'We owe our lives and victory to Dandak, and he will be the one king of all of Aryavarta. Dandak will usher in the Age of Asuras. Today, we stand bearing the flag of his kingdom.

'Tomorrow, we march to Hastinapur.'

~

The asura soldier watched Kaalnemi as he went around picking up and throwing things lying about the palace—idols, artifacts, paintings—whatever was left after the rampage. Kaalnemi tore them all down.

'Humans!' Kaalnemi hissed in disgust. 'Where is the king's body?'

'At the fort's entry, my Lord, it has not been moved yet.'

'Hang it from a tree in the centre of the city for those who have survived to see. Spread the word: Dandak has taken over Avanti.'

'Yes, my Lord,' said the shaken asura.

Kaalnemi moved around the palace hall towards the king's throne. He waved his palm and a small flicker of fire came alive at his fingertips, enough to light the hookah by the armrest. The asura soldier glanced nervously at him.

Kaalnemi seated himself comfortably like a king on a throne. 'Any word on the prince and his little sister?'

'They escaped, my Lord,' the messenger relayed the information with his head bowed.

Kaalnemi blew hard on the hookah and the flames rose higher. He put his hand inside the fire as if baking it, without flinching. Fire did not affect him. But Kaalnemi was fuming inside. It had been a blunder, letting the girl live when he could have killed her using sorcery. But he needed to get rid of Apasmitra first and so, he had left her to a bunch of asuras, while he fought the sage.

One girl. Three asuras. It should have been easy.

Incompetent bastards! He blew on the hookah, the white smoke escaping from his mouth and nostrils.

'Find the girl. At whatever cost. Kill the prince if you have to. But find the girl. I want her dead,' he roared.

22

An Unexpected Visitor

Ashwatthama was breathless, his body drenched in sweat. As he awakened, he realised what had been haunting him for the past few weeks. There was an unfulfilled promise hanging over his head. He had forgotten all about Rati, and Indra's curse. Like him, she had suffered too. He looked at the moon, which was directly above the roof now, shining brightly on the throne.

The torch had gone out while he was sleeping. Except for the shafts of moonlight, the hall was engulfed in complete darkness. Ashwatthama tried to wipe the sweat off his forehead with the back of his arm but to no effect. His arm too, was drenched in sweat. The pieces of the fake bow in his waistband poked him; he took them out and threw them on the ground next to the throne. There was no need for them anymore.

A thud near the entrance startled him. He looked around for the source but could see nothing in the pitch dark. Straining, Ashwatthama saw a figure bumbling around in the dark. Drona's son grasped his sword and in a swift movement, got up and approached a pillar to get a better look at the intruder. The torch hanging on the pillar was emitting a fireless smoke that wafted towards the roof. The stranger seemed to be moving slowly, struggling in the dark. Somehow, the walk seemed familiar. He tried to focus on the stranger's face in the dark but in vain.

Then as the intruder meandered into the moonlight, his face was revealed.

Ashwatthama sighed in relief. 'Vikram?'

The voice startled the intruder and he turned towards Ashwatthama, who still held his sword in an aggressive pose.

'Ashwatthama, my friend. I was not sure if I would find you but I had to take the chance,' Vikram said, moving forward.

However, Ashwatthama kept his sword up, moving it a little higher.

Vikram raised his hands in the air, 'Not a shape-shifter.'

'Prove it.'

'Um...well, Rana's poetry would act as a good cure for sleeplessness?' Vikram quipped, and they both chuckled.

'Indeed, it would. Someone should tell him that,' Ashwatthama replied calmly, lowering his sword and embracing the unexpected visitor. He offered water to his thirsty friend.

'Why are you here? Were you not supposed to be in Surparaka, gathering allies?'

An exhausted Vikram gulped down the water hurriedly.

'The city fell a couple of weeks back,' he said. 'I barely made it out alive with my family. We took refuge in the Mandara Forests, the abode of the Kimpurushas but the asuras attacked and tried to kill us there too. Many Kimpurushas were killed in the attack while defending us... many innocent ones. Then the Kimpurusha Chief asked us to leave. Not his fault. We went to Hastinapur, where we got information from Rana about the impending attack on Avanti. So, I asked Janam...'

'Wait...Avanti is under attack?' Ashwatthama asked, shocked.

'Apparently... From what I heard, the asuras were on their way to the fort. I am not aware of the present situation. Having no army of my own, I couldn't offer any assistance to Rana.'

'No,' Ashwatthama gasped as he smote his forehead with his hand. 'I should be there. I didn't realise the attack would take place so soon.'

'There's a lot more going on, Ashwatthama. Many kingdoms have accepted a truce with Dandak, so we have very few allies. Hastinapur and the Yeti kingdoms are the only two forces against Dandak now. Janamejaya mentioned that you were headed to Ayodhya. I figured you would be at the old palace, and was hoping to catch up with you before you went elsewhere. What brought you here?'

'We deduced Nyat was referring to Ayodhya when he said, "Yoddha," but it now seems...' Ashwatthama stopped talking midway. Something near the throne had caught his eye.

He walked closer as the silver moonlight seemed to morph into golden rays, the glaze bouncing off the throne. As he edged closer, Ashwatthama noticed a pattern on the seat. He looked at the wall of the palace from where the moonlight beamed down. It was the same patch of broken wall that he had crashed into, after being punched by Hanuman.

Ashwatthama examined the pattern. Vikram moved closer to look at it too. He was immediately intrigued.

'Is that a...?'

Ashwatthama nodded. 'Shivalinga. Accurate representation. I don't understand these two symbols, though.'

He pointed to the pattern. One pattern closely resembled a Shivalinga, complete with three sandalwood-filled lines.

The other two patterns by the side of the Shivalinga were a crescent and a full moon. Although the patterns were crude, they were accurate enough to not be dismissed as random symbols.

'A crescent and a full moon. What could these be?' Vikram murmured.

Ashwatthama shook his head, still looking intently at the pattern. 'We need to figure out what this means. There's only one person I know who can help; he is a master of symbols.'

Vikram looked intently at Ashwatthama, waiting for further revelation.

But Ashwatthama asked a question instead, 'Did you come here on a Yeti horse?'

Vikram nodded. 'Janamejaya lent me the one he had.'

'Perfect. We need to head out...' Ashwatthama paused.

'What is it?' Vikram asked, surprised.

Ashwatthama frowned. 'Vikram, you should get back to Hastinapur. Events are moving at a rapid pace. We had been fortunate with Raktavija and Vidyut but tackling the asuras is getting increasingly risky. I want you to return and look after the arrangements in Hastinapur. We may be at war sooner than anticipated.'

Vikram looked blank, then incredulous. 'I am here for you, my friend,' he said. 'I know that you can handle everything yourself but there are times when you might need another helping hand.'

'I know, Vikram,' Ashwatthama raised his hands in exasperation. 'But I cannot put you in danger. This war is going to get uglier.'

'So? I knew that even before I ventured into this, Ashwatthama. We have to think beyond ourselves. It is for the entire Aryavarta. If we back out due to fear and selfishness, they win. And *that* we must prevent, no matter what the cost.'

Ashwatthama shuddered as he recollected the encounter at Dwarka where they were almost defeated. Their lives had been in incredible danger. Each new war was getting worse than the last. He looked at the symbols again.

Would he have discovered the clues had Vikram not arrived? Who was sending these messages out?

With a heavy sigh Ashwatthama looked at Vikram. 'Fine, let us leave at the break of dawn.'

'Where are we going?'

'To Himavant. To the Yeti kingdom, again.'

23

Camouflage

Rana was restless in the humid night. He was neither asleep nor was he fully awake. His mind played out the scene of Janak Singh's death repeatedly. And in another vision, he saw Urmila standing close by and smiling as his father was being assaulted and killed.

He came out of his stupor with a sudden jerk. Realising that his nightmare bore a close resemblance to what had happened, he sighed. He raised himself against the wall in the light of the dim flame of the torch, and saw that Abhayajeet and Urmila were sleeping soundly. Weariness had peaked to an insane level in all of them. Wiping the saliva off his cheek, he checked on Shreya. The injury had thankfully spared her internal organs, since the blood had now clotted.

The wound had been stitched up properly by Urmila. However, it would take more than a week for it to heal. Rana's main concern was to protect her from further skirmishes. A slight pressure on the wound could cause it to rupture and then it would be beyond healing. Abhayajeet had guided them to a village near the border of Avanti, about forty miles from the palace in Ujjaini. The village was a small one, with less than fifty huts, a place of no real significance to the asuras. As a general, Abhayajeet knew all the remote corners of Avanti. It would be easy for them to camouflage themselves in the darkness.

Rana was not able to put his father's death out of his mind. A thousand questions plagued him. If his leg had not been pinned under the stone, it might have been a different story; if Urmila had tackled the asura who had struck from behind.

Why could she not have shown a little courage when it was urgently required?

A sudden commotion alerted Rana. He peeped out of the window of the hut, keeping his head low, and saw a few asura riders at a distance, carrying torches in their hands. He counted about twenty of them. They were shouting and randomly setting fire to the bundled crops. The scared villagers rushed out of their homes with folded hands, pleading but the asuras did not spare the crops.

Rana dropped into a crouching position and threw the torch on the wall onto the mud-plastered floor. He poured some water over it, and smoke hissed from the dying fire. The hut in which they were housed was at a little distance from the other huts in the village, and so, it was not visible in the dark. Rana peered at the scene outside again. The asuras, mounted on their horses, had their swords out and were threatening the villagers. They had come for Rana and his party.

Rana shook Abhayajeet, who woke up with a jerk. As Rana woke up Urmila, she clasped his hand. For a moment, Rana forgot his bitterness, looking at her serene face.

'We have to move. Now. They are here,' Rana whispered to her, pointing to the window.

Both Abhayajeet and Urmila peeked out of the window and saw the asuras going around the village.

'Shreya?' Urmila looked worriedly at Rana, then, at the injured Avanti princess. 'She cannot run.'

'I will take her,' Rana said in a low voice and beckoned to Abhayajeet. 'Get the horses ready at the rear of the hut. Which way do we go, Abhayajeet?'

'Towards the north. The kusha grass should provide us with a good cover,' the Avanti General pointed towards the north, putting his boots on.

Rana nodded. He recalled his journey with Ashwatthama and Vikram, and how they had escaped the monstrous goh. That had been just a few months ago but so much had happened since then. He felt as if it had taken place a lifetime ago.

Abhayajeet and Urmila tiptoed out to ensure the horses were not alarmed. They slowly unhooked the reins and prepared to ride away. Rana picked up Shreya, making sure there was no pressure on her wound. The *dhatura* (thorn-apple) Urmila had used as a painkiller had sedated her. Rana carried her out of the hut towards the back. He placed Shreya on his horse and sat behind her, ensuring she did not fall. Urmila and Abhayajeet mounted their horses and trotted into the kusha grass outside the village. As Rana looked back, he could see a few villagers pointing towards their hut. The darkness had been good camouflage and given them the cover they needed to escape.

The asuras were engaged in an animated discussion and the next moment, started moving towards the hut.

~

As the group moved through the kusha grass, Rana cautioned, 'Stay close, we cannot afford to lose each other.'

They heard the asuras reaching the hut and making a din on not finding the warriors. Faintly, they heard an asura giving orders to split up and head in different directions, one group coming towards the kusha grass.

'They are behind us,' Abhayajeet said, despondent as he realised that no less than ten asuras would be pursuing them. He cast a glance towards the others. All of them were moving slower than they should, due to Shreya's injury. A swift canter could rupture her stitches.

Abhayajeet looked at Shreya. One strike, and it would be over for her. He frowned, realising that it was time to take tough decisions. 'Rana, you take Shreya and Urmila and head left; continue going north, until you reach the next village. Keep moving every couple of days and camouflage yourselves to look like commoners. Travel during the daytime, and you should be safe from bandits. Get to Hastinapur.'

'Abhayajeet, no. We are not leaving you,' Rana stressed, shaking his head. He looked towards Urmila and signalled to her, speaking in a hushed tone. 'Take Shreya and move north as he said. I will deal with the asuras here.'

But Abhayajeet was adamant. He dismounted and stopped Rana from shifting Shreya to Urmila's horse.

'Listen to me, Rana,' Abhayajeet whispered urgently. 'It is imperative that you save Shreya because she cannot defend herself right now. If Urmila is alone, she can be attacked easily and it won't be possible for her to defend both Shreya and herself. We have to take tough decisions in war.'

The truth struck Rana head-on. He realised the weight behind the General's decision. Something about Abhayajeet reminded Rana of Valari. The latter had sacrificed himself for Rana, and now Abhayajeet too was doing the same.

How do warriors become brave? They do the right, not the easy, thing.

Rana looked at Abhayajeet helplessly. He knew in his heart that it was probably the last time he would see the

Avanti General. Rana couldn't fathom why in all recent situations he had been rendered so helpless, whether it was Janak Singh's death or Shreya's injury, the fall of Avanti and now his inability to prevent Abhayajeet from almost certain doom.

Rana gave Abhayajeet a grateful hug and held him a moment longer, something he wished he had done with Valari. With a heavy heart, Rana then mounted his horse and balanced Shreya carefully. He took a last look at Abhayajeet, with tears in his eyes. Abhayajeet nodded and thumped his fist on his heart. Rana looked at Urmila, who was teary-eyed too, knowing full well the significance of Abhayajeet's sacrifice. Avanti's General nodded to her and gestured that Rana leave before it was too late.

Rana nodded, tugged at the reins of his horse, followed by Urmila, and they rode away.

Abhayajeet glanced at the prince one last time and then turned around. He mounted the horse and started making sounds with his sword, drawing the asuras towards him and away from the young warriors who were riding away.

Moments later, Rana and Urmila heard the faint clash of swords and battle cries from Abhayajeet.

Rana closed his eyes, taking a deep breath. In one night, he had lost much more than he had ever anticipated. He felt like a puppet in the hands of destiny. Never in his dreams had he imagined that he would have to flee his kingdom. He missed his father; no matter their ideological differences; the king had always wanted the best for Rana. He was concerned if Shreya would survive the ordeal; she urgently needed better treatment and medicines.

And he missed his relationship with Urmila. He wished he could hold her hand and pour out his heart to her, put his head on her shoulders and cry. Rana's heart was broken. She was right next to him, yet she seemed distant.

The greatest distance between two people is the distance between their hearts.

For now, Rana was all by himself.

And so was Urmila.

24

Love Shatters

Rana and Urmila took Shreya and travelled from one village to another, moving swiftly as advised by Abhayajeet, not staying at any particular place for more than two days. They hadn't heard from Abhayajeet after their last meeting. Rana was certain Abhayajeet would have caught up with them had he survived the fight with the asuras. He was reminded of Vikram's words, back in the old days, before it all started: 'The cost of war is more than you think, my friend. You long for glory but along the way, you lose things that you took for granted. At that point, you look back and think, was glory worth it? Nature will not give you anything for free, Rana. Everything comes at a cost. And you must be ready to pay the price.'

But Rana hadn't wanted to bring this war upon his kingdom. Or had he, when he had opted to accompany Ashwatthama and Vikram to Himavant in search of personal glory? Maybe Avanti would have been spared and made an ally by Dandak. But would Janak Singh have allowed that? Would Rana himself have agreed to that? War would have been inevitable in any case.

Rana's head ballooned with questions he had no definite answers to. It also hurt from excessive thinking and stress, something he was not used to. It felt like his mind was being bombarded constantly by thoughts he had no control over. Despite trying not to, thoughts about Urmila's betrayal kept coming back to him. Rana longed for mental peace, something he felt had abandoned him. He wondered if physical injury was preferable to such mental turmoil. The former only destroyed one's body but the latter destroyed the body and soul, sucking the happiness out of one's life. Life was much more of a burden when one was constantly unhappy. Faith seemed to be the only way out of it but Rana wondered if his faith was a steadfast one.

On the fifth day of their travel, Shreya recovered enough to ride on her own. They traded some jewellery for another horse and rode towards Hastinapur, travelling only during the day to avoid bandits along the way. Since both Rana and Urmila had made the journey through the Ganges plains earlier, they knew the route. It spared them the ride through the arduous mountainous regions and kept them in the vicinity of small villages, where they could buy food and stay hidden at night.

After ten days, they were met by a team of soldiers from Hastinapur sent by Janamejaya, who gave them cover for the rest of their journey.

~

A few days later, they reached Hastinapur and were welcomed by Janamejaya, who was more than glad to see Urmila safe.

'Get some rest first and then we will talk,' Janamejaya said.

The travellers complied with relief. Janamejaya sent for the palace physician to examine Shreya's injury. After dinner, they all gathered on the terrace.

Janamejaya glanced at Rana who looked gloomy. 'What happened at Avanti?' he asked. 'We have had no news from that front, after your last message of an impending attack. We have been worried.'

'Avanti has fallen,' Rana said, leaning over the terrace, looking out at the city. 'Dandak's army has taken over the entire kingdom. They are massacring men, women and children, sparing no one.'

'The end of humanity as we know it,' Janamejaya remarked in a dismal, prophesying tone.

'Do you have any news of Ashwatthama?' Rana turned back to face the Hastinapur King.

Janamejaya shook his head.

'I have not heard from or of him since he left Avanti for Ayodhya. Vikram decided to head for Ayodhya to accompany him.'

Rana's eyes widened. 'Vikram is with Ashwatthama? What happened in Surparaka?'

'Vikram and his family reached here two weeks ago,' Janamejaya replied, eyes downcast. 'He had had a harrowing journey, similar to yours. His kingdom was attacked by mercenaries; when he went to find refuge with the Kimpurushas in the Mandara Forest, the asuras attacked there, killing many of the tribe. So, the chief asked them to leave their forest. He came here with his family and a few soldiers. On learning that Ashwatthama was headed for Ayodhya, he became restless, saying that if he stayed here, the asuras would come here, so he needed to get away. I'm not sure what he was talking about. He seemed out of his mind with worry, and increasingly restless. So, I lent him my Yeti horse, and he left about ten days ago.'

Rana ran his hands through his hair, squinting at a glum Urmila for a moment before shifting his attention to Janamejaya again.

'Ashwatthama had left for Ayodhya, to follow up on what we thought was Nyat's last clue for us. I wonder if he found something there. He was supposed to return after that but if he has not arrived, then I'm afraid, he might have walked right into Kaalnemi's trap.'

Janamejaya grimaced at the mention of a new name. 'Kaalnemi? Who is he?'

'The new general of Dandak's army. Said to be as fierce as the asura king himself. He was the one who led the attack on Avanti.'

'But Avanti had a large army. How many asuras were in the enemy camp?'

'Ten thousand asuras and four Giants. All four were incapacitated but apparently there are more.'

'Giants?' Janamejaya said with a gasp. He reached for a nearby bench to sit on and digest the information. The Kauravas had faced one Giant, Ghatotkach, in the Kurukshetra War, and he had wreaked havoc on the Kaurava army. If there were more than five Giants ranged against them, each one with only quarter of the strength of Ghatotkach, they were still doomed. The Giants were almost invincible, impossible to kill with ordinary weapons.

'How are we going to defeat the Giants? How did you incapacitate them?'

Rana flinched. 'We used aml. Although it killed many of our soldiers too, later. It was...gory. But nothing else would have worked.'

Janamejaya squirmed. He recalled how he had banned the use of aml in his kingdom for general industrial use as well as for warfare, when he became king. Due to its horrifying dangerous properties, many people had started acquiring it illegally and using it on their enemies. Some spurned lovers threw it on innocent girls, disfiguring their faces permanently.

It had become a horrendous weapon. Ultimately, Janamejaya had decided to ban production and ordered that all existing quantities of aml were to be destroyed. Not a single soul protested. They had seen what the effects could be.

'What is Dandak's plan?' Janamejaya asked.

'No one knows. There is hardly any news of him, which is confusing all of us. Why would an asura come out of hiding after thousands of years and then disappear? I believe he is planning something huge and will show up when the time comes. Nevertheless, I think the army is going to march to Hastinapur next.

'Given that the Giants will be coming with them and that the asura army might not launch an attack without the Giants, you have something like a month before they reach the Hastinapur gates.'

'I had better start the preparations then,' Janamejaya said, shaking his head in desperation. 'Oh, and Urmila, I will send a message to your father. He wanted to take you back to Indraprastha.'

Urmila nodded. She looked at Rana, who turned away. Over the last few days, she had sensed his aloofness but with events unfolding at such a rapid pace, she had not had the chance to clarify matters with him.

It was clear to her that Rana was miffed with her, for some reason.

~

After Janamejaya left, Rana stood at the terrace parapet, looking out at the vast expanse of Hastinapur city. Urmila came up from behind and put her hand on his shoulder. For a moment, Rana stood still, then, he brushed her hand aside.

'What has happened?' Urmila asked, a little nervously. 'Did I do something wrong? I know you are riled up about something. Is it related to me?'

Rana looked away, wishing there was a way he could avoid talking about it. But there wasn't.

He turned to face her and pointed a finger in her face. 'You. You are responsible for the death of my father. You could have saved him. He was just a step away from you. If you had taken out that asura, my father would still be alive.'

'What?' Urmila gasped as she widened her eyes, completely taken aback by the accusation and Rana's tone.

'I don't know what to say to you,' Rana turned his back on her.

Urmila stood stunned, unsure if she should offer an explanation. Finally mustering enough courage, she spoke, 'How can you accuse me like that, Rana? I fought in the war alongside you. I faced those asuras and I killed them.'

'And then you ran away,' Rana said with contempt in his voice. He looked her in the eye. 'You ran. In a moment that mattered the most. True friends don't do that.'

'But I was…I was…,' Urmila stammered as she felt tears gathering in her eyes. She was reminded of Shreya's words: *Please don't tell Rana dau. He won't forgive me.*

Urmila took a deep breath and closed her eyes. She stayed still for a few moments.

'I am not a coward, Rana,' she said defiantly, looking him squarely in the eye. 'I am a warrior, just like you. And I do not run away from the enemy. You have to start trusting your friends.'

'I trust my friends, Urmila. But can I count you as one among them? That is the question.'

Urmila stood dumbfounded for a moment, not knowing what to do. She hadn't cried for anyone in her life. Until now.

She turned around, tears flowing down her cheeks, and slowly walked away.

25

Yeti Kingdom, Again

Ashwatthama and Vikram walked through the familiar icy caves of the Yeti kingdom, led by Yetiraj.

'Glad to see you again, friends. I hope you have some news, positive news?' Yetiraj turned to look at Ashwatthama as he walked ahead of the visitors.

'I do. Let us meet Master Rudrasen, and then I can divulge it.'

They reached the library in no time, and Ashwatthama greeted Rudrasen.

'Ashwatthama, you have returned, son,' Rudrasen said. 'We heard about your fight with Raktavija and Vidyut. Good job, vanquishing them both, even though Dandak's resurrection could not be stopped.'

Rudrasen adjusted his chair as he gestured for the warriors to take their seats. 'But your work is far from over. And I believe it to be the reason for your visit now.'

'Yes, Master. Apparently, we lost the bow in the fight in Dwarka. And that's what brings me here.'

'I heard about that, too. It is disappointing but I believe that whatever happens will pave the path for future events. Strange are the workings of the universe. Anyway, I am just a blabbering old fool. How can I help you?'

'Master, do you remember how Dandak came to be in possession of both the Agneyastra and the Brahmastra?' Ashwatthama asked.

'He does have both and they are deadly weapons, Ashwatthama,' Rudrasen replied, clutching his staff with both hands.

'Yes, they are. We know that Shiva gave him the Agneyastra, and he got the Brahmastra from Brahma.'

Rudrasen nodded.

'And all along, we thought Dandak wanted the Kodanda because he was afraid it could be used to kill him.'

'Yes. I know there have been warriors who have had these three weapons and were practically invincible, and so...'

'Wait!' Rudrasen said. 'Are you...are you implying that Dandak still has the Kodanda?'

'Precisely' Ashwatthama replied. 'The Kodanda is the same bow, the Saranga that was given by Parashurama to Lord Rama. It was passed on from Vishnu to Sage Riciika, the son of Bhrigu. Then the bow went to Sage Jamadagni, son of Riciika, and from him to his son, Parashurama. It is virtually indestructible, impervious to attack by any weapon or mortal, given its celestial origin. Dandak now has all the three weapons that he needs to make him invincible in the world.'

Ashwatthama took out a piece of the broken bow and casually put it on the table in front of Rudrasen.

'This is a piece of the bow that Vidyut broke in Dwarka. This counterfeit was designed to mislead us into thinking that we have lost the Kodanda but it has been with Dandak all the time.'

Rudrasen picked up the broken counterfeit piece and examined it before putting it back. He leaned back in his chair, thinking for a while. 'What options do we have now?'

he asked. 'If Dandak has all three in his possession, we have practically lost the war.'

'Not yet. Please listen to me,' Ashwatthama continued. 'The celestial weapons of Tretayuga and Dwaparayuga had a specific property: they were mostly astras and not shastras. They could be summoned if the user just chanted some specific mantras. These mantras were unique to each warrior and needed to be remembered by him to invoke the weapon. The alternative was that warriors could carry the weapon in shastra form and use them but most warriors never did that for fear of losing the shastra.

'But what if someone had to hide these astras from all of humankind for an uncertain period of time, moreover, just before going into a state of physical uncertainty? He could not, and would not, rely on remembering the mantras after such a fierce curse.'

Yetiraj looked at Ashwatthama in surprise as the latter stared at Rudrasen who seemed to be silently weighing something.

Ashwatthama continued, 'And he would try to ensure he got them back when he resurrected. So, the best option is...' He paused for dramatic effect as he waved his open palms in a gesture signifying the obvious.

'...To convert them into actual weapons and hide them,' Rudrasen completed the sentence, nodding in agreement.

'Yes,' Ashwatthama thumped the table, and Vikram started with surprise.

'So, you mean that before Dandak went to Rasatala finally, he converted the two astras—the Brahmastra and the Agneyastra—to shastras and hid them somewhere? But where?'

Ashwatthama stood up and walked around the table, all the while gesturing impassionedly with his hands. 'I have been thinking about that for quite some time. We know that Dandak would not want any mortal to get hold of the weapons. So, he would hide them at a place where no one would find them, not for thousands of years.'

'That place could be anywhere on earth,' Yetiraj interrupted. 'Dandak had the Mansa chariot; he could have travelled anywhere to hide his weapons.'

'I know,' Ashwatthama replied, 'but think about it. Would he hide his weapons in a place where it ran the slightest risk of being discovered by humans? Or would he hide it somewhere where no human had ever set foot?'

'The ice mountains at the end of the world?' Yetiraj sighed, looking into the distance. 'I have always wanted to visit the place. Heard it is even colder than here. And many more fish...'

'No, no,' Ashwatthama waved, trying to bring Yetiraj back to Himavant. 'It is possible that someone will get there, eventually. Even I am unaware of any place where mortals cannot enter. But when we were in Ayodhya, we had a hunch.'

Ashwatthama pulled a blank sheet from a nearby shelf and put it on the table. He picked up a quill and started drawing a symbol, first of a Shivalinga, and then of a crescent and full moon by the side of it. He looked at Vikram for confirmation and the latter nodded.

'This is a symbol we came across in Ayodhya. The reason it intrigued us is...well...the Shivalinga was quite prominent. So, we came here to see if you could help us with it.'

Rudrasen pored over the symbols.

Ashwatthama continued, 'During our journey from Ayodhya, Vikram and I went through the list of all the major temples in Aryavarta where a full and crescent moon symbol might be found but we have not been able to zero in on any specific one. It has to be one where no mortal can ever go.'

Rudrasen gasped, 'Is it possible?'

He motioned for Yetiraj to fetch a terrain map of Himavant. Unrolling the map, the Master asked the visitors to look at the area beyond Himavant, towards the north. As Ashwatthama and Vikram looked closely, their eyes widened. There were two water bodies, marked in blue; one was in the shape of a crescent and another of a full circle.

'Are these the ones?' Ashwatthama looked at Rudrasen, wrinkles appearing on his forehead.

'Lake Rakshastal,' Rudrasen answered tersely. 'The only place where mortals fear to tread.'

'And the Shivalinga?' Vikram questioned.

Rudrasen pointed to a peak on the map. 'Forty miles north of the lakes. Kailasa—the abode of Lord Shiva.'

Ashwatthama and Vikram looked at each other, acknowledging the truth of what they had heard.

'That's it, then. This could be the place where Dandak has hidden the weapons. Anywhere else, and he risked losing them,' exclaimed Ashwatthama.

Yetiraj narrowed his eyes. 'So, you mean Dandak has hidden his weapons inside Rakshastal Lake, the one beside the Kailasa Mountain?'

Ashwatthama looked at Rudrasen for validation.

'In all probability, he will go to retrieve them,' the Master predicted, his eyes closed. 'The lake is cursed. Any human or animal that enters the water of Rakshastal Lake dies in a short time, almost within a week. Rakshastal lies just next to Mansarovar but an exquisite irony separates the two lakes. One is revered as a gateway for Shiva, the other famed for its curse. Rakshastal Lake was created by Ravana; it is where he performed his penances to propitiate Shiva. On an island on this lake, he offered his head, one each day, to please Shiva. Finally, on the tenth day, Shiva appeared and was moved to grant divine powers to Ravana. You will be able to identify the lakes easily since Mansarovar is circular and Rakshastal is roughly crescent-shaped. Dandak too was a devotee of Shiva's, so what better place to hide his weapons than at the foot of Shiva's abode?'

'But how could Dandak have hidden the weapons in the lake, given that mortals would die if they entered it? Would Dandak himself not have died because of the curse?' Yetiraj asked.

Rudrasen opened his eyes. 'I cannot be completely sure of it but I believe the curse only applies to mortals.'

Ashwatthama frowned. 'Could it mean that Dandak was immortal before he took a dip in the lake? We might need a new strategy then.'

Rudrasen replied, 'I believe that for some reason, the curse does not apply to him.'

The trio was silent, trying to figure out the ramifications of this information. Moments later, Rudrasen spoke, 'Ah, I think I get it. Since Ravana had created the lake, the curse might not apply to asuras.'

'Damn!' Yetiraj muttered. 'And I was thinking of a dip there.'

Rudrasen closed his eyes again and sat silently for a few moments. His eyebrows arched as if arriving at a decision. Moments later, he opened his eyes and looked intensely at Ashwatthama.

'There is something you should know, Ashwatthama.' Rudrasen now had worry lines on his forehead. 'Do you remember the last journey of the Pandavas, when they went towards Indra's abode through Mount Sumeru, and they all fell one by one, all except Yudhisthir?'

'Yes, Master,' Ashwatthama nodded.

Rudrasen paused as if speculating whether to divulge the information or not. He seemed to be calculating the repercussions. He looked at Ashwatthama, a soldier from out of time, fighting demons, who were also from out of time. They were all where they should not be and yet destiny had been ruthless in pitting them against each other.

Rudrasen pursed his lips, knowing that the information was dangerous to reveal but even worse to conceal. The warrior deserved to know.

'In their final journey,' Rudrasen said, 'the Pandavas were climbing Mount Sumeru. At that important turn of events, providentially, Bheema was carrying your gem along with him. This was an unfinished task, since he had been instructed by Krishna long before the final journey, to throw it somewhere where no human could ever find it.'

Ashwatthama settled down, listening hard. He had an inkling where the conversation was headed. His heartbeat increased in anticipation of the revelation.

Rudrasen continued, 'While en route to Sumeru, Bheema threw the gem away with so much force that it landed in Rakshastal Lake. We know about it because many Yetis witnessed the event. As far as we are concerned, we neither care about the gem nor would we reveal this information to anyone else. The place where Dandak has hidden his weapons is also the place where your lost gem resides.'

26

Brother Against Brother

Ahilsena stormed through the empty Hastinapur palace hall where Janamejaya was discussing the battle formation with his army general. The king had sent all ministers to prepare for war and to ensure the safety of citizens. His regular court sessions were suspended until further notice.

'Where is she?' Ahilsena demanded.

Janamejaya looked up from the map of Hastinapur, startled by the angry voice. He glanced at the general and motioned that the discussion could continue at a later time. The general nodded, bowed and left.

'Have a seat, brother,' Janamejaya said, gesturing at a seat nearby.

'Enough of this nonsense, Janamejaya', Ahilsena said tersely. 'I gave her permission to go to Himavant. Now she is going into battle without even asking me.'

'Let me call her,' Janamejaya clapped and a girl appeared. He asked her to fetch Urmila.

As Urmila entered the room, Ahilsena saw her crestfallen face and realised something was not right.

'What happened?' His tone softened.

'Nothing, father,' Urmila replied and hugged him.

'Enough of these adventures. Let us go home now.'

Urmila nodded. She looked at Janamejaya, who quickly deduced something had happened between Rana and her. He turned towards Ahilsena.

'Hastinapur is going to be attacked by the asura army; you know that, right?'

'I know,' Ahilsena answered calmly, moving towards the golden throne in the hall, past Janamejaya.

'Are you going to join us in the war? Will you be sending in your army?' Janamejaya asked as the two brothers stood with their backs to each other. He sensed the hostility in his brother, the King of Indraprastha.

'Yes,' Ahilsena said calmly. He paused for a moment.

'But not on your side.'

'Father!' Urmila gasped, wide-eyed. 'Would you side with the asuras?'

'The asuras have sent a peace treaty assuring us that they are not going to attack our kingdom, Indraprastha. The asuras want to live in harmony.'

Janamejaya turned around and found his kin looking intently at the Hastinapur throne.

'Don't you see, Ahil?' he asked. 'It's a trap. They are already attacking the kingdoms that are refusing to comply with them. The asuras are destroying them completely, killing all humans, not even sparing the elderly, women and children, meting out the worst fate possible to them. What promises do you expect these merciless beasts to keep?'

Ahilsena was silent for a while, then, he turned to face Janamejaya.

Janamejaya asked, 'What promises have they given you, Ahilsena? This kingdom? The Giants? How much more do you want, brother?'

Ahilsena looked away, towards the throne. 'I want what is rightfully mine,' he said. 'All these years, I have been a sidekick, a mere puppet on strings, while you, Janamejaya, have enjoyed all the glory of your ancestors. I want the share that was due to my grandfather Vrishaketu after Karna was killed. Was Vrishaketu not the eldest Pandava heir and rightful king of Hastinapur? How could they crown Parikshit instead of Vrishaketu? How could you be so ignorant as to not see it?

'What am I ruling? A kingdom with twenty villages. Does that even count? I will have Hastinapur, one way or the other. It belonged to my ancestors and I will set history right by stamping my name on it. Finally, the descendants of Karna will ascend the throne of Hastinapur.'

Janamejaya put his hand on Ahilsena's shoulder. 'You are not thinking clearly, Ahilsena. The asuras will never let the humans survive. This peace treaty that you so highly speak of is just a sham. Dandak is trying to make sure that the humans do not form a united front. He is dividing us first, and as long as we are divided, it makes his task easier.'

Ahilsena snubbed him, shaking Janamejaya's hand off his shoulder.

'Huh! This is the king who wants to hold on to his kingdom speaking. Consider my position, Janamejaya. Why is it that my ancestor got no glory in the war, while your ancestors became the supreme heroes? Did not the Pandavas cheat to kill every important warrior in the war? Every single one of them, Janamejaya. And what gets inscribed on the scrolls of history is that my ancestor was one of the villains in the war. History always gets written by the victors. Once this war is over, I will rewrite it. Karna's name will always be above Arjuna's, and that is how future generations will remember him.'

Janamejaya had no answer. All his life, he had tried to keep peace with Indraprastha, knowing full well its history. He realised that he had been greedy not to share Hastinapur with Ahilsena, despite knowing that the latter too was a claimant to the Hastinapur throne. And now, they were neck-deep in turbulent waters. This was the result of his greed. He would make amends.

'Let bygones be bygones, Ahilsena. You are making a big mistake. I realise I have not been fair to you. Let us fight this war together, brother, and I promise, I will share part of my kingdom with you.'

Ahilsena laughed harshly. 'Now, you think about sharing your kingdom, Janamejaya. Where were you all these years when I sat in that small court, with nothing to do all day; when my subjects called me "worthless king" behind my back as there was nothing to rule over? And now, when you see that I might have more power than you have, you are offering me part of my own kingdom. I do not accept charity, Janamejaya. It's just a matter of days and then Hastinapur will rightfully be mine.'

Ahilsena turned around and strode towards the door, motioning Urmila to follow. 'Goodbye, brother,' he said.

Janamejaya stood numbly as his brother marched out of the court.

As they exited the hall, Rana entered, glancing at Ahilsena. A distraught Urmila looked at Rana but he deliberately ignored her and went towards Janamejaya.

'What was that all about?' Rana asked a visibly shaken Janamejaya.

'Hard to explain all that's happening,' Janamejaya shook his head as he slumped on a minister's chair nearby and rubbed his forehead. 'And I thought I had seen the end of the feud between brothers.'

'What happened?' Rana asked again.

Janamejaya buried his head in his hands. He felt tired as he recalled the events of the past few months. Suddenly he realised the enormous mental pressure his ancestors would have gone through in the years leading up to the Kurukshetra War—the wax-palace, the game of dice, the thirteen-year exile, dealing with humiliation from Duryodhana, and finally losing their loved ones in the war.

Rana gently shook Janamejaya. 'What happened? What are you thinking about?'

'You might not believe it but you and your beloved are going to face each other on different sides of the battlefield,' Janamejaya said, looking towards the palace entrance. He saw Ahilsena mounting the chariot with Urmila behind him as they rode past the Hastinapur palace gate.

Rana saw Urmila disappearing in a cloud of dust and though he felt a twinge in his heart, he looked at Janamejaya again.

'How is that possible?' he asked. 'Is he fighting for Dandak?'

Janamejaya nodded.

'But why?'

Janamejaya walked towards the throne, looking at it from the vantage point of the courtiers.

'It's always about power. The more you have it, the more you want it. Partly, it is my fault, too. I pushed him, knowing full well that he was not happy. It was my responsibility to make sure he was respected, being a descendent of Karna.' Janamejaya smiled sadly and continued. 'We all have to pay for our sins, Rana. They will catch up with us, eventually.'

Rana looked at the seemingly helpless Janamejaya. It seemed events had spiralled out of control.

'How much of an army does he have?'

'Not much,' Janamejaya replied. 'Probably eight thousand soldiers, with four thousand horses and one thousand elephants.'

'Then why do you worry?' Rana asked curtly, turning around. His hostility towards Urmila was growing stronger with time, and now he didn't care which side she fought on.

'I will go and see Shreya,' he said. 'She mentioned something about having stumbled on a fact related to Dandak's weakness.'

27

The Lost Gem

Ashwatthama touched his forehead, where the gem had had
its home once. The spot still burned—the only remnant
from the curse that had not been set right during the
battle with Raktavija. Ashwatthama had been born with
the gem on his forehead, which made him more powerful
than all beings lower than humans. He could even kill a
full-grown lion with his bare hands. The gem gave him
control over physical needs such as hunger, diseases and
fatigue. It made him fearless, even from attacks by the
Gods, Nagas and rakshasas.

'What are you suggesting, Master?' he asked Rudrasen,
frowning.

'Retrieve your gem,' Rudrasen said. 'It is endowed with
divine powers. Your gem was the source of your strength
and your knowledge of the celestial weapons. Once you get
that back, you will regain your complete powers. You will not
be able to defeat Dandak without it. Someone like Dandak
cannot be killed unless you use the Brahmastra on him.
Forget killing, you won't be able to touch him. Contrarily,
if he gets the Brahmastra and uses it on you…believe me,
you do not want to be in that position. It would be like a
curse upon a curse.'

Ashwatthama could not absorb this fresh information. 'But...but how can I...I mean, I cannot use the Brahmastra again. And Krishna, how can I disobey his curse?'

'Ashwatthama, God has his ways. In his anger, he utters curses. But in his love, he gives you a remedy for them. If you put the gem back in its place on your forehead, you will become your former self and probably be able to counter Dandak. I am not sure if you would be able to use the Brahmastra again but you must try and who knows—maybe the restriction for the Brahmastra held good only for the former yuga.'

Ashwatthama sat motionless, staring at nothing, unable to decide whether to attempt this new task.

Rudrasen continued. 'There might be a catch here, Ashwatthama. You have tried for long to get rid of the ill-effects of the curse. You have prayed to Shakti, performed penance and sacrifices to get rid of your physical and mental suffering. The gem was thrown in the lake in accordance with Krishna's will. If you put that gem back, you might well see the ill-effects of your curse returning and...'

'And?' Ashwatthama looked at him in anticipation.

'And it is possible that you might be rid of your curse of immortality. The gem had protected you from Krishna's curse, and he ordered Bheema to take it from you. But once you are reunited with the gem, you might become mortal again. You would not have to suffer endlessly for thousands of years.'

'Only a few years, if what the Master is saying is true,' Yetiraj quipped.

'Oh,' Ashwatthama said, unsure of what to deduce from this piece of information. On the one hand, the gem would grant him powers to use the celestial weapons which could well kill Dandak. On the other hand, over a hundred years of effort to get rid of his physical and mental suffering would come to naught. It was possible that he might become mortal again but Rudrasen was not sure. That wasn't good enough. There were too many conjectures in Rudrasen's theories. If Ashwatthama did not regain mortality, it meant suffering for eternity. The burning sensation and mental turmoil that had started with the curse might return to haunt him forever.

Rudrasen observed Ashwatthama keenly. 'What are you thinking, Ashwatthama?' he asked. 'I am not trying to mislead you. This follows the sequence of events that happened on that fateful night. Your gem was your protection against evil and all curses.'

Ashwatthama's head was on fire now. He had come with a proposition to prevent Dandak from acquiring the weapons but it seemed that he might have also unwittingly found a way to be rid of his immortality, something he had been seeking over a hundred years. The wound on his forehead emitted heat as the pain grew unbearable.

Would my immortality curse be lifted? Would Krishna have made it possible to forgive me, so that I could die?

It could also imply a few more years of untold suffering but that would not be a problem. The years would pass in a flash.

Rudrasen understood his confusion. 'I know what you are thinking, son, but strange are the ways of God. There is no hurry. You can take your time to decide,' Rudrasen reassured him.

Ashwatthama placed his hand on the table. 'If I put the gem on, I become a mortal. But that is also the only way I can kill Dandak. I will get a minuscule window of opportunity to kill the asura king. But what if I get killed before Dandak?'

Rudrasen glanced at Yetiraj, who looked bewildered. He turned to Ashwatthama again. The Master shifted uncomfortably in his chair.

'Well,' Rudrasen sighed. 'Then I believe it will be the beginning of the dark ages, the end of humanity as it will be known. The asura rule will start with Aryavarta but slowly spread to other territories.'

Ashwatthama frowned, looking down at the scrolls on the table. He was not sure what he should do next.

'I need some time,' he said.

'Dying is easy, Ashwatthama. It's the burden of living that is harder. Sometimes we feel like giving up when the going gets tough but let your heart be the guiding light here. The moments will pass; what will remain is the strength we have shown during trying times.'

Ashwatthama once more felt the heat on his forehead.

'There is one more thing I wanted to warn you about,' Rudrasen said.

Ashwatthama looked up; his head was already heavy with everything he had heard. He hoped the next piece of information would be easy but warnings rarely were.

'Recall that Dandak had been given two weapons by Brahma, the Brahmastra and the Brahmadand. The Brahmastra, once he gets it back, can be hidden anywhere, separate from the warrior. It is an astra which can be recalled by saying the right mantras. The Brahmadand is an interesting weapon that can deflect any other celestial weapon, thereby protecting the warrior. Remember that once Dandak holds all three weapons together, he becomes an Atimaharathi—one who cannot be killed by anyone in war. To kill an Atimaharathi, he must be divested of at least one of his weapons.

'As for the Brahmadand, its specialty is that it must be worn on the warrior's body at all times. The wearer can choose a totem for wearing it: a ring, necklace, bangle, earrings or any object that he can carries with him. Before you can kill Dandak, you need to make sure that you take that object off his body. Otherwise, any weapon, even the Brahmastra, can't touch him. Do not forget this.'

Ashwatthama closed his eyes and shook his head. 'I thought the Brahmadand had to be fired by the one who possesses it?'

'Not necessarily. Brahma grants boons in different ways. As Bali had a locket given by his father, Indra, to absorb half the power of his opponent, and Karna had his shield and earrings that protected him from any weapon, the Brahmadand can be worn in the form of a totem on the body. In previous yugas, the records show that all Brahmadand possessors carried them around, disguised as a totem, to avoid its discovery. Do remember this. Otherwise, you might lose the only chance you have to kill Dandak. You must do it right, not necessarily fast.'

Ashwatthama sighed and said, 'Yes, Master.'

'One final instruction, dear Ashwatthama,' Rudrasen gazed into Ashwatthama's eyes. 'If Dandak attacks the Yeti kingdom, do not rush here. You must stay away unless we send for you.'

A shocked Yetiraj looked at Rudrasen, and so did Ashwatthama.

'But Master...' Ashwatthama tried to counter the elder Yeti's order.

Master Rudrasen raised his hand to quell all objections. 'I will say it as briefly as I can. We are a tiny kingdom, with about three thousand Yetis, and about a thousand soldiers among us. There was a time when the Yeti army used to be a formidable force, over ten thousand of us. I am not sure if we will survive this yuga, so if the asuras attack and we are not able to stop Dandak, you will be walking right into their trap. The Hastinapur army cannot survive the cold and battle here alongside us.'

Rudrasen paused for a moment.

'You, Ashwatthama, are the only hope of countering him,' he continued. 'To date, we do not have a way to counter Dandak in his current form. You must figure out a way to eliminate him. Dandak cannot be countered without sorcery. Unfortunately, nobody in the Yeti kingdom knows it. You will need to find someone who knows sorcery.'

Ashwatthama looked at Yetiraj, who seemed a bit dismayed but he nodded in silent affirmation to Ashwatthama.

'And we have ways to ensure our people survive the war, no matter the outcome of the fight with asuras. Is it not, Yetiraj?' Rudrasen looked at the Yeti chief.

'Yes, Master,' Yetiraj replied, 'We have protocols in place to ensure our women, children and elderly are safe from the results of war.'

'Good,' replied the elderly Yeti. He gestured at Ashwatthama, indicating that what Yetiraj had mentioned was right.

'Right, Master Rudrasen,' Ashwatthama answered, feeling disheartened at being asked not to fight alongside the Yetis. However, Rudrasen's logic made sense. The last thing anyone wanted was for Ashwatthama to be captured. Things would then go downhill for everyone, the Yetis included.

As Rudrasen got ready to leave, Ashwatthama spoke up. 'I have a doubt, Master. Why would Nyat send me to Ayodhya?'

Rudrasen sat down again. 'I had been thinking about the same thing. Was there a deeper meaning to Nyat's last word, or was he simply blabbering? I have concluded that perhaps Nyat knew about the attack on Avanti. He might have had deeper knowledge of Dandak's plans, which he could not reveal. You have to lose some battles to win the war.

'Nyat was a staunch devotee of Lord Rama and he must have known that you would find the path onwards from Ayodhya. No one who has faith in his God is disappointed. The Lord always comes to help his devotees and reward their faith in him. So Nyat's faith worked. Don't underestimate the slightest of clues on this journey, Ashwatthama. To fight and kill Dandak will require everything that we can gather. In the previous yugas, there used to be multiple warriors fighting against such demon kings. Unfortunately, Kaliyuga is going to be devoid of warriors.'

'Right, Master,' Ashwatthama realised that perhaps there was no way to know anything until they reached the end of the journey. Just what his father Dronacharya had once said: *'One can connect the dots only by looking back.'*

'Good,' Rudrasen said, slowly getting up from his chair with the help of his wooden staff. 'I must leave now. Time to teach the children.'

Yetiraj and Vikram moved forward to help the old Yeti master.

After Rudrasen left, Yetiraj approached Ashwatthama and put his hand on the brooding warrior's shoulders.

'I understand your dilemma, friend,' he said. 'I am sure you will find the way out of this morass. It might not be an appropriate time but it is important we speak of something. I need a favour from you.'

'Yes, Yetiraj,' Ashwatthama said, his elbows resting on his knees and his head buried in his hands. Vikram walked up to him and stood by his side.

Yetiraj continued in the same tone. 'If you manage to kill Dandak and get his Brahmadand, can I have it?'

Ashwatthama lifted his head, narrowing his eyes. 'What? Why on earth do you need the Brahmadand?'

'For my safety at home. From attacks by my better half,' Yetiraj said with a grim face.

The trio shared moments of heartfelt laughter after a long time.

28

Shreya's Misadventure

Rana knocked on Shreya's door but she was not inside. He went around the palace, looking for her, finally finding her inside the library.

'Here you are,' Rana said, seeing her absorbed in the old scriptures. 'What are you up to?'

'Oh, nothing. Just trying to find something on *shabda-vedha*.'

'What's that? Why?'

'The study of using sound to guide missiles. Just out of curiosity. How are you holding up?'

'Just fine,' Rana muttered, casually picking up a scroll from the table.

'Where is Urmila? I asked her to join me but she hasn't turned up,' asked Shreya absent-mindedly, absorbed in reading an old parchment.

'She has gone back to Indraprastha with her father,' Rana said coldly, feigning interest in the scroll.

'What?' Shreya was stunned. 'She did not even meet me before leaving.'

'Why does it matter?'

'What's the matter with you, dau?'

Rana was quiet. He tried hard to control himself but tears welled up in his eyes.

Damn!

'Dau, has something happened? Tell me.' Shreya walked towards him, looking him squarely in the eye.

Rana shook his head and sighed. He said in a low voice, 'We are not together anymore.'

Shreya stood rooted at the spot and her grin disappeared. She shook her head in disbelief as she threw the parchment down. 'Why? What happened? You two were so happy together.'

Rana's tears had dried up. The moment of emotion was gone and he felt stronger again, and filled with anger. He blurted out. 'Didn't you see what happened on the night of the battle at the Avanti fort? Didn't you see how she ran away while our father was being killed? She was just a few steps away from him and could have saved him but she ran the other way. She is a coward, Shreya. And I cannot be with cowards.'

'Oh, Vishnu!' Shreya held her head in both hands in disbelief, turning and walking away from Rana. 'This is so, so wrong.'

'What do you mean?' Rana looked at her, confused.

Shreya paced up and down the library corridor, walking haphazardly among the chairs and tables. She cupped her hand over her mouth and breathed hard.

'No, no…tell me you did not do that. You just don't know what has happened,' she gasped, waving her hands about agitatedly.

Rana had a sinking feeling in his stomach. 'Shreya, I do not know what it is that you wish to convey. If you have something to say, say it clearly. I am exhausted with this cryptic talk. For Vishnu's sake, tell me clearly or don't tell me at all.'

'All right,' Shreya nodded, raising her hands in surrender. She took a momentary pause, framing the words in her mind.

'You have to understand that it was not Urmila's fault, that night,' she said in a low voice.

Rana froze at Shreya's words as the uneasiness in his stomach grew. He felt his head spinning as he suspected what was coming.

'What are you talking about?' he asked.

'The night of the battle, when the asuras were attacking us after the wall was broken, do you remember that Father and you were on one side while Urmila and I were on the other?'

Rana nodded. 'And you disappeared.'

Shreya shook her head decisively. 'I had asked Urmila to cover me while I conjured an abhicara to kill the Giants.'

Rana's eyes widened as he repeated Shreya's words haltingly. 'What? Conjure an abhi...What?'

'Abhicara. It's an ancient dark arts mantra to conjure up a fiery Giant, a monster of our own that would have slain all their Giants in a moment. This mystical dark art was harnessed by Duryodhana in an attempt to kill the Pandavas while the latter were in exile. Together with Dussashana, Shakuni and Karna, he forced a holy sage to perform an abhicara which gave rise to a fiery monster who would have killed the Pandavas without fail. However, the monster, if it fails to find its target alive, comes back and kills the creator.

'So, when the monster set out in search of the Pandavas, it was the precise moment when all of them, except Yudhisthira, had drunk the waters of the Adi-Tirth Lake and were already dead. Yudhisthira was also unconscious due to the heat. This happened just before the thirteenth year of their exile in the Matsya kingdom, when Yudhisthira answered the eighteen questions of the Yaksha at the lake. Anyway, when the four Pandava brothers were already dead and Yudhisthira unconscious, the monster took them all for dead, returned and killed the sage.'

Shreya paused for breath. She looked at Rana with guilt in her eyes; he was watching her coldly, all semblance of affection having disappeared from his eyes. He remained calm for a moment, before bursting out.

'Are you insane?' he screamed. 'Creating a monster of your own? Have you gone mad? Who do you think you are? What if…what if it had turned back on you and killed you?'

Shreya replied meekly, stuttering. 'Uh…yes, maybe. Anyway, there was… there was too little time and too much distraction. I was not able to focus. What should have been done in moments, stretched on. I was behind a wall. And then, out of…out of nowhere, three asuras attacked me, even while Urmila was fighting the others. One of them stabbed me and picked me up. They planned to carry me away from the battlefield through the opening in the wall, which was less than ten steps away. Urmila saw them. And at that precise moment, another asura started moving close to Father. I noticed it but I was helpless. I cried out for help.

'Urmila had a choice—she could have either saved me or she could have saved Father. She chose to move towards me, running behind the asuras, killing them and saving me from that evil. Had she not been there, I would not have been alive today, dau. I would have been murdered in a manner most grotesque. She chose to save me, instead of Father. I mourn Father but Urmila made her choice. It's not about my life; you have to respect her choice, whatever it is. She is one of the bravest girls around, dau.'

Rana felt his knees give in and he broke into a sweat. Grabbing a chair, he sat down.

'Oh, Hari!' he cried out. 'What have I done?'

He remained seated for a while, staring at the far end of the hall while Shreya stood looking at him, covering her mouth with her hands. He buried his head in his hands, tears forming in his eyes again.

'But...but why did she not tell me that? Why did she have to hide it?' he asked.

'She hid it because I asked her to. I am to blame for my father's death. I did not dare tell you, for fear that you would hate me,' Shreya said, before bursting into tears.

'Oh Shreya, what have I done?' Rana cried, his whole body shaking.

The girl had followed him into the battlefield despite the dangers, just so she could be with him, and saved his sister from certain death. And he had thrown her out.

He sat motionless, clutching his stomach and taking deep breaths. His cheeks felt the wetness of tears, and he wondered if this relationship would ever be repaired again.

29

The Cursed Lake

Rakshastal was not what Ashwatthama had imagined it would be. He had envisioned a small enclosure of water, similar to the Naimisharanya Lake. But this was a vast expanse of water, so vast that he could not see the other end. Moreover, packed close together were big rough-hewn rocks jutting out of the water. The Prussian-blue tinge of the dawn sky added a touch of coldness.

Ashwatthama looked around him. In the distance, he saw the peak of all peaks, Kailasa, the abode of Lord Shiva, the un-climbable mountain. Kailasa was hedged on all three sides by deep moats, with the fourth side at an almost vertical incline. There was no sign of any civilisation in the vicinity, barring the one he could see on a nearby cliff—a temple with a trident at the top, a large bell attached to its side.

A Shiva temple. At the foot of God's hill.

Apart from that, the place was devoid of any habitation. Ashwatthama and Vikram looked down the small slope that led to the lakes. From afar, they could make out the crescent shape of Rakshastal, with the pristine, circular Mansarovar Lake by its side. The slope was covered with black pebbles and gravel, with a sprinkling of snow, quite like a salt-and-pepper landscape. There were the skeletons of a few animals scattered at a short distance from the bank of the lake. Vikram wondered if the water was harmful for animals.

After three days of travelling from the Yeti kingdom to the upper flatlands of Himavant, the cold was getting on Vikram's nerves. They were now about forty miles from the Kailasa Mountain. Both warriors prodded their horses down the slope of the lake and stopped at some distance from the water. Dismounting, Ashwatthama looked around but did not find anyone there in the early morning light. Vikram held the reins of both horses as Ashwatthama prepared to step into the water.

'This lake is much larger than we had thought. I am not sure if you will be able to cover its expanse easily,' Vikram said, cupping his hands and placing them close to his mouth, blowing hot air into them.

Ashwatthama nodded, reaching for his pouch on the saddle. 'It is going to take longer but we must do it before Dandak does.'

'What if he has already done it?' Vikram looked at Ashwatthama.

Ashwatthama was nodding his head continuously, and Vikram couldn't discern whether it was because of the cold or another reason.

'We discussed it at the Yeti kingdom too, remember? We have to take a chance.'

Vikram smiled feebly. 'The cold is freezing my memory, I think.'

Ashwatthama gave him a slight smile. 'Don't worry, my friend. We must have faith.'

Vikram smiled, recalling that he had said the same to Ashwatthama before they embarked on the journey to find the bow.

Taking the small underwater breathing device given by Yetiraj, which would allow Ashwatthama to remain underwater for up to thirty minutes at a time, Ashwatthama wondered if he would be able to cover the entire lake in a day.

'I will go into the water, Vikram,' he said, tying up his clothes. 'Light a fire here to stay warm. Don't touch the water of the lake under any circumstances.'

He wished Vikram had not come along but his friend had insisted. Ashwatthama had argued against it but Vikram had been adamant. The latter knew there were times when a helping hand made all the difference between success and failure.

'You might n...need help,' Vikram shivered as his mouth spewed cold vapour. 'D...d...don't condemn me for being a mere mortal.'

Ashwatthama acknowledged that as his breath blew out the condensed air. Each breath they took felt like ice piercing their lungs. After their adventure on Himavant, they knew that extended stays in cold regions could incapacitate them after a few days, as the water started to condense inside the lungs slowly, and within days, just by breathing the extremely cold air, a person could die as if by drowning. Vikram desperately wanted the sun to come out.

Ashwatthama fitted the breathing device onto his mouth and entered the ice-cold water which pricked him like a thousand needles. But there was no other way to do what he had to do. Once inside the water, he found the visibility severely reduced and he remembered Guru Apasmitra's herb. Back at Dwarka, the herb had enabled them to swim underwater easily, without the use of any breathing device and with the benefit of clear vision.

The lake was deep. Ashwatthama sank for some time before he touched the lakebed. Walking so deep inside the water was extremely hard as he soon found out. The bottom was muddy but even more difficult was defying the enormous pressure of water above and all about him. Add to that reduced visibility, and it required sheer willpower to remain inside the lake even for a moment. Taking each step was like walking with large weights tied to the legs. A mortal would have died of the extreme pressure, if nothing else.

Ashwatthama wondered how Duryodhana had done this on the last day of the war at Dwaipayana Lake, north of Hastinapur, when he was hiding from the Pandavas after all his brothers had been killed. The lake had been created by Sage Parashara, father of Veda Vyasa, and the former had meditated there for years. The icy cold waters of Dwaipayana had provided much-needed succour to Duryodhana who had been wounded badly in the war; the waters had soothed his body which was burning with the pain of the wounds he had received. The lake had hidden him, and he could come out of there only of his own volition. This he had done after the Pandavas found his hiding place and challenged him to a fight.

Ashwatthama lit the underwater torch given by Yetiraj, which provided sufficient light for looking around him. He moved about slowly, looking for any gleam being emitted from the lakebed. Any metallic object or gem would reflect light from the torch. But the bed was vast. This way, it would take him days.

Something surged past Ashwatthama. The entity disappeared before Ashwatthama could turn his head and look at it. He thought it was some underwater creature.

But no living beings existed inside the lake!

Dismissing his thoughts as a figment of an overwrought imagination, Ashwatthama moved forward. He inspected the area around, trying to find the weapons as well as the gem. He was still not sure if he would use the gem again. He knew the divine powers of the jewel would fuse it to his forehead and give him the same powers again. The gem as it was, could not be used by any other mortal, since no one else would be able to handle the amount of energy it emitted.

Ashwatthama mentally divided the lake into sections and started searching portions of it in real earnest. It was a tremendous amount of work but no one could have helped him. He would be able to feel the gem's proximity if he came close to it but he needed to make more of an effort to find the weapons, if they still were there.

Minutes passed but Ashwatthama could not find anything. He could feel his breathing falter. It seemed he would need to break surface to regain his breath.

Ashwatthama resurfaced and found Vikram waiting anxiously by the lake, warming himself by a fire. Ashwatthama gestured that he hadn't found anything, and dove back again to the depths of the lake. It was a strenuous effort but he knew there was no alternative. Morning slowly turned into afternoon and afternoon into evening. Even after multiple trips to the lakebed, he had traversed only a quarter of the lake, getting further away from the shore. Exhaustion was starting to set in. Ashwatthama started having trouble breathing, and each breath he took seemed to be more painful than the previous one. He realised he would not be able to continue for much longer.

As Ashwatthama went under once more, he felt a severe pain in his forehead. He felt invigorated as the pulsing indicated the presence of the gem nearby. With renewed energy Ashwatthama began to search for the source of the energy. As he started getting closer to the buried gem, the pain increased, to the level that it became unbearable for him. He felt as if his head would split. But to find the gem, he had to undergo the pain.

It was then that he spotted it. Buried in the lakebed, there was a clearing where the soil was arranged in circular patterns, with rings made around an object. Ashwatthama walked to the spot and moved the soil, using his hands. Buried deep within the soil, he felt it. A surge of energy ran through him as he touched the gem. He pulled it out of the soil, and held it in his palm. The gem radiated flashes of light inside the deep lake, lighting up the water all around.

Ashwatthama held the gem like a child holds his beloved toy. He thought of the moment when Bheema had taken it away from him, clenched his fist and gritted his teeth. This gem was his. No one had the right to take it from him. Ashwatthama stood up, his shoulders taut, his arms tense, his muscles clenched with renewed power.

Could this be the key to my freedom?

And then he felt another surge in the water, this time as if someone else was inside the lake too. It was time to leave. Ashwatthama placed the gem in his pouch and swam upwards, towards the surface. For now, he had forgotten that he had to search for the weapons, too. The gem had given him a lot to think about.

If Rudrasen was right, this was the key to his freedom. But if the Master was wrong, he was doomed. Everything Rudrasen had told him was based on assumption. It was akin to playing with fire. Ashwatthama went back to the surface, and felt the fresh air and the warmth of the evening sun. He waved at Vikram, who waved back. The latter understood that this time they would have something to cheer about.

Suddenly, someone tugged at Ashwatthama's leg and he was pulled underwater with a jerk. He was taken aback by this sudden attack. The attacker pulled Ashwatthama further and further down, deeper inside the lake. As they touched the lakebed, Ashwatthama felt his neck being held tightly by the attacker's hand in a lock—his left hand was on top of Ashwatthama's head and he was strangling the neck with his right hand. The attacker pulled out his breathing device, choking him. Ashwatthama tried to free himself by kicking out and punching but the impact of his punches was far lesser than the attacker's, more so inside the water.

Ashwatthama tried to move his attacker's hands but they were as solid as rock. Ashwatthama had the power of multiple elephants, even without the enhancing powers of his gem but he was unable to loosen the grip. He started running out of breath. The hand was pressing on his windpipe and without the Yeti's device, his breath was gone. He felt darkness overcoming him.

Then, his hand accidentally touched the gem in the pouch, and he felt a surge of power going through him. He grabbed the attacker's right hand, tearing his fingers apart. But he could hear no cry from the attacker. Instead, he felt the hand disappearing from his grip. However, the movement had given him time to push the attacker away with all his might.

The next moment, Ashwatthama felt a prodding on his shoulder. Moving his fist swiftly to punch, the hand stopped right next to the face of the intruder. A gasp in the form of bubbles left Ashwatthama's body as he looked at and recognised the face.

It was Vikram.

Instant dread filled Ashwatthama.

Where was the attacker?

However, they had to move fast, before they got attacked again. The duo swam upwards. As they came out of the water on to the shore, Ashwatthama confronted his friend.

'No, no! I warned you not to come inside, Vikram!' Ashwatthama yelled. 'Why did you have to do it?'

'Don't worry,' Vikram shivered, his teeth chattering. 'Many of these stories are folklore, with no truth to them. I won't die of some curse. But who attacked you?'

Ashwatthama swore and cursed himself. He shook his head as he felt his stomach twist, knowing that Vikram had entered the water to save him. He forgot about the gem for a moment and stepped away from the lake. The men gazed into the water, which now seemed as calm as the night.

'There is something else inside the water. Might be some underwater entity, something related to the curse perhaps. I need to get back in there, to search for the weapons. But why didn't you listen to me, Vikram?' Ashwatthama lamented.

'I would be wary of doing that if I were you, Ashwatthama. I do not think the figure is a human entity,' Vikram said.

Before Ashwatthama could respond, they heard a splash in the water. A figure emerged out of the water, floated above it and then slowly drifted to the shore. It held two long arrows in its hands, arrows which shone golden in the dying light.

Ashwatthama picked up his sword from the sand, the blade feeling colder as it stuck instantly to the skin on his numb hand. He was face-to-face with his nemesis.

Dandak had found the weapons.

30

Parmanu

Shreya walked fast, carrying a book in her hand. She knocked on Rana's door but finding no answer, pushed it and went inside. Rana was lying on the floor, with a bottle of *madira* (wine) by his side.

'Oh, Vishnu! Where did you get that?'

She put her book on the table, and lifted Rana, exerting some effort to place him back on a nearby chair.

'What is wrong with you?' she asked.

Rana was dazed and hardly able to comprehend anything. He just looked at Shreya and started laughing. Then, after a few moments, he started crying.

'Snap out of it. She will come back. It's not like she has got married and gone. Tell her you are sorry when you are crossing swords with her on the battlefield,' Shreya said.

'Huh?' Rana tried to comprehend Shreya's words.

'Get back to your senses now,' Shreya chided him.

Rana buried his face in his hands. 'You know, Shreya, I cannot explain...'

Shreya groaned in frustration before Rana could finish his sentence, clenching her fists. 'This is not the time, dau. We have a much bigger problem staring us in the face. We have to face an attack in a few days and we need your full concentration. You will not last long in the battlefield with a divided mind. As for Urmila, she will come back. I will personally see to it, I promise you that.'

With that, she picked up the jug on a nearby table and splashed water from it on Rana's face.

The reaction was immediate. The cold water did what Shreya's scolding could not. Rana immediately shook his face and the water promptly fell on everything in his vicinity.

'Why are you here?' he asked, wiping the water with a cloth Shreya handed him.

'To tell you something important. I might have found a way to subdue Dandak.'

Rana wiped his face. 'Tell me,' he said disinterestedly.

Shreya picked up the book and opened it at a particular page. 'See, do you recall, as children, we were taught sonic archery or shabd-vedhi-vidya? Shooting arrows just by hearing the source of the sound?'

'Yes, Arjuna used it on Jayadratha...' Rana was lost in thought as he tried to recall when they had last talked about this incident. 'Urmila was there when Ashwatthama told us...'

Shreya waved her hands in his face, and pointed her finger at the book.

'Right, right,' she said. 'Focus here. I found this book on shastra-bhautik-vigyan, the physics of weapons, in the library. It talks about many things such as the art of shooting an arrow in the dark, configuration of bows, sword design, among other things. This section on parmanu-bahutiki, atomic physics, says that if there are many different particles in a place which are bonded together, they can be disrupted by sound waves; this means that if the sound of a particular *aavritti* (frequency) is emitted, it is possible to break the bonding of the joined particles.'

Rana stared at her. 'So?'

'So, if Dandak is made of particles and his particles are bonded together, they would be bonded by force. By emitting the sound of a particular frequency, it is possible that we might be able to break the force between the particles, and temporarily or permanently disrupt his form. I tested it just now on obsidian, black volcanic glass, which Janamejaya dau had received as a gift from his friends in the East.'

Rana was bewildered by all the terminology but he carried on gamely, trying to avoid another vocal bashing from Shreya. He decided to play safe and ask generic questions.

'How did you do that? What did you do?'

'A simple set-up. I placed the obsidian wrapped in black cloth on a table. The cloth is just for preventing its shards from flying around. Then I took a veena. You can emit the sound of different frequencies continuously by tugging on the strings of the veena. As I continued to play at a particular frequency, with the help of several court musicians, the obsidian started to vibrate. On increasing the sound volume at that frequency, the obsidian began to shake vigorously and finally exploded.'

Shreya paced around the room, waving her hands excitedly.

'Now, use your brains, dau,' she said. 'If sonic frequency can make something as solid but fragile as glass vibrate, there might be a chance we can find a frequency to loosen Dandak's shape.'

'How will that help?' Rana mumbled.

'Are you not listening?' Shreya stressed on her words, looking into Rana's eyes. 'If we can temporarily disrupt Dandak's form, it gives us a chance to break him.'

'Shreya, he will join back or whatever, he is like a…I don't know,' Rana said, using his hand to form a shape, before dropping it disinterestedly.

'It's useless talking to you now,' Shreya said, slamming her book shut, and picking it up. 'You keep on sulking. I will wait for Ashwatthama dau to tell him this. He will surely understand what I am trying to say.'

She walked out of the room, unaware that at that very instant Ashwatthama and Dandak were in a face-off with each other.

31

The First Encounter

The figure stood in place for a few moments as if deciding its next course of action. Then it turned to face Ashwatthama who didn't know whether it was an illusion but felt that the figure grew slightly taller as it turned. Without taking his eyes off Dandak, Ashwatthama put his hands on Vikram's chest and pushed him backwards.

Vikram gasped, even as he realised just who the figure was, and pulled out his sword. The figure was completely covered in black and had red eyes. He was at least a foot taller than Ashwatthama, and clad in a fiery cape that emitted yellow sparks as it flowed like a living thing. Black smoke emerged from parts of his body which made it look like he was on fire, despite standing in the cold shadow of Himavant. He looked like the harbinger of death.

'Do not interfere, whatever happens, Vikram,' Ashwatthama cautioned his friend in a low tone.

'I thought I would have to expend more effort in finding and killing you,' the figure said in a cold, deep voice.

'This is between you and me, Dandak. Leave my friend out of it,' Ashwatthama swirled the cold sword and picked up the shield.

'I was told that niceties don't work with you,' Dandak held out his hand and a black sword emerged from it.

'Spare the people, Dandak. You are killing them without reason,' Ashwatthama told the demon in an even tone.

'Why does it matter to you, child-killer?' Dandak retorted.

Ashwatthama felt his face heating up, his ears getting warmer. He tightened his grip on his sword and said, 'You can take your forest and rule there. Spare innocent lives. Wars do not help anyone, Dandak.'

'And then what, Immortal? Someone like you will raise an army and attack us. The asuras have been suppressed for ages. No longer,' the asura king replied.

'We can make a pact; neither the asuras nor the humans will kill each other,' Ashwatthama said, hoping his nemesis would see sense.

Dandak shook his head. 'Where was this common sense a few months ago when Raktavija offered the same proposal to you?'

'I could not have handed the bow over.'

'Now I have it,' Dandak said, before realising his blunder. '*Had* it. And that's why you want to make a peace treaty. There can never be a peace treaty between asuras and humans. We are two entirely different sects which cannot co-exist. One will finish the other.'

'You have never given peace a chance,' Ashwatthama replied, though he realised the futility of this discussion.

'Enough!' Dandak yelled. 'The very smell of humans disgusts me. I will finish every last one of them, starting with you.'

Ashwatthama sighed. Violence, it seemed, eventually found its way into all solutions to conflicts.

He remembered Dronacharya's advice: 'Do not start a fight Ashwatthama. But if you are in one, make sure you finish it.'

'Then let us not waste time,' Ashwatthama answered, moving around in a circle, trying to take the encounter away from where Vikram stood.

Both warriors gave each other the death glare, not blinking as they circled around each other slowly. For moments, there was an eerie calm; it was as if one could hear the blood flowing in one's veins in those seconds. From far away, the shriek of an owl announced the onset of a moonlit night, and the waters of the lake shone radiantly black.

The asura king waited for a second, then, rushed in for the kill. He landed the first punch on Ashwatthama's face and it gave the latter the first taste of blood. Ashwatthama responded by landing a hard punch on his attacker's stomach but to his surprise, the punch went through Dandak as through air. Dandak looked at the powerless punch going through his body and jerked back his head. He landed another punch on his nemesis' temple. Ashwatthama was flung back.

Ashwatthama then threw all his might into the fight, trying to punch Dandak, slash him with the sword, throw large rocks at him. But nothing touched Dandak. It was as if he did not physically exist at all but was only a shadow. In return, Dandak pounced on Ashwatthama, threw him around, kicked and punched him, drawing blood savagely. What Dandak failed to notice though was that Ashwatthama was systematically landing a blow on each part of him.

Feeling frustrated, Ashwatthama thought about taking out his gem and putting it back on his forehead but there were risks involved. The gem, once back in his head, could never be taken out again. Ashwatthama might become a mortal and if Dandak killed him then and there, all hopes for humanity would be lost as Master Rudrasen had warned. Moreover, he might once again be gripped in the vice of unbearable pain for the rest of his life. Right now, it seemed

Dandak had the upper hand and Ashwatthama could not make any kind of dent on his enemy.

Ashwatthama stood up again, uprooted a boulder and threw it at Dandak, who disappeared from his place and then immediately appeared behind Ashwatthama.

Receiving a hard kick on his back, Ashwatthama lost his balance and tasted mud once again.

Dandak hovered over the warrior and mocked him. 'I thought you would have given me a better fight, Immortal. I am so disappointed in you.'

Allowing him to come closer Ashwatthama rose slowly, getting onto his knees. Waiting for Dandak to strike, Ashwatthama moved his shield to block as Dandak landed a right-handed blow on him. To Dandak's surprise, the punch did not reach Ashwatthama but was stopped by the shield. A furious Dandak shifted shape and appeared at Ashwatthama's back, landing a hard blow on the latter's head. Once more, Ashwatthama went down.

'Get up, Immortal. Let us see how your immortality saves you,' Dandak said, while conjuring a sword out of his hand again. The double-edged, serrated sword glistened in the moonlight.

By this time, Ashwatthama had run out of moves. Not only was Dandak turning out to be stronger than him, the asura king was making smart use of his newly-found powers. Dandak seemed content with what he could do. Till now, he had not tested his powers but now, within a few minutes, he had been able to subdue his nemesis. It gave an immense boost to his courage. He did not have these powers the last time but Shukracharya's curse had given him a new lease of power, albeit thousands of years later.

Dandak glanced at the sword he had created and then looked at Ashwatthama who was trying to get up, his body full of cuts and gashes.

'Ironic, isn't it Ashwatthama, that we are both devotees of Shiva?' Dandak sneered. 'I have always wondered that if God was impartial, who would he love more—the good son or the bad son? But what would he do when both sons were bad? I guess he would not interfere then. Gods have to rise above their preferences.'

Ashwatthama stood up slowly, picking up his fallen sword and raising it to defend himself. By now, it was clear that attacking Dandak was of no use. Defending himself was the only option he had.

Dandak continued speaking, feeling the edge of the sword in his hand. 'And I have always wondered what happens when an immortal is beheaded. Perhaps you will live the rest of your immortal days with a severed head? Well, I will get my answer today.'

Saying this, Dandak brought his sword down with full force on Ashwatthama's neck. Ashwatthama blocked the attack with his sword. Immediately, Dandak disappeared and reappeared at the warrior's back, not giving him enough time to react. After an exhaustive duel, Ashwatthama's reaction time had slowed down. In one swift blow, it would soon be over.

Dandak swung his sword, aiming for the warrior's neck. However, someone pushed Ashwatthama, and saved his head being separated from his body. He rolled over and Dandak's sword cut through the air, landing on the ground.

Ashwatthama looked up, gazing at the person who had saved him.

Vikram was standing before a furious Dandak.

'No,' Ashwatthama yelled, 'Vikram, get out of here.'

It was futile. Dandak glowered at Ashwatthama, who had got up and was staggering towards Vikram. Smirking over the futility of this action, in a swift move Dandak plunged his sword right through Vikram's chest and pulled it out.

Blood poured out of Vikram's mouth as he collapsed, with Ashwatthama reaching out to hold him.

'No, no, Vikram!' Ashwatthama cried as he slowly got down on his knees, supporting his old friend by the shoulders as the latter fell.

Vikram's eyes were full of tears.

Ashwatthama let Vikram's head rest on his lap.

'No, Vikram,' he cried, 'Not you, not you.'

Vikram knew the inevitable was near. He mustered enough courage and looked into the eyes of his friend. 'My friend...will you...my...my family?'

Ashwatthama nodded as tears streamed from his eyes, merging with Vikram's tears.

'They will be safe, Vikram,' he promised, knowing what Vikram needed to hear.

The words brought calm to the dying king and Vikram raised his hand as Ashwatthama clutched it. The next moment, the hand became limp and Vikram's head rolled to one side. Ashwatthama clutched Vikram and bent over his friend. The pain that had struck his heart in the war, over a hundred years ago, now returned. The pain of losing someone dear had found him again. He felt as if his heart had been stabbed. Ashwatthama held Vikram's body tightly in an embrace and the pain was unbearable.

However, Dandak was not done yet. After observing both from a distance, Dandak moved forward, to catch hold of Ashwatthama's head.

'Deep friendship, huh?' Dandak raised his sword, ready to strike at Ashwatthama's neck again as the latter bent over the body of his dead friend, the only person who had cared deeply for the Immortal.

But it didn't matter to Dandak that the warrior was sunk deep in a moment of grief. For him, there was only one motive, to win. He raised his hands and moved into striking position again to attack the warrior. The sword came down with full force.

At the same instant, the large bell of the temple on the hill rang out. The sword went cleanly through Ashwatthama as if the latter had become invisible or a shadow. Dismayed, Dandak looked down at the sword. It looked fine to him. Then the bell rang again, and Dandak saw that the sword had become wavy as indeed, had his own body. He was not able to maintain the complete shape of his body whenever the bell rang in sequence.

With fire in his eyes, Ashwatthama looked at the demon as the latter was locked in a visible struggle. It reminded Ashwatthama of the moment Nyat had described: Dandak's resurrection. He looked closely at how Dandak was struggling to keep his form while the bell continued to ring.

So far, it had been futile to attack Dandak. But then, there *was* a weakness and it had just revealed itself.

Soon, the bell stopped ringing and Dandak found that his body was stable and whole again. He swished the sword violently in the air to test it. With a stroke, he brought it down on a nearby rock, which immediately split in two with a loud crack. He then rushed furiously towards Ashwatthama again. However, before Dandak could reach him, a huge ball of fire encircled Ashwatthama. The ice blocks in the lake emitted large waves of steam, which made it impossible for Dandak to see clearly and he had to shield his eyes for a moment. The ball of fire raged on for some time and then slowly died down.

When the smokescreen cleared, Dandak clenched his fists and roared, 'No!'

Vikram's body had disappeared, and so had Ashwatthama.

32

Agnishringa

The cold air assaulted Ashwatthama's nostrils. He opened his eyes slowly, with some effort as his eyelids were frozen and sealed. As he came to his senses, he tried to get his bearings back. He immediately remembered that Vikram had died, even as he fervently wished it had been a nightmare. He looked around and found himself in a cave. For a moment, he wondered if the encounter with Dandak had also been a dream. On instinct, he reached for his pouch which had the gem. It was still there. His heart skipped a beat. It meant that they had encountered Dandak, and Vikram had been killed.

As he got up, he felt severe pain in different parts of his body, from his face to his torso, right down to his toes. Dandak's blows had been like iron on flesh. He did not know how many bones were broken but his ribs hurt badly and the skin covering them had reddened. He also felt the warmth of a transparent gel that had been applied all over his body. Ashwatthama took stock of his surroundings. It looked like he was in a cave in the mountains, going by the cold air around. There was a feeble fire burning nearby, which lit the cave with a yellowish hue. By the side of the fire, a white cloth shrouded a person's body.

Ashwatthama's heart sank as he looked at the corpse.

Why, Vikram, why did you have to come along with me?

Ashwatthama could not help but think about the moment Vikram had valiantly come to help him. He cursed himself for allowing Vikram to accompany him. No matter how hard his friend had insisted, Ashwatthama should have refused to take him along. But then, regret is always an afterthought. Never in his wildest dreams had he thought that Vikram would be killed, not as long as he, Ashwatthama, was around. He shuddered, wondering how he was going to face Manvita and Shrutika; the little girl would have no inkling that her father would not return, ever. Ashwatthama clenched his fists and breathed heavily, shaking. In spite of the trust placed in him, he had been unable to save his friend.

Moments passed as Ashwatthama sat by Vikram's body in the empty cave with a fire burning in its heart. Cold air blew in, trying to snuff out the flames of the dim fire on the ground but it endured, somehow burning stronger. Ashwatthama picked up the stick nearby, and limping on one leg, walked a few steps outside. An icy breeze hit him, almost knocking him down. He was in the snow mountains, presumably Himavant. He saw Arya standing close by, comfortable in the mountains. Ashwatthama went up and patted the horse, who looked happy to see his master. Nearby, Vikram's horse stood, looking downcast as if it understood the fate that had befallen its master.

A figure appeared on the horizon, bare-bodied and walking in the snow without a care. As Ashwatthama tried to peer through the falling snow, he could make out that the person looked like Guru Apasmitra. As the figure drew closer, Ashwatthama could see that the cold had no effect on the hermit and any snow falling on him just melted away. The figure motioned for Ashwatthama to step inside.

After sitting down on the same bed on which he had been lying moments ago, Ashwatthama got a better look at the figure. The man with his long white hair, matching beard and orange dhoti-*shela*, resembled Guru Apasmitra although he looked older.

'I know what you are thinking,' the hermit said, feeding more wood into the smouldering fire, watching the flames leap higher. 'I am Agnishringa, one of the Panchrishis. Apasmitra would have told you about me.'

'How do you know so much about me? Were you the one who pulled us out of the fight? How did you...how did you happen to be at Rakshastal Lake?'

'I will tell you everything. But first, have the ashvagandha broth; it's good for your injuries,' Agnishringa said, handing over a bowl of hot decoction which he had heated over the fire.

Ashwatthama took it reluctantly and set aside the bowl.

'I too am disheartened about your friend's death,' Agnishringa said. 'I wish I had got there sooner. But it was not until that demon had struck his sword upon the rock that I noticed both of you.

'Apasmitra must have told you that there are five of us Panchrishis. A few months ago, he set out to find all of us and convince us to join the fight against Dandak. Together, we could have put up a formidable resistance to Dandak.'

'Could have?'

'Like Apasmitra, the other three Panchrishis are in different parts of Aryavarta. It is hard to find them if one does not know about them but it is easier if one gets word about their whereabouts. Recently though, I discovered that all three have been assassinated. The assassins could not find me since I live in the mountains and nobody has any idea about my existence, except the Yetis, of course,'

Agnishringa said, waving his hand at the fire, which immediately glowed brighter.

Ashwatthama watched as the flames leapt higher. 'Can you conjure fire?' he asked the sage.

'Yes, there are mantras for that. I know them but I will not fight any more wars.'

Ashwatthama looked quizzically at the hermit as the latter continued.

'We fought lots of battles with demons, killed innumerable monsters. But there seemed no end to it. In all this, we forgot our basic humanity. Sometimes, demons and rakshasas were killed for no good reason, sometimes common folk were killed. A few years ago, I was using my powers on a rakshasa and by accident, a hut nearby caught fire. The two children inside were charred to death. I could not take the senselessness of that anymore and moved here...and decided not to participate in any more wars.'

'Did you know I was coming here?'

'I was aware of the Agneyastra hidden in Rakshastal Lake. But there was no cause for worry since no mortal would be able to take it out. But when I went for my evening worship at the Shiva temple on the hilltop, I saw Dandak battling with you. Seeing the form of that demon, I knew it had to be Dandak as Apasmitra had described his resurrection to me a few months ago. So, I tried to help you as I saw that your friend had been killed.'

Ashwatthama frowned and shook his head. 'I should have never let him come here.'

'It is difficult to predict the results of our actions, Ashwatthama. We are humans, after all. The best we can do is to learn from our mistakes and look at the path ahead.'

Ashwatthama let out a deep breath.

Some mistakes turn out to be simply too expensive.

'Dandak has all the weapons now,' he said.

Agnishringa nodded. 'Dandak has both the Brahmastra and the Agneyastra now. The Agneyastra is a power beyond measure, it can set the enemy on fire repeatedly. The only counter that works against this deadly weapon is the Varunastra but presently, no one possesses that. Apasmitra might have known what needed to be done.'

'And the Brahmastra?'

'There is no counter to that. If he uses that against anyone, that person is sure to die. If he uses it against you, well...I am not sure what will happen but probably something not much better than death. And as long as he has the Brahmadand, nothing can touch him, not even the Brahmastra.'

'Rudrasen did tell me that,' Ashwatthama said.

'I don't think I can help you any more than that; I have nothing that can act as a counter against the Brahmastra. Dandak did not use it against you yesterday because he did not get the opportunity as the clash ended before he had anticipated. But if you go to war with him and his army, he will not hesitate again, knowing that to leave you alive would be a mistake.'

Ashwatthama looked at Vikram's body and was overcome with grief.

'I must get back to Hastinapur,' he muttered.

'Ashwatthama, the battle is coming to Hastinapur. If you have to proceed to Hastinapur, you will need to pass through Himavant and then bypass Naimisharanya. It will take well over ten–fifteen days. Give your friend a proper burial here.'

'I was responsible for his safety and I failed,' Ashwatthama shook his head. 'I need to tell his loved ones myself. I will take the Valley of Illusions route. The Yeti horse can take me across in a day. I have to meet an old acquaintance too, inside the Valley.'

Ashwatthama got up to leave, ditching the stick, even as the fire in the cave leapt higher.

33

The Worst Pain

The Hastinapur royal flag flew at half-mast as everyone gathered around Vikram's body. Manvita laid her head on his chest, sobbing inconsolably. A little further from her, Shrutika held the little wooden soldier given to her by Vikram and looked confused. She was unable to comprehend why a crowd had gathered around her father while he was sleeping. She was waiting for him to wake up so that they could play together.

Ashwatthama stood in a corner in the Hastinapur hall, leaning against a pillar with his hands folded across his chest. He wondered where he had gone wrong. He was recounting the events of the fateful night and recalled that he had asked Vikram to stay put, far away from the fight.

Alas, Vikram, if only you had listened to me! Even then, the fault is all mine.

Janamejaya looked at Ashwatthama and walked up to him. He gently put a hand on Ashwatthama's shoulder. Ashwatthama's face was expressionless.

'Manvita's pregnant. She was about to inform Vikram on his return,' Janamejaya said despondently.

Ashwatthama gasped in pain.

And then he felt a burning rage against the vicious demon who had murdered his unarmed friend. Vikram had not been holding a sword when Dandak had killed him. It was against the rules of engagement.

Ashwatthama fumed. Dandak had made this personal. *At the end of this, only one of us would come out alive.*

The asuras didn't care about rules, a foretelling of the reign that would come into force. Brutality would be the law of the land.

'Do we descend into chaos to end this madness?' Ashwatthama asked Janamejaya, who seemed puzzled by the question.

'What do you mean?'

Ashwatthama kept looking at Vikram's body without blinking.

'This demon cannot be killed by ordinary means,' he said. 'We need to figure out a way to get past his barriers. Vikram's death is on my conscience.'

'On Dandak's conscience, Ashwatthama,' Janamejaya said as he looked into the warrior's eyes. 'If he has one. You have to accept it. This is war. On a different level. It is not like the Kurukshetra War, where the enemy was in front of you. Here, the enemy is killing us stealthily. Did you not hear about the three Panchrishis? The world of men is slowly being destroyed. It is a systematic cleansing of humanity. Finish the leaders first.

'There are so many events that seem random now but they all are linked. The fall of Surparaka and Avanti, the killing of the Panchrishis, the Giants in the war at Avanti, Dandak's presence at Rakshastal...'

'Wait,' Ashwatthama interrupted, looking at Janamejaya for the first time since the latter had approached him. 'Did you say Giants?'

'Yes,' Janamejaya said, 'they won the war at Avanti.'

Ashwatthama frowned. The Giants could plough through an entire army without giving it a chance to retaliate. He had seen firsthand what Ghatotkach and his Giant army had done in a single night in the Kurukshetra War.

But why did Dandak need the Giants when he had asuras in such large numbers?

Ashwatthama suddenly let out a gasp.

'Do you have an idea where the asura army is now?' he asked.

Janamejaya shifted uncomfortably and replied, 'About fifty miles from Hastinapur, near the Naimisharanya Forest. They will be here in about ten days, since the Giants move slowly.'

'No, Janamejaya. The asuras are not going to attack here. They are going to attack the Yeti kingdom,' Ashwatthama glanced at Janamejaya, who looked shocked.

'Oh, Vishnu! I was counting on the Yetis' help to counter the Giants.'

'Then you need a new plan for the Giants. Where are you sending the armies?' Ashwatthama asked.

'To the western border, towards Kurukshetra; that's where the battle will take place, right?'

Ashwatthama shook his head slowly and looked at the congregation near Vikram's body as more visitors poured in.

'Kurukshetra?' Ashwatthama sighed. He never wanted to see that place again. 'Send word to the Yetis. Tell them they will be attacked soon. Although I think they already know that.'

'Will you be going there?' Janamejaya asked.

Ashwatthama shook his head. He knew Janamejaya expected an explanation but he was not up to giving one right now. He desperately wanted to strategise how he could kill Dandak. This time, he wanted to get even.

He *had* to win.

'Can you call for a meeting this evening to discuss our next move?'

Janamejaya nodded, and sensing Ashwatthama's disinclination for further discussion, moved towards the congregation.

Ashwatthama looked at the people surrounding Vikram. He realised that the crowd was preparing for the king's funeral. A group of people were tying bamboo sticks together and stuffing it with straw to carry Vikram's body. A few others were arranging a white shroud on the bier; another group was rushing around, collecting material for the rituals.

Leaning against a pillar, Manvita sat still near the body, with her hands around her knees. Her face was blank, her eyes expressionless. It seemed as if she had gone in a trance, unaware of her surroundings. A few women sat close to her, trying to console her by putting their hands around her shoulder but Manvita was not moving. A little further, Shrutika was tugging at her father's body, trying to wake him up. Shreya was trying to distract the little child, desperately trying to get her away from the slain king's body, lest she discovered the congealed blood near his heart.

Rana stood silently at a distance, staring at Vikram's body. His face exuded pain, something Ashwatthama had never seen before.

Ashwatthama felt a deep emptiness inside him. He had forgotten the warmth of human bonding but it had come back to haunt him. No matter how hard one tried, life had a way of charting its own path.

Destiny...

34

The Fight for Survival

Kaalnemi moved about surveying the asura camp. Most of the asuras were asleep, after a night of raiding and looting nearby villages. They followed the same pattern every time they came near a village. The village folk were too weak or afraid to take up weapons against the intimidating asuras. Most villages had no security as that was the prerogative of the king's soldiers. Some kings who had aligned with Dandak turned a blind eye to these killings, lest they offend him. Other kings were helpless as they could not position soldiers at every village, and even if they could have, the sheer number of asuras moving in unison could slaughter any regiment in less time than it took for the latter to unsheathe their swords.

The treatment meted out to the common folk was most brutal. Most men, elderly folk and children were immediately killed, the women were raped and then killed, and the livestock was killed then cooked. The asuras would feast and drink up any available wine. They enjoyed their misadventures to the fullest.

Kaalnemi surveyed the asuras who had fallen asleep after a heavy feast of meat and drink. He had to put a leash on the fools.

As he started to move back towards his tent, he found a figure waiting inside. He drew his sword and moved towards the intruder, intending to kill. But then he realised the stranger seemed familiar.

'Master,' Kaalnemi bowed his head. 'How did you return so soon?'

'Task accomplished,' Dandak replied calmly. 'Could you do what I had asked you to?'

'No, Master, the girl escaped. She was accompanied by her brother and another girl...woman.'

Dandak clenched his fist. He hated giving important tasks to others but he had trusted Kaalnemi. 'It is important that we get the girl before the final battle. She knows too much.'

'Yes, Master, I will arrange for that,' Kaalnemi committed. 'Tonight itself.'

Dandak nodded.

'If I may ask, did you get what you were looking for?' asked Kaalnemi as he looked at Dandak pacing up and down the chamber.

'I also faced him.'

'Ashwatthama?' Kaalnemi looked up, interested.

'That wretched Immortal. He who just won't die.'

'I can understand how that feels.'

'No! You can't!' Dandak barked. 'Do not try to second-guess me, Kaalnemi!'

Kaalnemi kept quiet and walked to a chair in the room. He was taken aback.

'How are the troops holding up?' Dandak asked, without looking at him.

'Quite well. They have been looting the villages, helping themselves along the way to both food and people.'

'Good, good. Let them keep themselves refreshed. The big battle is coming. What about the Giants?'

'They…uh…they are a little tough to handle. First, we need large quantities of food for them, so they eat almost the entire village livestock and then do as they please. Sometimes, one of them will lie down to sleep and the others will follow suit. The entire procession has to stop then, waiting for them to get up. They act on instinct.'

'Handle that. We need them for the battle.'

'Do you expect surprises in Hastinapur?' Kaalnemi asked.

'We need the Giants to counter the Yetis. Do not underestimate the Yetis. Do you not remember the challenge they posted last time?'

'Where will you take position?' Kaalnemi asked, frowning.

'I will need to counter Ashwatthama. I do not trust that rascal. He might spring a surprise.'

'Why not send a spy to figure out what they are planning?' Kaalnemi suggested.

'Risky. If he is caught and reveals the plan about the Giants, the Yetis will be able to come up with a counter-plan. Also, nobody should know what we are bringing from Rasatala. I do not wish for any trouble on that end. The Yetis must die first.'

'Why is Himavant so important to you?'

'Himavant is the pinnacle of Aryavarta. The Hastinapur army is the largest in Aryavarta and they are going to put up a formidable challenge. There will be no doubt that we will lose a large part of our army, and maybe some Giants.

'We cannot conquer Hastinapur without conquering Himavant. The Yetis are too strong. They will attack us, sooner or later. So, we need to finish them off first, when we are strong. Humans are easier to kill than Yetis. We can finish off the human soldiers without help from the Giants but the Yetis…they are formidable. We nearly lost the last battle with them.'

'Now that you are much more powerful, why do you fear them? You can kill them all single-handedly. Why this extra precaution?'

'Only a fool does not take precautions, Kaalnemi. I can single-handedly destroy the entire Hastinapur army and the Yetis. But that will distract me from my main purpose and kings who get distracted are the ones who lose. If the different enemies join together, they could come up with a plan to defeat even the invincible. History is rife with examples of such incidents. Meghnaad too was invincible but together, Lakshmana and Hanuman were able to formulate a plan and defeat him. So, do not ever underestimate the enemy.

'Let servants do the job of servants. If the need arises, I will kill all the humans myself,' Dandak said with finality.

Kaalnemi nodded.

'Prepare the army,' Dandak ordered. 'Take ten thousand soldiers and five Giants towards the Himavant and divert the remaining towards Hastinapur. It is about a ten-day walk from here. Let them rest before they reach Himavant. I do not want a tired army. Give them whatever they want, even if it means killing everyone along the way. We are going to establish a new civilisation, Kaalnemi. Asuras will rule the entire Aryavarta. We will rout these humans, crush them as their Gods Rama and Krishna did with us. What makes them think that they, and not us, deserve to inhabit Aryavarta? The asuras have never had their time. One or the other avatar of Vishnu has always interfered with our existence. Devas and asuras, both were born of Diti. What makes only the devas so worship-worthy?'

'Maybe because they don't go around killing others?' Kaalnemi quipped.

Dandak shot an angry glance at him. 'Dharma, adharma, good and bad, all are matters of perception, Kaalnemi. For a lion, the law of the jungle is the right one. The stronger species always deserves the better life. Did Ravana not rule Lanka for hundreds of years? His citizens were happy under his rule. He did not kill his own people but only outsiders. That is what the humans too do, they kill outsiders. They domesticate and kill animals, the lesser species. So, what makes them better than us? This is the question of our survival.

'The stronger species always wins. It has been the law of nature from time immemorial. Humans would not allow us to flourish in alliance with them. I have seen it in the past; it does not need any validation now. I do not hate humans, Kaalnemi but I want us to get what is ours. For that, if we need to clear the way, let it be so.

'We are going to establish a new society, one that even the devas will envy. No human will dare set foot on this land. Our weapons will be so strong that even Vishnu will be wary of waging battle against us. Our rule will be supreme in all the three lokas, and even the Gods will recognise us as equals.'

'That will take hundreds of years, my king. We do not have enough women to populate the land with more asuras,' Kaalnemi said.

'Impregnate human girls and hold them captive. Keep them alive until they give birth. Hold out the hope of freedom for them once the asura children are born. You know what to do after that. You are not here for nothing, Kaalnemi.'

'I shall do that, Master.'

'Right now, I want you to find and bring the Avanti girl, alive if possible. If you cannot bring her, kill her. I do not want her on the battlefield. You should have killed her on that fateful night itself.'

Kaalnemi nodded and exited the tent. He set out to find Nirjar and Gujjar, two of his trusted assassins, ones who could shape-shift into humans and carry out orders to the letter.

Their task was easy—kill a young girl.

What they would not be told was that the girl knew a rare form of the dark arts.

35

The Battle Plan

'How did he know you would be at Rakshastal Lake?' Shreya wondered aloud, looking fixedly at Ashwatthama as they gathered around the table where they had met before their first journey to Himavant. Ashwatthama looked at the spot where Vikram had stood the last time. Manvita was standing in his place, sad yet attentive. Ashwatthama glared at Janamejaya and then back at her.

They had just returned from Vikram's funeral. Ashwatthama had placed Vikram's sword in the latter's hands before the last rites. The brave warrior had died a king's death, protecting his friend. Bucking tradition, Manvita had attended the funeral and Shrutika had lit the fire. The little girl had cried as never before as her father's body went up in flames. It was at that moment that she had realised he would never come back. Not a single eye remained dry at the heart-wrenching cries of the child.

'Where is Urmila?' Ashwatthama looked around.

'She has returned with her father, Ahilsena, to Indraprastha. They have allied with Dandak,' Janamejaya informed them.

'What?' everyone asked in unison.

'And it is all my fault,' Rana lamented.

'Pull yourself together for heaven's sake,' Shreya rolled her eyes as she nudged him.

'Ahilsena has been offered amity and peace by Dandak,' Janamejaya said. 'He has taken it. The contract promised him the reins of Hastinapur if he stands against us in the war to come.'

'Brother against brother,' Shreya commented.

'That's how Dandak would act,' Janamejaya said wryly. 'So Ashwatthama, what happened? How did you manage to come up directly against Dandak?'

Ashwatthama recounted his journey from Ayodhya to the Yeti kingdom to Rakshastal Lake. He described his encounter with Dandak, although he skipped the part related to his gem.

'Dandak has the weapons?' Shreya asked.

Ashwatthama nodded.

'Were you able to inflict any injury on him?' Shreya asked.

Ashwatthama shook his head. 'Though there was an incident that puzzled me. When the bell in the nearby temple rang, Dandak seemed rattled, and his shape seemed to...'

'Distort?' Shreya interrupted.

Ashwatthama looked at her in amazement. He asked, 'How did you know that?'

'That's it,' Shreya thumped the table hard with both her hands, vindicated. 'Remember I told you about this, Rana dau.'

Rana nodded gloomily.

'Listen to what I have to say,' Shreya continued. 'I have been reading about any and all possible weaknesses in Dandak. It is true that he is made of particles but there has to be a way to conquer him.'

'Tell me Ashwatthama dau, did you at all manage to hurt him?' Shreya asked.

'No. My hand, and anything I threw at him, just went through him. There is something I will share but perhaps you should finish telling us your findings.'

Shreya nodded. 'All particles are bonded together by a particular force. To break that force, we need a stronger force. Consider for example...' she took a stick lying in a corner of the room, used for pointing in maps. 'Now to break this stick, I need to apply a force greater than the strength of this stick. When I apply that force, the stick breaks.'

She broke the stick. Janamejaya looked on calmly, even as his heart skipped a beat. That stick had been used by the Kaurava commanders during the Kurukshetra War's strategy meetings.

There goes the legacy of my ancestors.

All eyes were on Shreya. She continued, 'Now, Dandak as a whole, is composed of particles. These particles are joined together by forces. When there is a greater force applied to him, he will break. Right now, it is almost impossible, since he immediately comes back into shape. There is more at work here than just *vigyaan*. It is something paranormal, or metaphysical, or...whatever...which helps him retain his shape. But the good news is that ultimately, he has a different structure, that of something like...say, a sandcastle. And like a sandcastle, he can be destroyed.'

Shreya looked at the blank faces in the room and decided to cut short her description lest she was asked to repeat everything.

'Now, particles, which are not strongly bonded together, like in Dandak's case, can also be rattled by sonic frequencies. The frequency of sound waves will be able to break his bonds temporarily, thereby weakening him. If we can find a way to...to...'

'Weaponise,' Ashwatthama filled in for her.

'Exactly. If we can weaponise this technique, we may well find a chink in his armour.'

Shreya thumped the table after finishing her proposal, expecting applause but everyone looked glum as if they had just heard an improbable ghost story. Nobody seemed convinced by her logic.

After a moment's silence Ashwatthama spoke, 'I think she has a point. Shreya, can you work on weaponising that? Take any help that you need.'

Shreya nodded happily and then sighed, unsure if Ashwatthama had said that merely to appease her. Not ready to let it go though, she chipped in with one last opinion. 'But there is still a catch. Dandak as such, is composed of uncountable particles. When he is to be killed, and however that has to happen, all his particles must be in one place.'

Ashwatthama said, 'Barbarik's arrows could have done that. I do not know of any other way in which he can be held together at one place, since a fraction of a second is enough for him to split himself up and escape.'

'This is almost next to impossible. How are we going to make sure all of him is in the same place?' Janamejaya asked.

'What is more important is breaking him apart and weakening him. From what I have seen, unless that happens, he will not give anyone a chance to strike at him. An entity like him will not die if we destroy only his body. His soul needs to be destroyed, too. So, we need an astra, not a shastra. An astra can strike his soul...' Ashwatthama paused. 'Or whatever he has in place of a soul.'

'But dau, how are we going to make sure he remains in one place when he is being struck and does not move during the attack? It is so easy for him to disappear,' Shreya asked.

Ashwatthama nodded. 'We need to make sure that all parts of him are in the same place. I don't have a foolproof plan for that yet...Now that was the scientific part. The metaphysical or paranormal or spiritual part, whatever you want to call it, is that Dandak has the Brahmastra, the Agneyastra as well as the Brahmadand. While the first two are offensive weapons, the last is a defensive one. No matter what you do—burn him, bury him, drown him or use a celestial weapon on him—nothing can kill him, not as long as he has the Brahmadand. He will be able to regenerate himself. The Brahmadand is the all-powerful celestial weapon.'

'Where does he keep it? How can we get it off him?' Rana asked.

'That's where we do have a clue. While fighting him underwater, I was able to feel a ring on his finger. While he shifted shape to free his finger from my hand, his ring, however, remained solid, indicating it was metallic. His body started losing shape momentarily. And then I noticed what parts of him did not lose shape. I noticed the ring on his right hand, a gold ring, the only piece of jewellery on his body, that he tried hard not to let slip. During the fight, I was able to block the ring with my shield. My instinctive feeling is that the ring is the Brahmadand. Before we kill him, we must take that ring off his finger.'

Ashwatthama took a step back as the others engaged in an animated conversation about this new development. He moved his hand over the pouch at his waist, feeling the gem. No one except the Yetis had known about it. What he had not told everyone here was his exact plan of killing Dandak. In that plan, there was certain death for one of them.

It was certain that only one of them would get through this battle alive.

36

Kill the Girl

Shreya finished reading the book and put it back on the library rack. Of late, she had been scouting material all around her, to find out everything she could about sonic frequencies.

Every demon has a weakness. History has proved it.

She knew what Dandak's weakness was and she was determined to use it. But for the first time in her life, she was afraid.

Dandak was making sure he destroyed all of humankind, and although the attacks appeared to be random and the asuras seemed chaotic, she was now beginning to believe that Dandak was successfully eliminating his enemies, and systematically at that. First, it had been Valari and Nyat, Guru Apasmitra, then her father Janak Singh, followed by Abhayajeet and now, Vikram. One by one, the men were falling. And she feared for Rana. If the leaders among the men were gone, the civilians stood no chance. However, Shreya felt she was quite close to figuring out the range of frequencies to disturb a close-knit particle formation, such as Dandak's.

Suddenly, she felt someone was watching her. She turned around but in the dim light of the large library, she could see no one. Dismissing it as a figment of her imagination, she picked up her notebook and walked towards the door.

And then she saw it. The library door slowly closed shut, even as she was a few steps away from it. She froze. Someone was indeed in the library, and she could sense there was more than one intruder. She tucked her notebook inside her waistband and took out her dagger. On tip-toe, she moved behind a rack and intently observed her surroundings.

At first, nothing happened. Then, at the far end, a shadow moved. Keeping her dagger ready, she slowly walked towards the door. However, a hand cupped her mouth and another held the hand in which the dagger was, by the wrist. She turned her head slowly. Her heart was beating faster than ever. But then, Shreya felt a huge surge of relief. Rana relaxed the hand over her mouth and held his index finger to his lips, indicating she was to remain silent. He slowly took the dagger from her and motioned for her to go towards the door.

Shreya nodded, relieved to see Rana. Whoever was in the library, they had far-from-noble intentions.

'Go through the door, sister. I will be right behind you,' he said.

Shreya looked at him and turned towards the door. And then she froze.

Rana never called her "sister".

She angled her shoulder scarf which had small mirrors embellished into it and looked into one of the mirrors. She saw the entity who looked like Rana hurling a heavy object towards her. In a quick motion, Shreya ducked even as she realised that the club flying towards her would have smashed her head in. The figure that had resembled Rana a moment ago, now turned into an asura.

Another figure joined him from the other side of the library. They grinned at a horrified Shreya, who was now flat on her back. Shreya felt at her waist but her dagger was in the hands of one of the asuras.

The two asuras looked lasciviously at her.

'She looks tasty,' Nirjar said, smacking his black lips.

'Master will roast and eat you first,' Gujjar replied. 'Either we take her alive or kill her. Those are our orders.'

Shreya knew that the asuras would follow orders or give up their lives. There was no use staying put on the ground or shouting for help. The library was far from the residential area of the palace and the asuras had probably killed the patrolling guards in the vicinity.

Shreya ran. She knew the library well and she ran in a full circle inside the circular hall. The asuras were taken aback by this sudden sprint, for they had imagined their task would be a simple one. They chased after the girl, splitting up so that they went in opposite directions. That way, one of them was certain to catch her from either side.

Shreya glanced at her attackers. As the asuras came towards her from both sides, she dashed from the centre of the library and ran straight towards the door. The two asuras realised their foolishness; they had left the door unguarded. Sherya yanked the door open and exited. Outside, she sprinted towards the residential quarters, where she could call out to Rana or Ashwatthama, though they were still about a quarter mile away. As she was running, Shreya noticed a patrolling soldier who had been killed, his body shoved behind a pillar on the corridor. She ducked, picked up the soldier's sword, and hid behind the pillar.

The asuras panicked on seeing their target run out of the door. The closed hall would have made the killing simple but outside, it meant that the task would be next to impossible if the girl reached the residential area of the palace. They would be massacred and worse, if captured alive, they would be tortured for information.

Shreya heard the sound of their footsteps getting close to the pillar. Even as the two asuras approached, Shreya jumped out in a swift motion, swinging the sword right into the gut of one. The effect was immediate—Nirjar doubled over and fell.

Gujjar slowed his run and stopped, aghast. He turned and looked at his fallen partner, then looked at Shreya and took out his sword. Taking her alive was not an option anymore.

Shreya twirled her sword like a seasoned warrior and challenged the asura to come forward. The asura lifted his sword and ran towards her and both engaged in an intense sword fight. With a quick movement, the asura shoved an elbow in Shreya's face. Her nose broke with the impact and blood spluttered out, staining her dress red. She stumbled and fell backwards. The asura swung his sword in a quick motion and moved towards her menacingly but Shreya picked up her fallen sword and was up in a flash, wiping the blood off her face. She already had the fight figured out in her mind. As the asura moved to strike, an arrow pierced his abdomen. He fell to his knees, the sword falling from his hand.

Shreya held the sword to the asura's neck.

Rana came running towards her and pointed an arrow at the asura's face.

'Why her?' he asked the attacker.

Gujjar looked angrily at the siblings as he breathed heavily. He knew he faced certain death but what he feared more than death was torture. Shreya slowly pushed the sword into the asura's neck and black blood spurted from the deep gash.

'The girl. He wants her dead!' he shouted as the blade started penetrating his neck.

Shreya looked in shock at Rana. She had never imagined that she could be of any importance to Dandak. But before she could ask anything else, the asura used the distraction to grab the sword and in a swift movement, moved his body onto it. The sword plunged into his neck. His eyes bulged and blood gushed out of his half-open mouth. As Shreya loosened her grip, his body fell on the floor with a thud.

Rana lowered his bow. By that time, there was a commotion in the palace because the news of the intruders had spread. Janamejaya and Ashwatthama came rushing and saw the two asuras sprawled on the floor, their blood staining the floor black.

'Do you know why they were here?' Janamejaya asked, looking at Shreya.

Shreya shook her head.

'He just said that Dandak wants the girl dead,' Rana said.

Ashwatthama stood calmly, his hands folded. He looked at Shreya, who was busy seeing to her broken nose. Shreya had discovered a lot of things about sonic frequencies but all of it was known only to those in the Hastinapur circle. And each one of them was trustworthy. What then could have prompted Dandak to send two assassins to kill her?

'Er...is there a reason why they came after Shreya?' Ashwatthama asked, frowning.

Rana shook his head and looked at Shreya. She shrugged.

Ashwatthama tried to put the pieces together. Rana had briefed him about the battle of Avanti and how Janak Singh had been killed.

Could Dandak be aware of her powers?

'The night of the battle at Avanti, did any of the asuras see you performing your...dark arts?' Ashwatthama asked.

'Uh…I think…I don't know, someone might have, yes.' Shreya tilted her face up to let the blood in her nose clot. As an afterthought, she added, 'I think Kaalnemi saw me but then he moved on.'

Ashwatthama did not speak further. It dawned on him why Dandak wanted Shreya so badly, alive or dead. He decided to talk to Shreya separately before they went to the battlefield. The battle strategy would need to be changed.

It might only be conjecture. But if it is true, then Shreya is in danger. The entire asura army would be after her.

37

The Battleground

The next afternoon, the warriors assembled in the meeting chamber again. Rana looked sober for a change and Shreya was happy about that. A map of Hastinapur and its surrounding areas lay on the table, showing the terrain around clearly. Ashwatthama took a map of the Himavant area from the shelf.

Rana looked at him quizzically.

Ashwatthama allayed the unspoken doubt immediately by saying, 'We are not going to fight at Kurukshetra.'

Everyone looked at him astonished.

'Where then?' Rana asked.

Ashwatthama moved his fingers right above Hastinapur, at the topmost kingdom before Himavant. 'Dwaitavana,' he pointed at it. 'Same distance from Hastinapur as Kurukshetra but instead of going west, we will go east.'

'Why?' Rana asked.

'Giants need a lot of space to move around. Dwaitavana has patchy terrain and large potholes. They will face difficulty moving around and it will break their momentum. We are not sure if they are going to attack the Yetis first or Hastinapur. In case they decide to attack Hastinapur, we will have a big advantage if the Yetis join the fight.

The Yetis cannot fight in the heat of Kurukshetra but they can in Dwaitavana, the weather will not exhaust them there.'

'But will they cross the Valley of Illusions?' Rana asked, doubtful about the prospect.

'They will,' Ashwatthama said. 'It's hardly a few hours run for them.'

Ashwatthama pointed at the Dwaitavana kingdom on the map again.'The path to the Kurukshetra ground would pass through Hastinapur. So, the real reason we must fight at Dwaitavana is to prevent the asuras from wrecking Hastinapur before they even reach Kurukshetra. Even if Dandak redirects five thousand asuras towards Hastinapur, they are enough to engage our army and kill many civilians once they infiltrate the city.'

'But how are you going to draw the asuras towards Dwaitavana?' Rana asked.

'Vacate the city and send them a message,' Ashwatthama replied calmly.

'Vacate the entire city?' Janamejaya gasped.

'Ashwatthama is right. Do you want them to get slaughtered?' Rana countered.

Ashwatthama understood Janamejaya's dilemma. Vacating a large number of men, women and children was no mean task.

'We still have time,' he said. 'About ten days, given that the attack on Avanti was about twenty days ago and the asura army is on its way to Hastinapur now.'

'Where will the people go? We can't send them to Indraprastha,' Janamejaya said. 'They won't be able to go far with aged people and children in tow. We need to find a safe and big enough shelter for them if we are going to be on the battlefield ourselves.'

'Send them to Indraprastha,' Ashwatthama suggested, 'Maybe Ahilsena is against Hastinapur royalty but he is not against its people. He will give them refuge. I will go and talk to him. Karna was my friend. Ahilsena won't refuse me.'

Janamejaya stroked his chin thoughtfully. 'That might work,' he said. 'With the peace treaty he has with Dandak, at least for now, Indraprastha won't be attacked.'

'It's a day's ride from here. I will ride tomorrow. Rana, you are coming with me,' Ashwatthama said, looking at Rana.

'Yes! Sure,' Rana said, trying to hide his happiness.

Shreya smiled at him.

'So, when do we move the army onto the battlefield?' she asked.

Ashwatthama pored over the map, studying the region around Dwaitavana. Looking up, he said, 'We have to inform the citizens of their impending move to Indraprastha. It will be a three-day walk for them. So, they must start on the third day from here, immediately after Rana and I return. The sixth day, we evacuate the city entirely and the army marches towards Dwaitavana. We set up camp there and then wait for the enemy.'

Everyone went quiet. It would be a defining battle for them, and all else.

'What are our odds?' Rana asked.

Ashwatthama gestured at Janamejaya, who cleared his throat. 'We have over fifty thousand foot soldiers, twenty thousand cavalry, and five thousand elephants. From the information I got from my spies, Dandak has over fifty thousand asura foot soldiers, ten thousand cavalry, two thousand elephants and seventeen Giants, out of which thirteen are battle-ready.'

'That gives us an advantage where the cavalry and elephants are concerned,' Rana estimated aloud.

'Not exactly. With Indraprastha participating in the war, Dandak now has about eight thousand foot soldiers, four thousand cavalry and a thousand elephants.'

'I think we must focus on the Giants first,' Rana grimaced. 'Their armour is impenetrable and their weapons heavy. With one sweep of their hand, they can kill hundreds of our soldiers. So, unless we have a plan to bring down the Giants, it is going to cost us heavily.'

He looked at Shreya and cautioned her, 'And no more abhicaras this time, understood?'

Shreya nodded meekly but she had another plan, which she had been working on with Ashwatthama. She knew the odds of them succeeding were low. They had only a slim chance and if they blew it, the war would be over for them.

38

Indraprastha

The guard announced the arrival of two visitors from Hastinapur. Ahilsena jumped from his throne and sprinted towards the visitor's room.

'Ashwatthama,' he exclaimed, striding towards the visitors. 'It is my greatest honour to meet my ancestor's friend and ally.'

Ahilsena hugged Ashwatthama, who returned the gesture.

'It is my honour to meet you at last,' Ahilsena repeated. 'We have a long history. I hope you are keeping well.'

Ashwatthama nodded, glancing at Rana whose eyes were busy scanning the interior of the palace.

'We need a favour from you, King Ahilsena,' Ashwatthama said, once the formalities were over.

Ahilsena had anticipated the proposal. He shifted uncomfortably as he prepared for the request. 'Anything, my friend. My ancestors fought with you, shoulder to shoulder. Ask me anything. If I can provide it to you, I definitely will,' he said, even as anxious lines appeared on his face.

'As you know, an attack on the soil of Hastinapur is imminent. This time, the war will be different. The asuras, led by Dandak, do not follow the rules of war. They are barbaric and will kill anyone armed or unarmed who stands in their way. They do not spare women, children or the elderly.'

Ahilsena nodded as Ashwatthama spoke, intending to listen to the proposal completely before politely refusing.

'Now, if the army enters Hastinapur, it will be a massacre of the citizens. So, I have come to ask that you give refuge to the citizens of Hastinapur for the duration of the war.'

Ahilsena heaved a sigh of relief. He had been very worried that Ashwatthama might ask him to join Hastinapur, something he could not do owing to the pact with Dandak, and it would have made him feel terrible to refuse Ashwatthama.

'Sure, I can do that. Although...I hope you do know whose...whose side I am on?' Ahilsena stammered.

Ashwatthama nodded. 'I have not come to convince you to join us,' he said. 'I think Janamejaya has already tried that, and I see no reason why you would listen to me. You are a wise king and I believe you are doing what you believe is for the best for your kingdom. I am merely asking for the safety of the citizens of Hastinapur.'

Ahilsena bowed his head, quickly making some calculations. Moments later, he looked up at the visitors again and nodded in agreement. 'I will make arrangements to set up refugee camps in Indraprastha,' he promised. 'We might be a small kingdom but our hearts are one with Hastinapur.'

Ashwatthama nodded in gratitude. He looked at Rana, who was despondent on not being able to get a glimpse of Urmila. Surely she would have heard of their arrival, or so Rana hoped.

'Be my guest for a day; you must be tired after your journey. Do have a look at our kingdom and see what your ancestors built,' Ahilsena offered.

Ashwatthama had never visited Indraprastha despite it being close to Hastinapur. After Duryodhana visited it and was humiliated by Draupadi, relations had become worse between the Kauravas and Pandavas, and there had been no more social visits. And then the exile of the Pandavas had happened. A visit to the kingdom might have made sense when the Pandavas were alive.

'Uh, some other time maybe… We have to hurry back,' he said.

A look of disappointment darkened Ahilsena's face but he persisted. 'Leaving so soon? You have barely arrived. Do allow me to offer you some of my hospitality.'

'There is something you can help us with. Rana wanted to talk to Urmila. If you could call her…' Ashwatthama drew out the last part of the sentence to make it look like more of a humble request.

Ahilsena glared at Rana but then his expression softened. He knew about Urmila's fondness for the prince. He was meeting Rana for the first time and despite Rana's princely looks, he was not too impressed. However, the request had come from Ashwatthama and so he could not refuse.

'Of course. No reason not to. I will send for her,' he said, before turning back to Ashwatthama. 'Are you sure there is nothing else I can do for you?'

'I'm sure, King Ahilsena. The protection of Hastinapur citizens from the asuras is of prime importance now. Once Dandak gets hold of Aryavarta, he will not allow humans to survive, whether they are allies or enemies. Sooner or later, all will fall.'

The words hit Ahilsena hard. His face showed momentary guilt and doubt. It felt as if Ashwatthama was hinting that he would be wiped out by the asuras if he joined Dandak and won; if not, then Hastinapur would take over Indraprastha.

'I...I will call Urmila,' Ahilsena got up from his seat, feeling ten years older after the conversation.

Ashwatthama looked at Rana, who was relieved and barely able to contain his excitement. He put his hand on Rana's shoulder.

'It will be all right,' he promised.

Rana looked at him and nodded, pursing his lips in anticipation. For the first time in the last few days, he felt his heart become lighter, his mind at peace.

Moments later, much to Rana's relief, Ahilsena came back. Rana had been counting the seconds. Never had time seemed to pass more slowly for him.

'She is calling you...' Ahilsena said.

Rana got up excitedly.

Ahilsena held up his hand. 'Er... no. Not you, Rana. She wants to talk to Ashwatthama.'

Rana had felt pain many times in his life but this one hurt him most. When a loved one stops talking to you, there can be no bigger punishment. Conversations are bridges that keep relationships intact and this bridge seemed to be on its way to doom. He looked heartbroken at a surprised Ashwatthama.

'Are you sure, Ahilsena?' Ashwatthama arched his brows.

Ahilsena nodded. 'Yes, she specifically asked for you.'

Ashwatthama got up and shot an apologetic glance at Rana, who slumped back in his seat.

'I will be back,' he said.

39

A Tough Enemy

The black asuras moved like a swarm of ants on the white snow. They moved in large groups without order, just following each other. Their spears and swords clanked against their armour, making a loud din as they moved along. Apart from that, their constant grunting and shouting would have put even mad monkeys to shame.

The Giants, trained only to kill and eat, moved behind them slowly, at their own pace. They were conditioned to receive massive amounts of food once they had demolished the enemy in battle. Any Giant in a battle was disastrous for the enemy. They crushed and kicked the enemy soldiers, many of them at a time. But the bigger damage they did was to break the enemy's morale; on the battlefield, morale lost was half the battle lost.

Dandak knew this and it was primarily the reason why he had brought the Giants into the battle. The current generation of soldiers had not seen Giants at war and so were intimidated by the sheer size of the beasts. That gave the asura army a great advantage and minimised their casualties. Dandak also had metal armour made for the Giants, which gave them ample protection against spears and arrows, minimising their injuries. It was a well-thought-out plan and had worked so far for the asuras.

And so, the asuras trekked on the snowy plains of Himavant. As summer had set in, most of the areas usually snow-logged during winters had now become traversable. The asura army was able to trek for miles each day, getting closer to the Yeti kingdom. They had also brought with them large boulder-throwers and catapults that could hurl ten-foot spears, enough to kill a Yeti with a single shot.

~

A young Yeti messenger walked briskly towards the central hall where Yetiraj was busy having an animated conversation with one of the ministers.

'My Lord, the southern post has sent an urgent message,' the messenger spoke up.

'Go ahead,' Yetiraj gestured.

The messenger held up a scroll and read the words slowly.

'Army of asuras, ten thousand, with five Giants. Prepare army. Three days.'

Yetiraj stood up, dropping the map he was holding. He knew the first attack on the Yeti kingdom was coming, just as Master Rudrasen had anticipated. He instructed the ministers to get the army ready, activate the traps along the kingdom boundary and start preparations for building the protective wall outside the kingdom. The evacuation protocol was to be followed and communicated to the Yeti women, children and the elders. The king knew the battle was going to be a bloody one, bloodier than the one their tribe had seen over five thousand years ago, when they had fought the same nemesis. He dismissed the council and walked towards the library to deliver the news to Rudrasen.

~

On the third evening, the asuras camped at the border of the Yeti kingdom. They were led by Kaalnemi, who had seen to it that the Giants reached the battleground on time. The Yeti kingdom was not an easy one to find, given the camouflage the tribe had employed over the last few centuries. It was so artful that even people wandering in the vicinity of the kingdom would never be able to guess there was a tribe of rare exotic beings living in the region. But Dandak had been there before and he didn't forget.

Kaalnemi looked at the near invisible boundaries of the kingdom, slightly larger than the usual ice wall, designed to look like a natural formation but unscalable by mortals. The kingdom lay beyond but the asuras had to break the wall first. Kaalnemi's asura army was tired after the long trek to the Yeti kingdom. He asked the troop commanders to let the armies rest for an hour. The asura chief then walked towards the wall. He was careful not to step on any trap, and took measured steps in the dim evening lights. He came near the wall that protected the Yeti kingdom. Standing at its base, he jumped, and in one spring, landed on top of the wall. The asuras watched him in awe.

Standing on top of the wall, Kaalnemi surveyed the entire Yeti kingdom. He could see the Yetis bringing a large number of weapons and troops on the other side of the wall.

He smirked.

Nothing could save the Yetis...

40

Rati

Urmila stood by the palace terrace, staring blankly as the evening sun glinted on the Yamuna which flowed some miles away from the palace. She stared at the sparkling diamonds on the surface of the water absent-mindedly. And then the floodgates burst open. She gave way to tears; she had let her anger get the better of her emotions so far but was unable to hold up any longer.

Moments later, she heard the footsteps approaching. Quietly, she wiped away her tears, lest the approaching figure became concerned. She then squinted at the figure walking towards her.

'Are you okay?' he asked, calmly.

Urmila nodded.

Ashwatthama went and stood next to her, looking at the horizon. For some reason, his presence soothed Urmila and she felt relieved. They stood in silence for a few moments.

'Talk to me Urmila, if there is something you wish to say,' he said.

Urmila stayed silent, unsure if she should confide in Ashwatthama. Under the current circumstances, her worries seemed trivial. There were much bigger things happening that needed attention. And yet, her heart was restless.

After waiting for a while, Ashwatthama spoke up, 'I do not wish to intrude upon your solitude but Rana and I need to leave, to prepare for the war. We must get going.'

Ashwatthama walked back towards the terrace door. As he neared the door, he felt a hand on his arm. Urmila's eyes were wet. For a moment, Ashwatthama felt pity for her situation, whatever it was.

'Dau!' she spoke feebly. 'Stay with me for a moment, won't you?'

Ashwatthama nodded as Urmila held his hand and led him back to the terrace.

After a quiet moment, Ashwatthama asked, 'Rana?'

Urmila shook her head and started to sob. Her eyes were filled with pain.

'I cannot believe Vikram dau is gone and that, at this moment, I am not with Manvita,' she said. 'It is killing me from inside. What must little Shrutika be going through?'

Ashwatthama shifted his glance, avoiding eye contact with her.

I am to blame for his death.

'I wanted to tell you something, dau,' Urmila continued. 'I know you were there, fighting with Dandak when it happened. I know what you are going through. People tend to blame the one who remains but they do not know the exact circumstances. One has to make tough choices in war, and you cannot know those choices beforehand. Only when the battle is over, can you sit back and reflect on the choices made. But a warrior's dharma is to make the choice and detach himself from its consequences. There is no middle ground. All that happens becomes part of the choice we made and we must learn to live with it, without holding ourselves responsible.'

Ashwatthama was silent. He could not help but recall the similar words he himself had spoken to her at Himavant.

'You have grown wise,' he said calmly.

'I want to meet Manvita, dau. It is hard for me to be here and do nothing.'

Ashwatthama assured her, 'I will convey your feelings to Manvita. I know it is difficult for you to leave the kingdom at this time.'

Urmila sniffled as she wiped her eyes.

'Shall I send Rana to you?' Ashwatthama asked.

'I don't wish to talk to him,' Urmila said, her eyes welling up again.

'Do not worry overmuch, Urmila,' Ashwatthama said calmly.

Urmila was silent. Then she burst into sobs again. 'How is it my fault, dau? A moment could have saved Rana's father's life but the same moment could have taken Shreya's. I had to make a choice and I did. There were no two ways about it. Even though Rana's father was needed more in the war, Shreya is like a sister to me. I had to save her. How do you choose between two paths when both mean the doom of someone important to you?'

Ashwatthama understood her dilemma. He knew her choice had been hurting her ever since.

Even though one makes the right choice, the mind doubts its correctness.

'You let your heart make a choice,' Ashwatthama answered quietly, before adding, 'I too might have made the same choice. I do not see any reason for you to be upset.'

Urmila nodded and then out of nowhere, she asked, 'Have you ever been in love, dau?'

Ashwatthama froze. He had never expected this question from anyone, especially in a situation like this. No one had ever bothered asking about his personal life. And he never even wanted to talk about it. He had forgotten all about it.

In the aftermath of the Kurukshetra War, he had forgotten what it meant to love someone.

And it was precisely at this moment that he realised what had lodged in his heart ever since the night Raktavija was killed. He glanced at Urmila, wishing for once that he had a sister like her to share his emotions with. There was nothing that Ashwatthama had hidden from anyone. Nothing but this. And he never thought he would share it with someone. He was confident Urmila could be trusted.

'Her name was Rati,' he spoke in almost a whisper.

'A girl from your village?'

'No. She was a…celestial nymph…an apsara. It was a different time. Indra used to send heavenly nymphs to obstruct the worship of rishis, so they would not become stronger than him. Among his four favourites were Rambha, Urvashi, Menaka and Tilottama. Rati was a newer one among them, sent to places the four refused to go. One day, she was sent to disrupt the meditation of Sage Mandavya and she mistook my father for the sage. To disturb his meditation, Rati went near him and started caressing his legs as dictated by Indra. Shocked, my father moved back, hitting his head on the tree trunk.

'A nervous Rati giggled, feigning innocence as she was supposed to. But my father was furious. He abused her for disrupting the meditation of a sage. Rati was terrified, pleading with my father not to curse her, telling him she had made a mistake in identifying him. However, before my father could curse her, I calmed him down and whisked her away from the vicinity of my furious father.

'I had never seen someone as beautiful as her. I was afraid to even talk to her. But slowly, we got to know each other. She lived in a hut in the forest near our home. She had a soft corner for animals and would put out fruits, leaves and water for them outside her hut. Whenever I used to visit her, the place would be surrounded by deer and birds as lively as a waterfall after the rains. We would go out for long walks in the forest, talking about anything and everything. Even the silence between us would feel like a blessing.

'Time just flew by. Days turned to weeks, and weeks to months. A few months later, we were madly in love and spent all our time together. Then, fate decided to turn against us. Indra found out that she had not completed her task and was frolicking around. He grew angry and cursed Rati with disfigurement and a life destined to roam in hell indefinitely.'

Ashwatthama paused. Urmila looked at him, and placed her hand on his.

'Dau, I am sorry…' she said.

Ashwatthama spoke again, 'Overnight, Rati developed boils all over her body, and her skin became wrinkled. The glow from her face disappeared and she looked much older than her years. Flies started buzzing around her wherever she went. Her body emitted a foul smell, so much so that nobody wanted to be close to her. I tried to calm her down but she was inconsolable, and as Indra had ordained, transcended to hell in a few days. I was furious with Indra but I had no powers then. I cursed him but in vain.'

Ashwatthama pressed his lips together, taking deep breaths. Silence hung in the air for a while.

'In life, we cannot choose what happens to us but we must have faith,' he said after a pause.

'Do you have faith, dau? In Krishna?'

Ashwatthama looked at the horizon. The sun had set and the sky had turned dark blue. The yellow lanterns of the city made for a picturesque scene.

'People think I hate Krishna. Well, I used to. For years, my mind was filled with hate, anger and disgust for him.

But I have learnt to accept my fate. If you cannot change something and accept that you can't, you free yourself. Accept reality; keep trying to make your situation better and you will embrace a happier life. I have to atone for my karma; no matter how much good I do now, it cannot change the wrong I did to others.'

Ashwatthama's grip on the terrace railing tightened as he spoke, 'I do not hate Krishna either. What will my hatred achieve? I feel I lost a huge opportunity by not recognising him, acknowledging him. Arrogance, anger, hatred, jealousy… call it whatever you want. The Gods do not walk the earth now; that age is over. I wish I could talk to Krishna, once, just once, and ask him…'

Ashwatthama paused.

Urmila looked at him. 'Ask him what, dau?'

'All my life, I wanted glory and power. And now I realise how transient these are. The biggest treasure in a person's life is peace of mind. That is what I saw in Rati. Her face brought peace to me. It was something that reassured me that no matter how bad the situation might be, love would make it better. Love is the only force that transcends space and time. For me, Rati was lost innocence, the exact opposite of me and I loved that contrast.

'There is also something else that I haven't told anyone. The night I got my powers back and Raktavija was killed, it brought back my old pain and memories, memories which I had long forgotten after the curse. Rati left me just a few years before the Kurukshetra War and through these years, her memory had been subdued. But they returned and made it seem like it was yesterday again.

'Let me tell you something, Urmila. You and Rana might have your misunderstandings but don't let little fights spoil great relationships. There will be many who love you but few who love you more than they love themselves. Do not let those people go since they are the ones who will strive to fill each moment of your life with pure joy. Your heart will find a home with them. And as far as I have seen, Rana has that kind of love for you.'

Urmila glanced at him. Ashwatthama looked at her and gave a half-smile. 'In life, we cannot choose what happens to us but we can choose how to react to the situation.'

'How do I explain to him why I couldn't save his father, dau? He refuses to forgive me for that,' Urmila said in a low voice.

'Shreya has already told him about that and he has realised his mistake. You have the upper hand now, the golden opportunity to torment the young rascal a little. Cheer up. Right now, we have other issues that demand urgent attention... Shall I send for Rana?'

Urmila smiled and nodded, wiping her tears. Ashwatthama's words had soothed her and her heart felt lighter. Ashwatthama smiled back at her, patted her shoulder and walked away. He felt concerned as he realised that Urmila was going to fight the war from the enemy's side. He wondered if he would be able to raise his sword against her if it came to that. At that moment, he also realised Arjuna's dilemma, and how it must have been so difficult for that warrior to raise his sword against his relatives and friends in the Kurukshetra War.

He moved towards the visitor's room to give the good news to Rana, deciding to deliver it from a safe distance, lest Rana jumped up in joy and rushed to kiss him.

41

The Battle on Himavant

The attack began at the stroke of midnight. The cold was troubling the asuras but they had lit large bonfires which served a dual purpose—warming them and throwing light on their weapons. Making the first move, the asuras loaded their spears, the tips covered with inflammable cloth. The tips lit up and the large spear-catapults on wheels sent them flying towards the wall. Soon, the wall started to melt and emitted large quantities of steam.

Kaalnemi, sitting on his heavily-decked grey horse, narrowed his eyes even as the thick steam clouded his vision. He anticipated a response from the Yetis any time now, even as the thick wall melted like butter. He did not have to wait for long. From across the wall, a boulder appeared. At first, it seemed like a large white snowball and landed with a thud amid the asuras. As the curious asuras gathered around it, the snowball exploded, taking out dozens of them. Soon, more snowballs landed from across the wall, each killing several asuras.

As the frequency of the incoming boulders increased, Kaalnemi shouted, 'Shoot at them mid-air.'

The asura soldiers complied. They quickly put their smaller slings in position, put small boulders in them, aimed the boulder at one of the incoming snowballs and fired. The snowball exploded mid-air, preventing any further asura casualties. The strategy worked. The asuras kept repeating this, mostly meeting with success. Each snowball was targeted and destroyed mid-air. A lonely one made a landing occasionally, taking out a few asuras but overall, they had found a counter to the first attack by the Yetis.

'Burn the wall,' Kaalnemi ordered a fellow asura commander, who scrambled to carry out the order. Kaalnemi knew the design of the wall. He had seen it before. The Yetis would have dug a metallic frame deep in the ground which allowed for large amounts of ice to be put vertically across the height. Once the frame was dug deep and the ice placed on the shelves of the frame, the entire frame would be plastered with several layers of rock and ice. The combined strength of metal, rock and ice usually proved to be a deadly combination. No matter how hard one hit at the frame, it would not budge from its position. It was a foolproof design.

The asuras braved the incoming arrows from across the wall using their shields, and quickly moved a large amount of cloth and hay in large sacks to the base of the wall. Even as innumerable asuras carrying sacks fell in battle, their followers took the load over and continued with their task. The entire path from the frontline of the asuras to the wall was coloured black and red. The relentless asuras continued their task and finally threw the sacks at the bottom of the wall. As they retreated, they loaded flaming arrows on their bows and shot them. The arrows hit the target, lighting the entire battlefield. In an instant, the entire front of the wall hissed with steam. The fire looked so intense that it seemed even the metal of the wall would melt in moments.

'Fire,' shouted the Yeti closest to the wall as they felt the heat across the area. The wall was their first and last line of defence and almost impenetrable by a normal army. However, the Yetis knew this was no ordinary enemy.

The soldiers swung into action. They pulled out thick metallic chains and tugged at it. In an instant, the topmost part of the wall tilted and a large volume of snow fell on the fire set off by the asuras on the outer side, with a deathly hiss, filling the entire region with fumes of silver smoke. The fire was immediately put out.

Kaalnemi gritted his pointy teeth. The asuras had taken a lot of effort to come up to the snow-mountains. Neither they nor he would go back defeated by a mere barrier made of ice, metal and rock. But he could not move ahead with that wall standing along the periphery of the entire Yeti kingdom. The Yetis had strategically built it in a matter of days; they were prepared for events like these, thanks to the lessons they had learnt from experience.

As the snowballs and arrows kept raining down, the asuras could do nothing but fire boulders back. However, they were slowly getting tired and their boulders were diminishing. They were having much difficulty in dragging the boulders in the snow and it was getting difficult to get more of the big stones now. Kaalnemi looked at the tired asuras. He knew that unless he found a way to breach the wall, it would all amount to nothing. He had hoped to keep them as a last resort but it seems they would be needed to break the first line of defence.

'Bring on the Giants,' Kaalnemi ordered the troop commander standing near him.

The heavy Giants thudded their way through the snow, their feet submerged till their shins but they had been given thick animal-hide boots to counter the cold, along with winter clothing for their bodies. Their thick skin could withstand some amount of cold but nothing like what was on Himavant. Dandak had ordered the Giants to be used sparingly, and to save them for the final battle at Hastinapur. However, Kaalnemi could not wait till Hastinapur. If the Yeti kingdom was not captured, the Yetis would come out in full force and join Hastinapur in battle.

Dandak had no doubts about defeating the humans but it was the Yetis who worried him. The intelligence of these snow-monkeys as he called them, was far superior to humans. And Kaalnemi realised that, too. From across the wall, the Yetis were making life miserable for the asuras, without losing a single soldier of their own. So, he had to do whatever was necessary to succeed.

As the Giants appeared on the scene, the asura morale rose. They cheered in unison. For a moment, the snowball shower stopped.

'What is it? Go find out,' Yetiraj told a fellow Yeti soldier.

The soldier ran towards the interior, where, far from the battle zone, on top of a camouflaged tower, a Yeti sat holding a long metallic tube, with glass pieces fitted at both ends. Using gestures, the soldier asked the Yeti on the tower for an update, and immediately got a reply.

'Giants! It's the Giants!' he blurted out as he ran back to Yetiraj.

'Giants!' Yetiraj repeated, worried.

The asuras were smaller compared to the Yetis and the latter could easily beat them, unless the former used dark arts. But the Giants were twice as large as the Yetis and had even thicker skin. They were tough to kill, a winning card for anyone who had them in their army. The next instant, the Yetis were under attack from the Giants, who started pounding the wall from the other side. Five Giants, in unison, ran and put their shoulders to it jointly. The Giants might look dumb but when it came to war, they knew what to do. The wall shook repeatedly; cracks started appearing in the thick ice and even in the rocks, which would normally have been impenetrable.

'Throw the chakras,' Yetiraj shouted, raising his voice to be heard above the din of the falling rocks.

The commander complied and signalled to the troops. The chakras were large rotating wheels, fitted with over a hundred thin spikes on its periphery. They were launched from a customised launcher and rotated swiftly as they flew towards the enemy. Once they landed, the spikes flew in all directions at high speed, immediately killing or severely injuring the enemy. Soon, the chakras started flying towards the other side of the wall. Yetiraj could hear the commotion made by the asuras as the spikes started clashing with their shields, many of the spikes impaling the asuras. Desperate cries filled the air.

There was a loud thud. One Giant had fallen. The spike had gone into his eye. Unfortunately for the Yetis, the Giants were well shielded by the armour that covered their arms, torso, legs and head. Dandak had spared no effort in making sure the Giants were safe during the war. Despite facing multiple chakras, the Giants continued to pound the wall.

Yetiraj moved around impatiently, trying to figure out another way to counter the beasts. It would be a disaster if the Giants broke through. The asuras would be able to infiltrate the kingdom and the Yeti women and children would be in danger.

Reluctantly, he gave the final order. 'Bring the tar.'

The soldiers complied. Separate from the stack of all explosives and weapons, huge cauldrons of black tar were smouldering on top of the fire. The black tar boiled and made a gurgling sound as it emitted thick black fumes. It was something Yetiraj didn't want to use on the enemy. Despite being a weapon of war, using it was an inhuman act. The tar as it fell on the enemy, burnt them severely. Not only did it stick on the skin, the first-degree burn results were also untreatable as the tar solidified and remained stuck. The victims had absolutely no chance of recovery.

Wars were inhuman; still, there were some ethics involved in creating and using weapons. Then again, when it came to protecting one's land and loved ones, humanity was usually shelved. The cauldrons, mounted on rails, were hauled to the top of the wall. Through an intricate mechanism of the pulley, they were lifted from their rails and moved to the top, towards the approximate position where the Giants were standing on the other side. Some Yetis in camouflage had climbed atop the wall and corrected the position of the big vessels holding the black liquid of death.

It had to be immediate. If the enemy saw the cauldrons, they would back off or change position. The Yetis waited till the Giants started making their customary run to attack. When they were about twenty paces away, the Yetis signalled and the cauldrons were lifted.

The Giants, busy in their run-up with their heads down failed to notice the cauldrons.

'Watch out,' shouted Kaalnemi at the top of his voice.

But it was too late. As the Giants went at the wall one more time, the cauldrons were tilted and hot black tar poured onto them. The tar fell on the face and hands of the Giants, incapacitating them. There were loud shrieks as the injured Giants cried out in pain. Two of them got the tar in their eyes and were running around madly. Another one fell like a dead log on the snow as the tar melted through the opening on his head-armour and penetrated his head.

The injured Giants ran back towards the asuras in fear, ploughing through their lines, trampling many of them.

The plan had worked. The Yetis had stopped the Giants in their tracks.

~

The wall remained intact. The Yetis heaved a sigh of relief. Had the Giants pounded at it a few more times, it would have come crashing down. Kaalnemi looked angrily as the injured and howling Giants rushed past him, back to the asura camp, continuing to trample many of them unwittingly.

Furious, Kaalnemi rose and moved his hands in a circle. Then, to everyone's amazement, he rose up in the air and hovered even higher than the wall.

In a dazzling move, he gestured with his hands and a red fire emerged from them, heating the ice-wall in an instant. It grew red hot as the ice immediately gave way to steam and the heat melted the rocks and metal inside. The Yetis could do nothing but watch helplessly. The next moment, the wall exploded, opening a pathway into the Yeti kingdom.

Yetiraj gasped helplessly. They had no counter to the dark arts.

Through the broken parts of the metallic frame, the asuras and Yetis stood face to face, breathing in anger, confronting each other yet again after five thousand years.

~

'Archers,' shouted both Yetiraj and Kaalnemi at the top of their voices.

The Yetis picked up large crossbows with wooden arrows, their tips dipped in the juice of purple vatsanabha flowers. A single brush of the arrows could paralyse the victim for a few hours, giving the Yetis sufficient time to take prisoners or kill them.

The asuras, meanwhile, had bows and wooden arrows with iron tips, with inflammable material on them. The iron tip ensured it would pierce any armour, in this case, the thick ones of the Yetis. The fire at the tip ensured maximum damage.

The next instant, the night sky was lit by the fire on the arrowheads. The pointed darts from the two warring sides crossed each other, some of them colliding with their counterparts in mid-air, others hitting the shields of both the asuras and Yetis. A few of them hit their mark, piercing the victims' heads or bodies and killing them instantly. Volley after volley of arrows hit both factions. A few Yetis fell to the asuras' bows and many asuras perished.

With a loud battle cry, the asuras ran through the snow, tripping and falling over the snow and dead bodies alike but still making their way through the broken wall. The Yetis continued showering the asuras with arrows and killed scores of them but the army was large—over ten thousand asuras—and they were attacking in waves. When the first batch of asuras fell, they were immediately replaced by the ones behind them. A few hundred dead did not matter much to the asuras.

As the enemy reached the Yetis, the latter drew their double-edged swords and maces. When the asuras drew closer, the Yetis dealt the first blow and the snow turned dark with asura blood. They hardly stood a chance against the taller and agile-as-leopards Yetis. A single blow from the mace of a Yeti sufficed to bring half a dozen asuras down.

Kaalnemi asked the commander who was in charge of the reserve troops to find the remaining Giants and bring them back. As the commander left to do that, Kaalnemi ordered that the bigger machines be brought in. He would end this today. If dawn broke, the asuras would be depleted of their power severely.

A little later, the big machines retrofitted with large round black balls were rolled to the front of the asura rows. They had picked the machines up from Avanti's armoury. Compressing a lot of firepower in a small area did the trick. Once aimed at the enemy, the black balls exploded on contact, covering a large area in fire.

'Shower it on them,' roared the asura chief.

The commander hesitated. 'Master, many asuras are also there. They too would...'

But before he could complete the sentence, Kaalnemi gave him a deathly glare. The reluctant commander bowed his head and ordered the asuras to mount the attack. The large swings released the balls. In an instant, loud explosions rattled the Yetis' lair. Some Yetis immediately succumbed to this new weapon. The heat of the explosion was so intense that everyone in the vicinity of the explosion was incinerated immediately.

Yetiraj was worried. The wall had been their great defence and he had hoped that it would last through the night but the asuras had got past it in the first two hours of the battle. Worse, the asura army was being replenished at a terrifyingly swift rate. They could not win this war in a conventional manner. The one-thousand small Yeti army had held the fort so far. The mighty snow-warriors were smashing the asuras like a pack of cards. The only downside was that there were too many of the barbaric brutes. And now with the exploding fireballs, Yetiraj was facing a bigger challenge. The balls were claiming a number of Yeti soldiers at a time. Their dwindling numbers would be a matter of concern soon.

Yetiraj signalled to two of his able warriors to ride with him. Slashing and bludgeoning the asuras in their way, the trio made their way to the inner side of the wall, into the kingdom. Known only to themselves, the Yetis had built an opening in the wall, sufficient for them to pass. There was no way the passage could be discovered from the outside. It was meant to be a strategic and emergency exit.

'Raghavraj, go back to the village. Wave the blue flag, evacuate the citizens through the back gate. Lead them towards the back of the Rikshat ranges. There is a large cave there…you know it…hide them there,' Yetiraj spoke rapidly.

'But what if the asuras find out, Yetiraj? And they come after us?'

'Don't worry. The asuras want the decimation of our species and we will not let that happen. I had already sent word to Hastinapur before this battle. The asuras would be aware of that and will be more interested in defending themselves from the strong and mighty Hastinapur army than tracking our civilians. Ashwatthama is the one they fear. Dandak is interested in making sure the Yeti army is destroyed, which is what he is attempting right now. Let us give them a fight they will remember and save our women, children and elders. The women, the children, they will ensure the continuation of our race.'

'Master!' Raghavraj bowed and hurried down towards the Yeti valley, where scores of female Yetis and children had gathered at the rear of the kingdom, in preparation for an emergency exodus, if it were to happen. Many of them had linked their arms to protect the children. Master Rudrasen had packed two large bags of books and loaded them on the backs of two Yeti horses, who thus burdened, were staring angrily at Rudrasen. Two Yetis had been assigned to look for the arrival of any soldier with a coloured flag. A green flag would mean victory was complete and a red one would mean the asura attack was imminent. The arrival of Raghavraj with a large blue flag indicated that the exodus was to begin quietly.

The exodus plan was not a new one. It had been developed ages ago by the Yetis, in the event of a sudden attack by another tribe or army. The plan ran thus—the soldiers would march towards the battleground, about a mile from the Yeti kingdom, where the wall was constructed. If the wall fell and the Yetis were vulnerable, a soldier would ride back to the kingdom waving the blue flag, signalling an exodus. A select group of ten soldiers carried all three flags with them but the order for the exodus had to come from the highest war commander on the battlefield. This detailed planning had been put in place over the years. Several such scenarios were practised by the Yetis once every year to make sure there would be no gaps when a real-life threat came along.

That threat had come, and years of smart planning was paying off.

The sentries unlocked the large wooden back-gates of the kingdom which led towards the Rikshat ranges, a day's trek away. They had stocked the large caves in the range with food, medicines and supplies for two weeks. The children and elderly were seated on Yeti horses and led away from the kingdom in a single file. Yetiraj knew the massacre that would happen if their soldiers lost; the asuras were merciless. In the previous age, Dandak had taken the Yetis as slaves. The Yetis had snatched the kingdom back from the asuras when Dandak had been cursed. He would not repeat the mistake; he would ensure that every Yeti the asuras could find would be killed.

When the last civilian Yeti exited the kingdom, the sentries locked the door from outside, sliding large bars of iron across the door to prevent it from being broken easily. They mounted their horses, held a large piece of cloth in their hands which had a wooden bar attached at the end. In unison, they wiped the bar over the footprints leading from the door towards the Rikshat ranges. Without any clear footprints, it would be next to impossible for anyone to track the Yetis.

Raghavraj locked the door from inside to confuse the asuras and leave a false trail. He then scuffed the footprints over the entire area and created a false trail towards the west of the kingdom, which led towards the Naimisharanya forests. Dropping off items like pieces of Yeti food and a piece of clothing or a utensil here and there, Raghavraj knew that the asuras, not being too smart, except for their chiefs, would be misled.

The Yeti soldier took a long look at the village which had once been his home as he prepared to drop the last artefact and ride back to the battlefront.

Our homes. Our village. Our kingdom. You can't...just...take them from us. There will be someone who will stop you, and punish you for what you have done.

~

Yetiraj and his fellow warrior, Chitrangada, peeped out from behind the trees at the large asura army that was idling at the foot of the plateau where the battle was happening. The two Yeti commanders could not see the end of the asura gathering. The entire white mountain range was now a black mass of asuras.

'There must be about ten thousand of them,' Chitrangada frowned as he communicated the number to Yetiraj.

Yetiraj knew what the numbers meant. He looked towards the wall where the frontline of asuras was battling the Yetis madly. Kaalnemi was watching the proceedings from afar as the asuras bombed the Yetis with black balls of firepower.

'What is that weapon?' Chitrangada narrowed his eyes to get a clearer look.

Yetiraj frowned.

'Some new explosive. Explodes on contact. The asuras must have grabbed it from the Avanti kingdom. They had developed a *rasayan* (chemical) that was capable of doing something like this.

'Forget about that. We know the asuras are large in number and killing a few sections of them will not help. However, in war, victory is often the outcome of the leader's vision. Kill the leader, and you have a headless snake, scary but harmless. Then we can bring the avalanche down on them. But as long as Kaalnemi is alive, he will foil any technique we use on the asuras,' Yetiraj said as he eyed Kaalnemi.

'Are you implying we kill their leader, the one in the green armour?' Chitrangada looked at Yetiraj, worried where his chief was going with this.

'He is Kaalnemi. We know little about him and it is rumoured that he has come from Rasatala. We don't know the extent of his powers but we have to take a chance.'

'How do you propose to do that? He is surrounded by asuras on all sides, except in front. Also, you have seen what he can do.'

Yetiraj pondered for a while, watching the battle. 'Then we will take to the trees,' he announced after a moment.

Chitrangada looked at the white birch trees with their thick branches. They were strong enough to hold a Yeti. Nevertheless, the plan seemed suicidal to him.

He dismounted. 'Let me go. You need to lead the troops.'

Yetiraj shook his head in disagreement. 'No, Chitrangada. You are the second in command, as able as me. Being the commander of this army, I must be the one to undertake any unconventional step to win the battle. Go back inside the wall area and get fifty soldiers ready for attack. As soon as I behead Kaalnemi, prepare to bail me out from that area. I will fend off the other asuras but you will need to be swift.'

Chitrangada looked doubtfully at the location where the asura chief was seated. There weren't too many choices before them at the moment. They had to find strategic ways to cut the head off as it were. Ten thousand asuras meant that sooner or later, they would overpower the Yetis.

'Be careful, Yetiraj,' Chitrangada cautioned his partner, 'Some of these asura chiefs are shrewd. It could be a trap.'

Yetiraj dismounted from his horse, getting ready to climb the trees. He patted his horse and watched it go right back through the gate.

'There seems no other way to end this war, Chitrangada. We cannot win with our small numbers.'

'May Hanuman be with you,' Chitrangada said and rode back towards the wall, keeping an eye on his battle commander who was already shinning up the nearest tree.

~

Yetiraj moved stealthily up from tree to tree, right up to the branch directly above Kaalnemi. The asuras could not hear his movements due to the commotion of war. He looked at Kaalnemi who was busy monitoring the war below.

It might be wrong to do it this way, attacking him without warning but then, when was war fought the right way?

He told himself that killing the enemy from behind was cowardly but the brutalities that asuras committed on civilians did not classify them as normal enemies.

Yetiraj took out his sword and pointed it towards Kaalnemi. It had to be a clean strike. The Yeti leader stood up on the branch, carefully balancing himself on it. Then, in one swift movement, he jumped on his adversary, over thirty feet down below.

And then it all happened too fast for Yetiraj to register. The next moment he was lying on the ground, surrounded by asuras who were pointing their swords and spears at him. Kaalnemi looked triumphantly at him with his cold eyes, still seated atop his horse. The distance had not been too great for Yetiraj to miss and he was sure that his sword had gone through Kaalnemi's neck but how had the latter dodged it?

Kaalnemi dismounted from his steed and brandishing his spiked silver sword, walked up to the fallen Yetiraj.

'You know, Yetiraj,' he snarled. 'There is a difference between bravado and foolishness. There is a thin line and only the wise know how not to cross it.'

A hard blow bloodied Yetiraj's face, knocking out a few teeth. Kaalnemi was even stronger than he looked. He then motioned to the asuras to assault Yetiraj, and they beat him with their maces and clubs. At first, Yetiraj successfully fought the first few asuras, blocking their attacks and sending a few of them flying. One-to-one, the asuras were no match in individual strength with the chief of the Yetis; he could even have handled ten of them together. But the equation was different with over a hundred asuras crowding around him. A couple of asuras attacked his leg from behind, piercing it with their spears and forcing him onto his knees. The hapless chief of the Yetis tried to defend himself but in vain. On his knees, his strength was no match for over a hundred asuras, who tossed him around to be beaten by yet others.

Moments later, Yetiraj lay face down, his blood staining the snow around him a bright red. The asuras parted way to allow their battle commander to come up. Kaalnemi moved forward with his sword in hand.

Yetiraj knew his end was imminent. With difficulty, he turned his body around. Letting out a loud groan as his broken hands took the weight of his body, Yetiraj sat up.

'Why? Why do you bother to get up, chief of Yetis? You know what is inevitable is going to happen.'

'A Yeti…a yeti…must not die lying down.'

Kaalnemi taunted him, twirling the sword in his hand. 'Foolish ideals to live by and foolish ideals to die for. Fools… you believed you could take on Dandak and beat him. He will conquer the entire Aryavarta. This time, we will wipe out Yetis from the face of the earth.'

'There is…there is someone who will stop you,' Yetiraj spat out with difficulty, well aware that his statement would anger the asura commander but he was not counting on mercy from Kaalnemi now.

'That Immortal!' Kaalnemi sniggered. 'Don't worry! Master has a plan for him. The coward escaped last time but he and his motley group of friends will perish in the coming battle.'

Yetiraj felt blood flowing down his nose and cast a final look at his kingdom. He turned his head slowly and could see Chitrangada and his fellow Yetis trying hard to reach him but the asuras were virtually an unsurmountable barrier. It would be impossible for anyone to ride out to his rescue without being killed. He lifted his gaze towards Kaalnemi as the latter twirled his sword again, clearly relishing the pain of the Yeti chief. Yetiraj did not have the strength left to move his hands or legs for the asuras had broken them.

And then Yetiraj noticed the gold ring on Kaalnemi's finger. An astonished gasp escaped his mouth. He wondered if Ashwatthama knew this fact. He spoke with difficulty, 'I...I think I know who you are now. You can fool many with your appearance. But you do not know...whose world you...you have rocked...one of the greatest warriors on the battlefield. You have killed Vikram...you...can kill me. But you have no ...no idea what's coming for you. Your Brahmada...'

Kaalnemi's smirk vanished. He gave an angry grunt and in a swift stroke, slit Yetiraj's neck before the latter could complete the sentence. The Yeti chief's body stayed in position for a couple of seconds before falling motionless to the ground, his blood reddening the snow.

Kaalnemi looked at Yetiraj's fallen body for a while and then signalled to his army to clear up the area. The Yetis had seen their leader's demise from afar and had been madly trying to reach out to him unsuccessfully but the asuras had heavily clogged the wall. Kaalnemi saw a group of Yeti soldiers fighting wildly to ride to their fallen commander but the asura chief was not worried anymore. He had decimated the head of the enemy. It was just a matter of time now. The sheer number of asuras this time was enough to ensure their victory.

The war was effectively over. Kaalnemi had seen to it. The asuras were slowly killing the Yetis, one by one. His boots stained with Yetiraj's blood, Kaalnemi left red footprints on the snow as he walked back to his horse to prepare for the final battle. He looked on as the asuras overran the Yeti kingdom, routing the Yetis, killing them in cold blood. There would be no prisoners this time. That lesson had been learnt.

Kaalnemi looked towards the west as the sun approached the horizon from the east and lit up the sky. The other army would be marching towards Hastinapur, ready to take over the city. He needed to hurry.

The final frontier in the quest for the rule of Aryavarta, Hastinapur, awaited him.

42

The Plan That Cannot Fail

'Bad news. Yetiraj is dead. The Yeti kingdom has fallen,' Janamejaya strode towards Ashwatthama as the latter stood inside the Hastinapur war room with a quill in his hand, marking places on a map of Dwaitavana and the Valley of Illusions.

Ashwatthama closed his eyes, anger reddening his face. He leaned on the table, his fingers clenching the stone, which gave way. Part of the table broke, his blood smearing it.

Not again.

He turned to face Janamejaya, his eyes ablaze.

Janamejaya was taken aback by the warrior's anger but he tried to calm Ashwatthama down.

'Get a hold of yourself, my friend,' he said. 'Decisions taken in haste are never the right ones.'

Ashwatthama's blood rushed to his head. His breathing grew loud and his heartbeat quickened so rapidly that anyone standing close by could have heard it. He felt that his head would explode. This war had taken away two people with whom he had formed a deep bond over the years. The physical pain hurt his body but the loss of two close friends gnawed at his soul.

Ashwatthama moved swiftly around the room. If the gem had been in his forehead, he would have incinerated someone with his anger. He felt the gem in his waist pouch and wondered for a moment if he should put it back on. The gem would bring all his powers back but it might take away his immortality. Furthermore, if his old curse, that wrenching pain, came back, it would make it difficult for him to fight effectively in the upcoming battle. Then again, it might rid him of his immortality. And all this pain too might disappear in a few years. Memories of those whom we lose are the most painful ones to endure, and Ashwatthama did not wish to suffer for eternity. He wanted death...he deserved death...as much as anyone else out there.

Ashwatthama looked at Janamejaya and then calmed himself down. He recalled Master Rudrasen's words: 'You want to do it right, not necessarily fast.'

'What happened to the Giants?' he enquired. 'How were they killed at the Yeti kingdom?'

'Hot tar. Dropped from the ice wall.'

Ashwatthama thought hard. He felt disturbed by the massacre of the Yetis, one of the most intelligent races to live on earth. It was a tough task to kill one single armoured Giant in a battlefield and the Yetis had managed to subdue five of them. But with Yetiraj gone, he had lost his other remaining friend.

'And what about the other Yetis? Can we help them?'

'No idea. The Yetis never share the location of survivors with anyone, lest they are caught and forced to divulge the location. The location where the civilians would take shelter changes before every war and is decided just before the battle starts. It is a secret they guard with their life and even among their ranks. Only a handful know it. Except for the Yetis, no one knows about it. The male Yeti soldiers are all dead. So, right now, it's best to leave the civilians where they are. They will be safe.'

That sounded like a piece of good news after all the bad bits. The Yeti race would survive but only if Hastinapur was able to decimate the asuras. Otherwise, sooner or later, the remaining Yetis would be hunted down, with disastrous consequences.

'Whatever needs to be done, we have to hurry,' Janamejaya said. 'The word from the spies is that the asura army is already marching towards Hastinapur. It will take them roughly four days since the last eight Giants are with them.'

Ashwatthama was taken aback. 'How is this possible? To cover the distance from Himavant to Hastinapur is going to take more than a week, I think?'

'That would have been the case if it was the same army which was travelling,' Janamejaya replied. 'Dandak is not pulling out from the Yeti kingdom. He has split the army into two parts and sent the second unit towards Hastinapur. So, we are now looking at a time-frame of about six days.'

'Six days? That means they will be here on the fourth day.' Ashwatthama sounded worried. 'Is our army ready?'

'We will do whatever possible in the next two days. I was hoping to recruit more men as well as forge more weapons but it seems we won't have time for that,' Janamejaya replied.

'Janamejaya, prepare the army for immediate departure,' Ashwatthama suggested. 'Let us not wait for the asuras to come to Hastinapur. We will meet them at Dwaitavana. Start the evacuation of the city immediately and send them on the road to Indraprastha. The city must be evacuated by tomorrow evening.'

Janamejaya nodded and prepared to leave.

'Er…Janamejaya,' Ashwatthama said hesitatingly.

Janamejaya turned around. 'Yes?'

'I am not sure how to put this but given Manvita's condition, I do not think she should be out on the battlefield.'

Janamejaya waved his hand, indicating helplessness. 'I hold the same opinion and I had Shreya talk to her about this but Manvita is adamant. She mentioned a promise she had made to Vikram that no matter what, she would join the fight if she had to. She will not budge from her position.'

Silence hung in the room for a while as both men stood contemplating the matter.

Finally Ashwatthama shook his head and sighed, taking a deep breath. 'Let us respect her decision. We must try to keep her safe on the battlefield.'

Janamejaya agreed. With a nod, he turned towards the door.

Ashwatthama called out to Janamejaya just as he was exiting the room.

'Also, can you send for Shreya? I need to talk to her,' he said.

Janamejaya nodded, even though he was puzzled about Shreya's role in the war. Among all the warriors and masters, what made Rana's younger sister so important? She looked naive, did not seem to know the nitty-gritty of war and yet, somehow, she was important. Even Dandak had sent two assassins to take her out. He wondered about this.

What was it that she knew, apart from breaking ancestral sticks?

~

Ashwatthama fumed. First Vikram and now Yetiraj.

However, he decided the best way for revenge was to ensure that they won the battle at Hastinapur. Though still in a disturbed frame of mind, he resumed the markings on the map as Shreya entered the room.

'Yes, dau?'

'Shreya, there is something I want you to find out. You talked about sonic frequency disrupting particles, right?'

Shreya nodded.

Ashwatthama looked at the map and gestured for her to look at the markings he had made on it. 'There is something more to that,' he said. 'I suspect we are being trapped. In battle, there will probably be two fronts, one with Dandak and another with Kaalnemi. This is what I want you to do.'

As he outlined the plan to Shreya, her eyes widened.

'Collect all the equipment you need and we will leave for Dwaitavana to set things up,' he instructed her. 'Rana and about thirty soldiers will come with us. Make sure the equipment is not visible to anyone and is concealed properly. Arrange for large chariots covered on all sides with black cloth. I will talk to Janamejaya about it. Let no one else know.'

'This is dangerous, dau. You are taking a big gamble,' Shreya bit her lip as she thought about the execution of the plan. One wrong move and they would all be dead.

'There is no easy way to do this, Shreya. We cannot win with Dandak in a one-to-one fight or even with our entire army. It will go one of two ways—we will all win or we will all perish. But you must make sure word of this plan must not get out. Each step of this is dependent on the preceding one and if the enemy gets even a slight hint of this, we are sure to lose. So, tell no one about what you are going to do or why you are doing it. Trust only Rana and Janamejaya, and ask them to keep our departure a secret.'

Shreya nodded. For a moment, he felt sorry for putting her in danger but there was no one else who could execute this plan. The strategy he had in mind was based on assumptions and untested theories. If Dandak even got the slightest hint about Shreya's action, he would do anything to kill her. The asura king might have an inkling that Shreya would figure something out to outsmart him. And that made it dangerous. But given the time and situation, they did not have any other way to counter someone like Dandak, who could not be defeated or killed by ordinary means. By killing the Yetis, Dandak had shown his fell intent. He was no longer constrained by any higher deity or guru who could hold him back. The Gods had retreated from the earth and it was upto the humans to face the demons.

Ashwatthama stroked his chin as he pondered over the strategy he had in mind. 'There is one unknown factor in all this—Dandak's secret weapon from Rasatala. Nobody knows what it is, and it is rumoured that Dandak has not appeared so far in any of the battles because he is personally bringing the weapon and does not want it exposed before he unleashes it.

'Despite all our spies, we have not been able to find out the nature of the weapon. I assume he will be bringing it to the battle at Hastinapur, given that he views this army as the biggest challenge to him. Right now, we cannot do anything about it.'

Shreya tried to figure out combinations in her mind, speculating aloud. 'If this is a divyastra, along with some dark arts, it can wreak havoc.'

Ashwatthama nodded. 'Yes. He has the Kodanda, too. So it might not be impossible for him to use the divyastra.'

They remained silent for sometime, then Ashwatthama said with finality, 'Leave that be. We will decide on the battlefield how to deal with it. For now, you will need to hurry; Dandak and the asura army will be at the Hastinapur gates in four days, which gives us three to get our task done. So let's get started.'

'When do we ride out?' Shreya asked.

'Tomorrow evening. I hope it will give you time to gather the equipment.'

Shreya nodded in agreement and left the room.

Ashwatthama kept thinking about the different weapons that Dandak could bring from Rasatala. Dandak already had the Agneyastra and Brahmastra from his previous avatar, so why would he go to the depths of Rasatala to get more weapons? Then again, he would not use Brahmastra on a simple target and the Agneyastra, though deadly, could be countered. So whatever Dandak was trying to acquire must be related to a weapon capable of inflicting large-scale casualties.

Such weapons were barred from use in the Kurukshetra War. This time, there were no rules. It was a free-for-all war.

43

Ready to Ride

The two asura generals stood dumbfounded at the gates of Hastinapur. They had been handpicked by Kaalnemi to lead the sixty thousand asuras from Dandakaranya to Hastinapur. In the course of events, the sheer number of asuras was enough for any kingdom to surrender without a fight. Along with that, the eight Giants who walked with them added to the intimidation. Most kingdoms who had initially opposed the alliance with Dandak had surrendered after seeing the massive size of the army.

The only formidable opponent would be the Hastinapur army which was almost a half akshauhini strong. One akshauhini was twenty one thousand eight hundred and seventy chariots, twenty one thousand eight hundred and seventy elephants, sixty five thousand six hundred and ten horses and one lakh nine thousand and three fifty infantry. To Dandak's dismay, there were hardly any asuras left in Aryavarta and he had had to bring out the asura army from Rasatala. Starting with over a hundred thousand, after all the battles, he was now left with sixty thousand for the Hastinapur war. Ten thousand had been killed in different battles and the remaining twenty thousand were stationed in different kingdoms to prevent any possible rebellion. The remaining ten thousand had been sent to the Yeti kingdom.

'How did we miss this, Keerin?' Vartak asked, glaring at the asura leader who stood next to him, scratching the dirty hair on his head.

'No idea, Vartak. We never thought they would evacuate the city. We thought the battle would take place again at Kurukshetra. However, we have seen no human all along our route. It seems they have all run away in fear.'

'I am tired of all this travelling. Let us rest here...' Vartak stopped speaking as he looked at the trees.

'What is it?' Keerin asked. 'Are you tired of talking, too?'

Vartak shook his head and pointed to the trees. Keerin saw that each tree had a knife stuck in its trunk, and there was a piece of cloth jammed between the knife and the trunk. As the duo looked around, they saw at least a hundred trees around with similar knives.

'What is it? Is it a message?' Keerin wondered aloud.

'Let us find out...' Vartak said as he kicked a nearby asura and told him to bring the knife and cloth across.

The hapless one went to a nearby tree and pulled the knife. He brought it back to Vartak. Keerin brought his horse alongside Vartak's and peeked. As they opened the cloth, a message glared at them.

द्वैतवन

DWAITAVANA

Vartak and Keerin looked at each other as they realised the implication. The venue for the final battle had been declared.

~

Janamejaya had ordered large tents to be set up for the massive Hastinapur army on the Dwaitavana battleground. It was almost as big as the Kurukshetra one, although being near the Valley of Illusions, it had numerous rocks and dead trees on it, some of them massive, enough to hide tens of horses. The surface was uneven and made running on it difficult.

'I hope the wretched asuras all trip on the potholes, hit their heads on the rocks and die,' Rana commented on seeing the state of the venue.

They all wondered why Ashwatthama insisted on having the battle at Dwaitavana instead of Kurukshetra. The talk among the soldiers was that Ashwatthama dreaded going onto the same battlefield again.

The Hastinapur army had stationed itself with its back towards the Valley of Illusions, to deter any ambush from the rear, which would otherwise be a real threat. The oncoming army would have to come up from the front and so the battle commanders would be able to coordinate their attack in a planned manner without worrying about flank or rear attacks.

~

A day later, a loud bugle sounded the arrival of the asuras. In the dim late afternoon sunlight, the asura army stood face to face with the Hastinapur army. Janamejaya sounded the war bugle as the soldiers got into formation.

The Hastinapur war formation was structured in layers as was done during Kurukshetra War. At the front were the chariots, which usually were helmed by the kings, princes and battle commanders of different units. Some of the chariots were wide and drawn by four or more horses. Many different kinds of weapons were stocked to hand, such as multiple spears, swords, bows with hundreds of arrows and maces. The soldiers had fitted all chariots wheels with thick animal hide for smoother movement. Following the chariots were the horsemen, heavily armed with swords, bows and quivers full of arrows. The horses selected for the cavalry were young and were often fed a little liquor just before the battle, to make them agile and able to bear pain better.

Behind the cavalry stood the mighty elephants and atop them, a few archers, spearmen and a mahout each. These elephants were battle-trained and heavily armoured to guard them against attack from spears and arrows. Their temples, tusks and legs were clad with pointed blades to impale any enemy that came their way. Armoured elephants were extremely difficult to kill, and the only way to neutralise them was to kill the soldiers sitting atop them.

Finally, the last formation was that of the infantry, the foot soldiers. The infantry was divided into different sections: archers, swordsmen, spearmen and mace-wielding wrestlers. Each soldier also carried a small knife hidden in his armour as a contingency, in case he lost his primary weapon. This knife was usually hidden near the wrist and could be pulled out in the blink of an eye. This made the foot soldier an unpredictable foe in battle.

Hastinapur was feared for precisely this. It had perfected the art of war. Thousands of years of conflict had made the army quite efficient and battle-ready, and so the kingdom commanded much respect among others. For this battle, all the royal warriors—Ashwatthama, Janamejaya, Rana and Shreya—had opted for horses, because their agility would be an advantage when moving on the rocky terrain. Manvita was in a chariot, to make the ride less bumpy for her.

As the asura army moved into position, many soldiers in the Hastinapur camp looked on in dismay. The Indraprastha army was standing alongside the asura army; some of the soldiers had relatives in the opposite camp and were understandably apprehensive.

Ahilsena looked across at his cousin Janamejaya as Kaalnemi came and stood beside the King of Indraprastha.

'I hope you do not get an *Arjuna moment*. There is no Krishna here to deliver a sermon to you,' Kaalnemi taunted.

Ahilsena narrowed his eyes as he located Janamejaya among the warriors in the Hastinapur army. 'Emotion has no place in wars. The throne is to be mine,' he said calmly, putting his hand on the hilt of his sword and feeling the coldness of the weapon. He felt it was ready to taste blood in war. It would be brother against brother again, after over a hundred years.

'Good,' Kaalnemi moved to the front ranks of his army.

Urmila was beside Ahilsena on her horse, listening to everything quietly. She had turned down Rana's proposal to join Hastinapur, when Ashwatthama and he had come to Indraprastha. She owed her allegiance to Indraprastha, being the crown princess. Now she was facing her friends on the battlefield. Seeing Ashwatthama, Janamejaya, Rana and Shreya, her thoughts were split now. On the one hand, she had an obligation towards her kingdom; on the other, it was about doing the right thing. She had to choose and she decided to make the choice which her ancestor, Karna, had made long before her. She had to stand with her kingdom regardless of who was right and who was wrong.

And then Urmila saw someone she least expected to see—Manvita.

Dressed in warrior's attire, Manvita had trouble holding the bow on her shoulder, along with a sword on her waist. Shreya was beside her on the horse, instructing her.

Urmila was stunned. It was barely ten days since Vikram had been killed. In a flash, Urmila was reminded of the noble king of Surparaka, how he had decided to take her along with them to Himavant, and how he had treated her throughout as a younger sister, just like Ashwatthama had. And now, Vikram had given his life for this cause. It pained her heart to see Manvita; however, she still could not bring herself to turn her back on Indraprastha. Her heart burned with the difficult decision.

But she made up her mind.

Her duty lay with her kingdom, Indraprastha.

~

Ashwatthama led his horse Arya to the front of the Hastinapur army. He rode across the ranks, his sword ceremoniously clanging with the swords of the horsemen in the first row. After completing a full round, he circled back and stopped in the middle, facing the Hastinapur army.

At the top of his voice, he roared, Arya moving a few steps ahead and then behind.

'Soldiers of Hastinapur! Today, we stand against an enemy who will show you no mercy. They have shown no mercy to anyone all along the way, right from Dandakaranya, to Avanti, to Hastinapur. You may be afraid of their ferocity, of their brutality but the person who can fight when he is afraid is the true warrior. So when you take up your weapons today, remember that this fight is not just for you but for your family, your home and for all those whom you hold dear.

'As you run across this battlefield, facing and fighting the asuras, remember that this is the battle of your life. And you have to fight it, by not dying but by killing those who have come to take everything from you. Let this be the moment of your reckoning, the day—the only day — when you fight like true warriors.'

The Hastinapur army cheered, thumping their sword hilts to their shields and thumping their spears on the ground. The ground shuddered with rocks and stones shaking with each thump.

Kaalnemi sniggered as he looked towards the evening sun, which would leave the battlefield dark in moments.

Fools. They will all be dead soon. Do they have even the slightest idea what is coming their way?

44

The Secret Weapon

Another bugle sounded on the asura side and a warrior in shining armour, mounted on a black horse, appeared alongside Kaalnemi. From afar, they both looked similar. The new entrant took a prominent position among the asura ranks. Ashwatthama's nose flared and his face went red as he recognised the asura.

Dandak.

The asura king was robed in black and golden clothes and his cape had the same fiery red touch to it, with yellow sparks coming out of them. It was not draped on his back like the warriors but was floating behind him as if it had a life of its own. Dandak's face glowed golden in the dying sun's rays and his eyes looked like they had a thick black kohl lining to match his dark curved moustache and thick beard. He had a mist of black around his body in the way smoke lingers over smouldering coal.

Rana gasped as he looked at the asura king. Even before he looked deeper into the demon king's eyes, he knew they would be red as he had seen in his vision, long before this chain of events had been set in motion.

'I have...I have seen him before,' Rana gasped.

'What?' Janamejaya looked at him, amazed. 'You have never met him.'

'Where have you seen him?' Ashwatthama asked.

'In my...dreams,' Rana said, lowering his voice as he realised the incorrect choice of words.

'Come on, dau. I thought you would be seeing someone else in your dreams,' Shreya chuckled, even as Rana's ears went red.

Ashwatthama shook his head.

'Make as much fun as you want,' Rana narrowed his eyes, 'I saw it before it all started. Him...and...'

Rana paused as he tried to recollect his dream, the one he had seen months ago, before the visit by Vikram and Ashwatthama to Avanti the first time. He had never thought about it again but the black robes and red eyes of the asura king reminded him of that very vision.

'...A golden bowstring with a bluish-gold arrow,' Rana finished recollecting his vision but realised that the others were not interested in listening to his sleep adventures.

Rana looked at Ashwatthama, who seemed absorbed in his own thoughts. Ashwatthama was replaying his plan in his mind and pondering on the best way to execute it. It all depended on Shreya's theory and her execution of the same. They had set it all up as per Shreya's calculations but it was a tricky situation, it had not been tested. They did not know if it would work.

This was no ordinary enemy. It had taken Karna the Vasavi-shakti to kill one demon with magical powers. Here was an asura king, master of the dark arts, and Ashwatthama had no weapon with which to counter him. There were no Barbarik arrows around this time. And he could not use any celestial weapons without putting the gem back into his forehead. And that could be disastrous.

There were loud shouts of joy in the asura army as if they had received a lifeline. The din made the earth rattle but it was the combined effect of the asuras rejoicing and the heavy tread of the eight Giants who had just appeared on the scene.

'Eight it is.' Janamejaya announced. 'Our blades are ready for them.'

'What about their secret weapon? I don't see anything yet. Is Dandak wielding something?' Rana struggled to survey the entire asura army as it had started to grow dark. The asuras had timed their arrival so that they reached the battleground at dusk, to ensure they fought at night when their powers were amplified multiple times.

The Hastinapur army started to light torches around the battlefield, bathing the area in an orange-yellow hue. Ashwatthama too, scanned the area but he could not see any unexpected lethal weapon. They already knew about the Giants. If Dandak had brought a new divyastra with him, they would know about it during the battle. But a celestial weapon from the depths of the netherworld was not something anyone had ever heard of. Celestial weapons could not be transferred from one warrior to another and had to be earned. And there were no Gods in the netherworld, only demons.

Suddenly, the asura bugle sounded again.

'How many times do they have to do that? How many of them need a special entry?' Rana asked, irritated.

And then from the asura side, a chariot came forward with a dark-skinned, thin figure in it. He had a blindfold on his eyes. The chariot moved forward slowly and came in line with Dandak and Kaalnemi. In the dim light as everyone strained to see the new entrant, Shreya and Ashwatthama gulped in horror and looked at each other as they recognised the figure. Their eyes conveyed the same message.

We are not prepared for this.

'Now what? We fight a blind warrior?' Rana waved towards the asura army, annoyed.

'He is Bhasmaksh, the fire-demon,' a voice from the back startled them.

As they turned around, they saw an old man with a white beard and white clothes emerging from among the soldiers standing near the Valley of Illusions.

Ashwatthama recognised the old sage. 'Guru Agnishringa!' he bowed to the master of fire. 'I thought you said you would not join this war!'

'I thought you might need help and as I am the last of the Panchrishis, it is my duty to join the fight for dharma.'

Ashwatthama acknowledged this and introduced the Guru to the others, who were most happy with his arrival on the scene.

'Know this—Bhasmaksh is the secret weapon,' Guru Agnishringa said calmly as the others looked at him in shock.

'What can he do?' Janamejaya asked.

'Whatever he sets his eyesight on, turns to ashes instantly. It's a boon given to him.'

'But you can counter him, right?' Rana asked, 'With your fire…er…control… power?'

Agnishringa shook his head. 'I can stop fire with fire but not this. He does not shoot fire; his gaze does the damage. It is beyond my control.'

Shreya gasped. 'The one who could burn everything with his eyesight! I have heard myths about him but never imagined he would turn up like this.'

'How bad is it?' Rana had worry lines on his forehead now.

'Very bad,' Guru Agnishringa replied. 'Anything that he looks at bursts into flames. Nothing that moves, survives.'

'What if he looks at his own hand or...' Rana drew out the last word.

'We don't have time. Let's move,' Ashwatthama interrupted and moved his horse as he surveyed the surrounding areas for possible cover.

'This looks disastrous,' Shreya said as she turned to guide Manvita's chariot.

'Take cover behind rocks, trees or whatever else you can find,' Ashwatthama ordered the few battle commanders near him. 'And send word through the army to do that. This is going to hurt us hard.'

45

Nick of Time

Chaos spread through the Hastinapur army. The soldiers started running for cover, hiding behind anything they could find. The rocks and trees would not save them if Bhasmaksh decided to take a tour of the place but at least they would have some level of protection.

~

At the asura camp, a delighted Kaalnemi watched the ensuing chaos in the Hastinapur camp.

'They know about him,' he looked calmly at Dandak, who was gazing at the Hastinapur camp with both interest and contempt.

'What happened, Master? You look alarmed,' Kaalnemi asked.

'I can't find Ashwatthama; I need to keep an eye on him.'

Kaalnemi surveyed the Hastinapur camp and said, 'I can't, either.'

'Send him out there,' Dandak ordered.

Kaalnemi nodded and turned to Bhasmaksh. 'Take the chariot to the middle of the battlefield and when it stops, you know what to do,' he ordered.

Bhasmaksh nodded, prodding his charioteer to move ahead. A special metallic extension in front of Bhasmaksh prevented the charioteer and horses from being in the direct line of sight of the fire-demon.

~

Amidst the chaos in the Hastinapur camp, Ashwatthama called out to Shreya, 'Stay with me.'

Shreya nodded and moved her horse in line with Ashwatthama's. Rana guided Manvita's chariot behind a large rock and the other warriors took positions behind trees and boulders. As they looked on, at a distance in the asura camp, Bhasmaksh's chariot started moving forward slowly, and at the same instant, Dandak and Kaalnemi moved their horses back, melting into the asura army.

Ashwatthama understood. They were saving themselves from accidental incineration.

The fire-demon's chariot slowly moved towards the centre of the battlefield, even as Hastinapur's soldiers ran for their lives. The boulders were massive but they couldn't accommodate everyone. Ashwatthama, Rana and Janamejaya ran around the camp guiding soldiers and trying to make sure they could save as many as they can. However, the situation was grim. Fifty thousand soldiers needed a large number of rocks and trees to hide behind, and the battlefield did not have enough. It pained Ashwatthama and the others to see the plight of the hapless soldiers, all of whom could not be helped.

As Bhasmaksh's chariot came closer to the centre, it crawled. Ashwatthama signalled to Rana and Janamejaya, who took position behind rocks. As soon as the chariot came to a halt, Bhasmaksh moved his hand and slowly removed his animal-hide blindfold. In an instant, the ground shone with the light of multiple suns. It was not the light that came from the demon's eyes but the flare of the thousands of bodies that were instantly burned. Thousands of soldiers were reduced to ashes in seconds. The soldiers' bodies dissipated in fiery particles as soon they came in the direct line of sight of the Rasatala demon.

Bhasmaksh moved his gaze from left to right and all the soldiers who could not take cover or were still rushing around turned to ashes instantly. Elephants, horses and men—the fire emanating out of the demon's eyes spared none. Those who hid behind rocks and trees fared better since his gaze did not reach them. But an army of over fifty thousand could not hide instantly and there were not enough places for everyone to hide. Unfortunately, elephants and charioteers became the biggest casualty, incinerated immediately.

Rana and Shreya hid behind a large rock. Rana peeped at the carnage and looked on in horror as the Hastinapur soldiers perished without a fight. He felt a churning in his stomach. He looked at Shreya helplessly even as he felt the rock protecting them heating up. The heat scalded their backs and they shifted uncomfortably. A moment in the line of fire would be enough for immediate death.

'This war will not last even ten minutes,' Rana said wryly.

As Bhasmaksh continued his merciless onslaught, one that threatened to destroy the entire Hastinapur army and warriors in mere moments, Dandak and Kaalnemi were relishing the massacre of the enemy army.

'That is truly a masterstroke,' Kaalnemi said joyously.

Dandak was silent, still seeking his adversary. He decided to make a move as soon as Bhasmaksh had done his part.

Where are you, bloody Immortal?

The fire-demon had been instructed to take the battle deep into enemy territory and that was what he did. Once thousands of soldiers had perished by his gaze, he prodded the charioteer to take him deeper into the enemy camp.

Ashwatthama gasped. He signalled to Rana, Shreya and Janamejaya to start firing their weapons. Hiding behind the rocks, the trio used their shields as mirrors to figure out which way Bhasmaksh's gaze turned but it turned out to be very difficult to shoot arrows accurately in such a short time-frame. A moment of exposure would turn them to ashes in the blink of an eye. So, most of the arrows they shot at Bhasmaksh missed him by a mile. Ashwatthama's arrows went near Bhasmaksh but the constant movement of the chariot made him a difficult target. He could have used a mild astra at this point like the one he had shot at Raktavija but he needed to see the target clearly to fire the arrow. It was getting darker and the asura armour plates were glowing orange with enhanced powers.

Ashwatthama was worried. It seemed that Bhasmaksh by himself would finish off the entire Hastinapur army. Even the other warriors wouldn't stand a chance.

He shouted out to Rana, 'Do we have a mirror?'

Rana asked Shreya the same, who glared back at him angrily. 'Why on earth would I carry a mirror to a battlefield?' she asked.

Manvita, however, shouted that she found mirrors at the base and handle of the chariot. The mirrors were there for warriors to be aware of their surroundings and to be on the lookout for someone attacking from the back. Pulling out the pieces of the mirror from the clamps, she handed them over to Shreya who passed it on to Ashwatthama.

Realising that the only way to kill Bhasmaksh might be to make him look at his own reflection, Ashwatthama combined all the mirrors to create a large one, almost half his height. He then joined different shields to protect himself from the fire-demon's gaze once he stepped out.

~

Back at the asura camp, Urmila looked on in horror as the Hastinapur soldiers and commanders were incinerated and vanished in a cloud of ash. Her heart cried at the sight of soldiers running desperately from certain and instant death, all without shedding a single drop of blood. This was not the death the soldiers deserved. There was glory in martyrdom but this was not it; this was a massacre.

Bhasmaksh was not done yet. He had been instructed to finish the entire Hastinapur army. So, he ordered that the chariot move forward, the charioteer steering the horses slowly.

Urmila could not take the bloodshed anymore. And in that brief moment, she took her decision. It was not just about Rana. Vikram, Nyat and Janak Singh had been killed and the entire city of Avanti, and all the villages along the way, had been destroyed by the asuras and their inhabitants slaughtered in the most inhuman way. They had not even spared women, children or elders, from whom they faced no danger. She recalled Ashwatthama's words: was she ready to kill those who were fighting for a just cause?

If I have to, let me die fighting for dharma.

Urmila looked at Ahilsena, who too, seemed shocked at the massacre unleashed by Bhasmaksh.

'Forgive me, Father,' she said, gathering her courage. 'Someone told me once that I can do things either the right way or the easy way. Today, I choose the right way. I will not kill those who are fighting for dharma.'

Urmila prodded her horse to canter ahead, towards the other camp.

'Urmila,' Ahilsena shouted, 'Come back here, now!'

Urmila turned around. 'I will never leave you, Father but you are not fighting a righteous fight. A father is the first man in a daughter's life and I have looked up to you all my life. But today, I feel that there are those who are fighting for much more than money and power. There are those who are fighting for their family, home, people and kingdoms. They are fighting to uphold all that is good in this world and I cannot stain my sword with their blood. Father, forgive me but I have now chosen my side.'

Urmila galloped towards the Hastinapur army as Ahilsena shouted angrily.

'Urmila, come back here this moment!'

'Let her go,' Kaalnemi hissed, fully expecting Urmila to be incinerated by Bhasmaksh's glance. 'One more warrior is no worry for us.'

Ahilsena looked on in shock as Urmila sped towards the chaotic Hastinapur camp. One glance from the fire-demon and it would all be over for his daughter.

In the Hastinapur camp, the shocked warriors watched Urmila cantering towards them.

'Holy Vishnu! Is she crazy?' Rana gasped. 'I have to go and help her.'

Shreya and Janamejaya tried to dissuade him as he would not last even a second if caught in the fire-demon's gaze.

'Walk with me,' Ashwatthama shouted at Rana, who quickly formed a barrier of shields for himself like Ashwatthama had done. The shields joined together to form a shape larger than Rana and would take the impact of Bhasmaksh's glare while protecting his body. They would need to bind another shield fitted with a mirror at their back to guide them towards the fire-demon. It was a complicated and cumbersome set-up but there was no option.

Rana and Ashwatthama stepped out as even Bhasmaksh's glare hit their shields. Holding their positions for a moment, they heaved a sigh of relief to find that the shields worked. From afar, they could see Urmila was fast approaching them. In mere moments, she would cross the fire-demon and if he took a look over his shoulder, it would be over for her.

Ashwatthama and Rana moved as fast as they could but realised with horror that Urmila would reach Bhasmaksh's location much before they themselves would, on foot. In the loud din made by the Hastinapur soldiers, Bhasmaksh had not heard the galloping of Urmila's horse. He had been strictly instructed not to look back at the asura camp.

An angry Bhasmaksh was looking at the warrior duo moving towards him. He picked up a bow and arrow, and stringing the bow, mounted the arrow on it. With one precise stroke, he took aim at Ashwatthama and released the arrow. With a swift swish, the arrow hissed past Ashwatthama behind the shield, crashing into the mirror he had been carrying carefully. In the next instant, Rana's mirror too was in pieces on the ground. The mirrors had been destroyed before they could be used against the fire-demon.

Ashwatthama looked at Rana in frustration. Without the mirrors, their strategy was useless. They were caught in a bind now, whether to continue or return and think of another strategy. Ashwatthama looked into the broken mirror as he could still see Urmila's reflection in it. She was just seconds away from Bhasmaksh's chariot. He wondered why Urmila was moving so close to the demon's chariot, and then his face brightened.

'Keep moving,' he signalled to Rana, 'We need to keep him distracted.'

Ashwatthama and Rana kept moving forward as Bhasmaksh watched in fury, confused about the duo's plan. He focused his gaze on them, trying to locate any exposed part. Rana winced as his shield started to heat up.

As Urmila's horse came nearer to Bhasmaksh's chariot, the warrior princess took out her sword. Urmila was not too good at jumping from horses but with this fire-demon, there would be no second chance. Bhasmaksh was busy trying to annihilate the enemy with his death rays. He had not expected someone from Dandak's camp to go rogue.

Urmila took Vishnu's name and summoning all her energy, jumped from her horse as it came right behind the fire-demon's chariot. Landing just behind Bhasmaksh, she did not wait for a moment. Even as the demon realised someone was behind him, before he could turn his eyes, Urmila separated Bhasmaksh's head from his body with one quick stroke, ending his reign of terror.

The carnage was over.

Urmila looked at the lifeless body of the asura to see if he had any boon that would cause his head to join his body again but mercifully nothing happened. Looking back at the asura camp, she saw the shocked faces of the asuras as complete silence descended over them. Then came shouts of anger, followed by a volley of arrows targeting her. Jumping back onto her horse which had moved alongside the chariot, Urmila galloped towards the Hastinapur camp to escape the arrows and spears that were following in her wake.

Ashwatthama and the others in the Hastinapur camp looked on in disbelief; the princess had done something which no one else had even thought of. The Hastinapur camp erupted in cheers for her as she rode into the camp. The Indraprastha princess took her horse close to Manvita's chariot which was now between Shreya and Urmila, and the trio of women looked every bit as fierce as any other warrior on the battlefield. Rana glanced at them, his chest puffed up with happiness. He tried hard to ensure no one saw the tears of joy in his eyes.

As everyone in the Hastinapur army got wind of the netherworld demon's death, they were relieved and came out of hiding. Soft murmurs of how the demon was killed began to fill the air. The warriors regrouped and the Hastinapur army regained its formation, realising as they did so that almost four-fifth of its total strength had been depleted. It was a big loss, considering that the big war had not yet started.

As Janamejaya looked around, he took in the massive loss they had suffered, all because of a single demon. Bhasmaksh had killed over forty thousand of his men, riders and elephants, at a rough estimate. The Hastinapur king could see hardly any manned chariots or elephants. He groaned in desperation. The battle seemed already lost to him.

Janamejaya looked at Ashwatthama with bewilderment; he, along with Rana and the others, was also trying to take stock of the strength of the remaining army. It seemed they were woefully short in terms of number. The Giants would finish the war off in the next hour.

'Too many lives lost,' Urmila rued. 'I wish I could have done it earlier but I couldn't risk coming in his line of fire.'

'Many lives saved. A mother saved,' Shreya commented as she looked appreciatively at Urmila.

They glanced at Manvita who had been rattled by this attack and was sitting in her chariot, trying to catch her breath. She had never seen so many dead before. Both women got down from their horses to comfort the queen.

Guru Agnishringa came up from behind them and hailed Urmila's heroic deed. 'That was a brave act, Princess.

Indeed, you have the heart of a lioness. Bhasmaksh was a long-time battle-winner for the Rasatala king, the most fearsome demon out there. Many warriors of fame have fallen before him. Dandak will be furious at this loss. He would have been sure that Bhasmaksh would win the war for him. No wonder he wanted to reveal the fire-demon only in the last hour as a surprise.'

'But Bhasmaksh has put us in a tight spot,' Janamejaya said ruefully as he surveyed his army. 'I estimate we have less than ten thousand soldiers and horsemen left.'

'We cannot win with those numbers,' Rana mounted his horse. 'Five to one is a bad...a horrible...ratio in a war.'

'Probably the reason why Dandak brought him out first,' Shreya said.

Ashwatthama was looking towards the asura camp, where he noticed a slight commotion taking place as the enemy prepared for attack. 'We have no choice,' he said as he looked back at the Valley of Illusions. He wondered if he would be able to execute his plan. Events had become further complicated with Bhasmaksh's entry.

The warriors lined up on their horses and prepared to face the enemy. The light from torches lit up the battlefield. Multiple torches had been strategically placed along the periphery and in strategic positions for the enemy to see each other. Asuras were known to be nocturnal creatures and hence had a natural advantage in the dark.

As the warriors regrouped, the soldiers fell in line and the initial four-fold formation started to take shape once again. The army organisation felt different this time, with almost no elephants and chariots. There were only horsemen and foot soldiers, scattered far apart. Each soldier knew the outcome of the fight. In war, even a ratio of three to two was considered uneven, so five to one was a totally different game altogether, a losing game. But a soldier's destiny was to fight, kill or be killed.

With the sound of bugles filling the air from both sides, the armies ran towards each other. The Giants ran and the ground shook like there was an earthquake. Several asura soldiers were thrown off balance and crushed under the feet of the uncaring Giants. The large ones howled and ran blindly towards the Hastinapur soldiers as they had been instructed to. With a loud noise, the armies clashed. The battlefield came alive with the shouts and cries of asuras and humans alike. The horses too, clashed with the enemy cavalry. Ashwatthama raced along on his horse, along with other warriors. Unlike the Kurukshetra War, this one had no rules; this war could rage on night and day without a break and nobody would bat an eyelid.

Kill the enemy. That was the only motive.

The Giants started killing the horsemen and soldiers as they moved along. The already scant number of Hastinapur soldiers was dwindling faster with this attack by the Giants. Some horsemen were smartly bleeding the Giants by swinging alongside them and slashing them multiple times, looking for a chink in their armour. Eventually, they hoped, the loss of blood would weaken the Giants but it did not seem that it would happen soon enough.

Ashwatthama plunged his horse into the enemy camp, killing as many asuras as he could. He had asked Shreya to hold back until the time was right. Moreover, he had asked Rana and Guru Agnishringa to look after her. Everyone was still in the dark about why Shreya was being protected this heavily. The immortal warrior moved swiftly, decimating the asuras around him. The asuras didn't have time to react as Ashwatthama deftly killed scores of them with just a few strokes of his sword. The pathetic Rasatala soldiers had not seen this form of warfare before.

Manvita gamely took out a bunch of asuras. She had been a princess and had learned sword-fighting skills but had given it all up when she became a mother. But now, she displayed her valour, and proved to be as capable as any other warrior in the field.

Ashwatthama paused to catch his breath and looked across at Dandak, who had been standing with Kaalnemi. Ashwatthama found that the Giants had killed a large number of soldiers, probably half their remaining army. He realised he had only moments to get this done. But as long as the asura soldiers blocked him, he would not be able to reach Dandak.

~

'Do you see her, Master?' Kaalnemi asked.

Dandak nodded. 'Kill her. I am going to handle the Immortal,' he said as he led his horse towards Ashwatthama.

~

Ashwatthama frowned as he realised Kaalnemi was moving towards Shreya. He tried to hack his way out from among the asura soldiers but there were too many of them. It would take him much longer to reach Shreya. He looked around. Urmila, Janamejaya and Manvita were all surrounded by asuras. Everyone fought as if it was their final battle. The number of asuras was large and the might of the Indraprastha army added to the misery of the Hastinapur soldiers. The entire ordeal would be over in another hour.

A loud bugle sounded towards the far end of the battlefield, alarming everyone. Dandak and Kaalnemi stopped in their tracks. The sound took even the Giants by surprise; they stopped trampling the Hastinapur army and looked at the source. A large Kimpurusha, dressed in gold, with swords in both hands, led an army in. The yellow flag, with the sigil of a Kimpurusha with its front leg raised and sword in hand in the backdrop of the sun, shone brightly in the golden hue of torches and the silvery moonlight.

As the Kimpurushas entered the battlefield, passing by the asuras, a deafening silence descended over the field. The asuras were clueless about the intruders and so were the Hastinapur soldiers.

Ashwatthama sighed in relief as the Kimpurusha Chief, Druma, came forward and bowed before him. Druma looked at Manvita and bowed to her from a distance. The queen acknowledged his obeisance.

'Your friend, Vikramsena, once requested allegiance,' Druma said. 'I turned him down. But now, I realise gravity of situation. Fight of humans, fight of Kimpurushas. Asuras, enemy of Kimpurushas. We fight as friends. To defeat a common enemy.'

Ashwatthama nodded his head and said delightedly, 'You are most welcome, brother.'

A huge roar of joy erupted from the Hastinapur army, who was suddenly replenished in strength. The Kimpurushas were known for their poisonous weapons which could take down the biggest of enemies. It seemed the army had found a countering force for the Giants.

The asuras, facing this new enemy, panicked. Then, with a loud shout, they charged at the exotic tribal soldiers. The Kimpurushas, being extremely skilled in war, slashed the asuras left and right and brought out bows and arrows to fire at the Giants.

Ashwatthama was now free to take on Dandak. He turned his horse back to see his nemesis, looking furious at this turn of events. Any soldier or Kimpurusha who tried to approach Dandak was immediately rendered dead, disintegrating into particles, with a slight gesture of the asura king's hand. Dandak had no qualms about displaying his powers. He knew this was the last battle he had to win and it was not going according to his plans so far.

Nor was it proceeding according to Ashwatthama's plan.

He glanced at Kaalnemi resuming his way towards Shreya. With a few Kimpurushas blocking the asura chief's way, it would buy Ashwatthama only a little time. He moved towards Dandak. As the asura king saw the old Hastinapur warrior approaching, he conjured silver spears out of his hands and threw them towards the oncoming man but Ashwatthama dodged them deftly. The spears then turned and merged back into Dandak's hands again. Ashwatthama pulled out a few spears from the dead asuras he passed, and threw them at the asura king, who was able to move his horse and himself at lightning speed as if teleporting both.

Ashwatthama glanced back. Kaalnemi had not yet reached Shreya but was close to her. The Kimpurushas who had fought Kaalnemi had fallen. Rana and Guru Agnishringa were getting ready to defend her. That wouldn't be enough. With a move that surprised Dandak, Ashwatthama turned Arya around and galloped back towards Shreya. He moved fast on his able Yeti horse, slashing asuras along the way.

A furious Dandak, who was waiting to finish the Immortal, sped up to pursue him at incredible speed. A few Hastinapur soldiers and Kimpurushas attempted to oppose Dandak but with a flick of his hands, he ensured they met the same fate as the other braves who had attempted to check the asura king. As Dandak moved along the battlefield, the soldiers around him started falling dead, disintegrating into thin air; this despite the fact that Dandak was not actively focussed on killing them. He waved his hands, killing hundreds of soldiers instantaneously, clearing the path for him to pursue Ashwatthama. Dandak had anticipated that he would be able to catch up with Ashwatthama in moments but the large melee of soldiers of both armies restricted him, forcing him to kill the human soldiers first. He decided against disappearing as it would have meant exposing the weapons he was carrying.

As Ashwatthama moved through the battlefield, he signalled to Janamejaya, who then gave the cue to Urmila. All of them turned at once and started moving towards Shreya. However, Kaalnemi had already reached Shreya and had taken out his first arrow, which glowed orange at its tip. Ashwatthama rushed to Shreya, with all the warriors rallying behind him, their actions spurred Kaalnemi to swiftness. He pulled the arrow on his string and with a mantra, shot it at Shreya. Instantly, the arrow unleashed a hellfire which enveloped the entire area.

The Agneyastra.

Guru Agnishringa moved his hands and released fire from them, countering the fire from Kaalnemi's weapon. He then packed his fire into a circular cone and absorbed Kaalnemi's fire inside it. In a quick move, he directed the fire back towards Kaalnemi who flicked it away.

By now Ashwatthama had almost reached Kaalnemi and the latter turned to fight him; to his surprise, though, the warrior did not stop. He passed by the asura chief, his sword extended in the direction of Kaalnemi, and called out to Shreya, 'It's with him!'

Shreya nodded in response, and the immortal warrior hurried along the path that led inside the place he had feared once, the Valley of Illusions.

For Shreya, the clock had started ticking.

46

Kill Them All

Kaalnemi looked with contempt at the assembled warriors and released a second arrow, chanting the mantra again. He realised that the Agneyastra would be ineffective with Guru Agnishringa countering it. The other warriors moved forward and engaged in a fierce duel with him. Shreya, still standing apart, was observing all this calmly. Rana, Urmila and Janamejaya were perplexed by her behaviour. They failed to understand why she was being so passive at this crucial time.

As Ashwatthama rode deeper into the dark of the Valley of Illusions, aided only by the light of intermittent torches along the way, Dandak felt chagrin overcome him. If Ashwatthama escaped again, it would be a serious threat to the asura king, given that the Immortal's existence would always hang like a sword over his head. The best recourse would be to incapacitate him.

So, Dandak moved swiftly behind Ashwatthama, following him into the Valley of Illusions. As he passed by Shreya, he considered killing the girl but with the Panchrishi by her side, he decided it would be a time-consuming, long-drawn conflict. The girl was a mere mortal and Kaalnemi would take care of her. The asura king could not let Ashwatthama escape.

Dandak pointed his sword at Kaalnemi, shouting, 'Kill the girl; kill them all.'

47

The Last Stand

Dandak moved at a rapid pace along the narrow valley, although the jutting rocks made it difficult for him to manoeuvre his horse as easily as he could have in more open spaces. As he moved swiftly, a figure came out of nowhere and with lightning speed, grabbed the front legs of his horse. The horse went down and Dandak was thrown off. However, instead of falling to the ground, Dandak floated. Regaining his composure quickly, he turned to face his attacker.

Ashwatthama stood fearless in the night with his shield and sword, and faced him like a lion.

Dandak levitated a foot above the ground, his cape glowing fiery red in the night. Black smoke emanated from his body, cloaking him over his armour. The light of the torches coloured his face orange on one side; the moonlight lit it silver on the other side.

'So, this is where you choose to die. No sages to save you this time,' Dandak conjured up a dual-edged serrated sword. It looked every bit lethal as the one in Ashwatthama's hands.

In a swift motion, both warriors charged at each other. Ashwatthama was able to block most of Dandak's sword attacks but nothing could stop the deadly punches and kicks that went right through the shield. In contrast, nothing seemed to touch Dandak. He was impervious to touch, like air.

A frustrated Ashwatthama kept attacking Dandak with all his might but it was futile. As soon as Ashwatthama landed a blow, Dandak disappeared in a smoky fog and reappeared elsewhere. On his part, Dandak repaid him with hard punches and sword cuts and blood flowed freely from Ashwatthama's body. In a few moments, Ashwatthama had become a wounded lion. Blood oozed from every part of his body where Dandak had inflicted injuries and the latter seemed to be enjoying it.

Dandak circled a fallen Ashwatthama arrogantly, taunting him. 'Do men have no strength? Is this the best of the warriors from the previous yugas? Shame! I will not kill you here. I will take you to your friends, if they are still alive, and behead you in front of them. But first, I must break you.'

Dandak moved his sword and struck hard at the fallen warrior's torso. Ashwatthama was hardly able to see anything, with one eye swollen and blood filling the other. Dandak swirled his sword in a victorious gesture and moved to Ashwatthama's side, ready to plunge it through the fallen man's heart.

Ashwatthama looked at him but did not have much strength left to do anything.

Shreya, if you have to do it, now is the time.

~

Outside the Valley of Illusions, all the other warriors had engaged Kaalnemi, who was proving to be more than a match for them. He was easily able to fight off as many as five of them. They were able to land blows on him but nothing seemed to hurt him. He was more than a match for all of them combined, even dodging attacks from the fire weapons Guru Agnishringa aimed at him.

Shreya kept observing him for a while. She wondered if Ashwatthama was ready. But delaying it too much could also mean failure. There was no way to find out and she had to take a chance. She tightened the long thin silk rope in her hand and then, in a swift motion, galloped towards the entrance of the Valley of Illusions. The moment she reached there, she took aim and threw her sword towards the entrance. The sword swirled in the air, before hitting a camouflaged rope at the entrance.

In one single movement, several enormous bells broke out of the walls of the Valley and rang in unison. These bells had been plastered inside the rocky walls and spurious rocks had been put over them to hide their presence.

A horrified Kaalnemi looked up and felt the vibrations. To everyone's shock, his body started disintegrating with every vibration produced by the ringing bells, though he did regain his shape in the interval between two consecutive rings.

Shreya did not waste time. As soon as the next bell sounded, she focused on Kaalnemi. As the asura chief again disintegrated into particles, she noticed the gold ring on his finger. She moved her hand like lightning, flicking the long silk thread towards Kaalnemi's hand. The thread got entangled in the gold ring, pulling it from the asura chief's finger. The ring resisted as if reluctant to leave its master. Kaalnemi looked at Shreya's hand and in the moments of his disintegration, shifted his gaze to the ring in his hand. He tried to clutch the ring with his other hand but Shreya exerted even further force, closing her eyes and muttering a hymn.

Kaalnemi looked on in horror as the ring started its journey from his finger to Shreya's hand. He stretched his hand unsuccessfully to grab at the departing ring but the sound of the bells had not died down yet. They kept tolling loudly. Finally, the ring reached the Avanti princess who clutched it tightly.

Shreya now had the Brahmadand.

'No!' a horrified Kaalnemi yelled. Before he could react further or regroup himself completely as the sound of the bells started dying down, Guru Agnishringa created a large barrier of fire covering the entire area with smoke and dust, making it impossible to see anything. Shreya turned and galloped away on her horse, with Rana and Janamejaya close behind her, providing her with the protection that she might need, and the short window that Ashwatthama was, right at this moment, so much in need of.

~

At the same time, inside the Valley, an equally shocked Dandak was unable to comprehend what had transpired. As he tried to collect himself, Ashwatthama rose. He had instructed Shreya to keep the bells ringing continuously, since Dandak would remain weak as long the bells rang. They had a tiny window to keep the asura king weak.

As Ashwatthama looked within the disintegrating Dandak, he could see Lord Rama's bow, the Kodanda. Ashwatthama then stood up, staggering a little. He stumbled, taking steps like a drunkard, and came face to face with Dandak. The latter tried to stab Ashwatthama but to no effect. Dandak, just like Kaalnemi, was weakened by the ringing of the bells. Ashwatthama stared at Dandak coldly, and the latter gave him a death glare, though clearly unable to hold even a blade of grass. Ashwatthama extended his hand, put it right into Dandak's torso and grabbed the Kodanda. In one fluid move Ashwatthama pulled the divine weapon out of the demon's body where the latter had camouflaged it.

Dandak was raging mad by now. There was no way he was going to let Ashwatthama get away with the Kodanda. Just then, to Dandak's relief, the knell of the bells started becoming feeble. He closed his eyes and meditated for a moment. As Ashwatthama stepped back, Dandak held on to the bow and slashed Ashwatthama on the chest with his sword. Blood sprayed on the divine bow but Ashwatthama held on to it, crying out in pain, yet knowing that this was the very last opportunity to take back the Kodanda.

~

Outside the valley, Kaalnemi realised just what had happened. He looked at the bells which had been installed at the entrance of the Valley of Illusions and at regularly spaced intervals inside. He could not see anything in front of him as a large storm of fire and dust engulfed the battlefield. There was no sign of Shreya or any of his other adversaries.

Kaalnemi gasped in horror as he realised that Dandak had been tricked. The only solution would be to kill Ashwatthama before the latter got to use the Brahmastra. Gathering all his strength as the tolling started dying down, Kaalnemi rose and moved towards the bells, swiftly hacking them down, one by one. The bells were linked together through a mechanical line and placed all along the Valley of Illusions, right up to the area where Ashwatthama and Dandak stood. With each bell destroyed, the sound lessened and Dandak started to regain his strength.

Ashwatthama was left with only a few moments before the ringing completely stopped. If he put on his gem and became as powerful as before, Dandak was good as dead. However, if he did put the gem back on and the old burning feeling with the restlessness of mind came back without mortality, his life would be one long living hell. He had only seconds to decide.

As Ashwatthama struggled to hold on to the bow, Dandak, unable to kill Ashwatthama due to the vibrations still going through him, brought his face close to his nemesis.

'You will never kill me, Immortal,' he snarled.

Ashwatthama held on to the Kodanda and looked at it. He glanced at Dandak again with his bloodied eye. And then, Vikram's dying face flashed before him, and so did the entire sequence of events of Vikram's killing by Dandak.

This is for you, Vikram.

'How about a mortal, then?' he asked and swiftly moved his free hand to pull out a shining object from the pouch at his waist. Without losing a moment, he thrust the gem into his forehead. A blinding light came out of his forehead as the gem fused with his body. The impact threw Dandak some distance away from the Kodanda as Ashwatthama glowed with a lightning-like blue-white energy. The Kodanda was flushed with rays of energy slithering like quicksilver all over it as if it had been hit by lightning.

In an instant Ashwatthama recalled all his weapon training, all his mantras and all that he had been. He was able to recall the hymns that Dronacharya had taught him, including the power to conjure and wield the Brahmastra. He didn't feel pain any more as the gem had given him power over all ghosts, fear and physical pain. However Ashwatthama could feel the intense burning he had felt when Krishna had cursed him on the fateful night. He felt his mind going berserk with anger and restlessness. But the moment at hand needed him to focus with every bit of his being.

Dandak was horrified at this turn of events. He knew that he had to use his final weapon before Ashwatthama could use any he had. He looked at his hand but the ring or its shadow, had disappeared. There was no protection now.

Meanwhile, Kaalnemi entered the Valley of Illusions, destroying each bell systematically as he rode towards the location where Ashwatthama and Dandak stood, facing off each other. Dandak split himself into innumerable replicas of himself, each exactly the same. With each knell of the bells, the shadows too quivered but the sound was becoming more muted as Kaalnemi progressed, cutting them down.

And then, Ashwatthama observed that Dandak had meditated briefly and an arrow had appeared in his hand. He did not have to guess that the arrow was the Brahmastra, since it was clear Dandak wanted to finish the fight. Ashwatthama knew he merely had moments to live; the Brahmastra would finish him, given his mortality with the gem back on, and bring his loneliness and suffering to an end. But then, if he died before Dandak, he would be leaving the world to the mercy of an asura who would ensure the downfall of Aryavarta, an asura whose rule would plunge the world into darkness, leaving no hope for humanity, no goodness left anywhere.

It would be the end of the world as everyone knew it. And the start of a long Age of Darkness.

By this time, Kaalnemi had reached Dandak. As he destroyed the last bell, Kaalnemi glared at Ashwatthama and moved in a swift motion, splitting himself, just like Dandak, into multiple figures. The replicas of Kaalnemi then merged into Dandak's figures.

'Your end is near Ashwatthama. No matter how hard humanity tries, it is going to lose,' Kaalnemi's voice echoed.

Ashwatthama felt vindicated. His doubt that Kaalnemi was but a shadow of Dandak had been proved right.

Dandak raised his hands and let out a burst of green fire towards Ashwatthama, intending to incinerate him. However, the fire was absorbed by the Kodanda in Ashwatthama's hand. Ashwatthama looked in confusion at the innumerable shadows surrounding him. All the shadows looked like Dandak, and they raised their hands in unison and spoke in a deep voice that reverberated.

'How will you kill us Ashwatthama, when there are so many of us? You can use your arrow only on one target. If you fire your weapon on the wrong target, you lose forever. Even if a part of me survives, you will lose. And then I will unleash hell on you and your loved ones. They will get the kind of death no one has ever seen before,' Dandak's voice boomed.

Ashwatthama looked at all the identical shadows but it was tough to make out who the real Dandak was among them. There was not an iota of difference between them but he was sure that all parts of Dandak would need to be present if the latter wanted to use the Brahmastra.

Dandak smirked. 'You are weak now. You have no power left.'

Ashwatthama spat out the blood filling his mouth and said, 'But I still keep my promises.'

He raised the Kodanda high above his head and twanged the divine bow, which emitted an ear-deafening sound as if hundreds of lightning bolts had struck one spot all together. White fog started emerging from all sides of the valley, from the rocks, the dead trees and the air around them. It soon started taking the shape of soldiers and horses with red eyes. They encircled Dandak, who stood wonderstruck at the strange smoke circling him. The smoke warriors started enveloping all the shadows of Dandak. The asura king glared in shock and anger as the smoke warriors started penetrating Dandak's shadows.

'What...what is this?'

Ashwatthama closed his eyes and raised his hands, silently invoking the incantation for wielding the Brahmastra. He was sure that after putting his gem back on, he would be able to acquire the celestial weapon. But the Brahmastra did not appear. Dronacharya's word that it could be used only once seemed to be true, and Ashwatthama had apparently incorrectly assumed that he would be able to use it again.

Nervousness swept over the now-mortal warrior as he struggled to think straight. As far as he knew and from what others had told him, Dandak could not be killed without a Brahmastra. And no matter how hard Ashwatthama tried, the Brahmastra did not appear.

As the smoke warriors started circling Dandak, the asura king seemed baffled by what was happening. He realised he did not have much time before Ashwatthama used his weapons, whatever they were. The only counter that would work against him would be the weapon of the Gods, the Brahmastra that could never miss its intended target. Dandak lifted up his hands, and all the figures resembling him now had a red glowing arrow each in their hands. His target was in front of him, confused and clueless.

Ashwatthama did not have the Brahmastra. He realised he had made a mistake in believing that he could use the divine weapon again. This was not the time for learning either. Ashwatthama recited the celestial hymn again to summon up the mightiest weapon but it still did not appear.

Meanwhile Dandak, livid at the attack by the smoke warriors who had started merging inside him and taking over his shadows, prepared to fire the Brahmastra. He just needed to say the mantra and victory would be his, killing his one and only nemesis. He would deal with the white smoke later.

Ashwatthama was sweating in the cold night as blood and sweat fell from him to the ground. And then as if out of the blue, he recalled Rana's words just before the battle had begun.

A golden bowstring with a bluish-gold arrow.

Rana did not know what the bluish-gold arrow was but Ashwatthama knew what it was: the Narayanastra.

This divyastra made a definite kill: it only killed the one who did not submit to it. And he was dead certain that asuras were arrogant, never one to bow down to a weapon of the Gods. It was not the first time Ashwatthama would be using the bluish-golden arrow either. Right after Dronacharya was killed, he had become livid with anger and released the Narayanastra on the Pandavas.

It would have killed all of them too, had Krishna not realised the danger and asked each one of them to get down from their chariot and surrender to the weapon. Bheema, the hot-headed Pandava, did not comply and decided to fight. He seemed to be destined for death but Krishna had run and pushed the mighty Pandava to the ground, forcing him to surrender. The weapon was infallible, like most other divyastras.

Ashwatthama meditated for a brief moment on the name of Vishnu, imploring that the weapon become his to use and sure enough, the bluish-gold divine arrow appeared in his hands. The silver bowstring of the Kodanda acquired a golden hue in the presence of the Narayanastra in the moon-lit night.

Dandak was still battling the smoke around him; he noticed that the smoke was taking shape while merging inside him, the shape of soldiers on horseback, each one jumping onto a different shadow. Slowly, Dandak's illusory shadows started disappearing, with only one remaining; and then a smoke warrior, with a golden crown on his head, threw a quick glance at Ashwatthama, came and jumped on Dandak, merging inside him.

The melee was over, the white fog lifted, and with it, the illusionary shadows of the asura king vanished. A furious Dandak raised his red arrow and uttered a mantra. He could not take any more chances. The arrow glowed and swiftly sped towards Ashwatthama.

In the same instant Ashwatthama had already mounted his arrow on the bow and shot it, whispering.

'May you be at peace, Ashtak. By Lord Shiva's grace, I free you all from your curse.'

Ashwatthama fulfilled the promise he had made to the Smoke Warriors, when he had crossed them the first time with Vikram, Rana and Urmila.

The weapon of Vishnu shot through the bow of Rama. The two arrows, Brahmastra and Narayanastra, moved past each other. They were not meant to counter each other but to kill. As Ashwatthama's arrow hit Dandak, there was a loud boom and lightning crackled all around. When it stopped, there was nothing left but some silver-grey shadows ascending upwards.

Before the Brahmastra could strike Ashwatthama, he saw a blue entity throwing an object towards him. Right before the deadly arrow could hit his chest, he saw a wooden object deflecting it, so that the arrow hit the gem on his forehead instead. There was a huge crackling sound, and Ashwatthama felt like his head had split into two.

The last thing he saw as he fell, was the wooden stick that had deflected the Brahmastra.

Or was it a flute?

48

Orphan with a Family

The Kimpurushas had managed to bring the Giants down. Their poisonous arrows had worked on the Giants, leading to their immediate death. They slashed asuras by the hundreds at one go, even while the asuras were clueless how to attack the new tribe. The horse-like bodies of the tribe gave them an impeccable advantage over the mighty asuras, allowing the use of both hands at once. Their tough skins and battle armour were difficult for the asuras to penetrate and injure.

Shreya and the others had stopped running when they found Kaalnemi had disappeared. They knew he had gone inside the Valley of Illusions, and so they would have to wait for Ashwatthama to come out, not knowing if the warrior had been able to execute the plan he had worked out. Shreya was sweating in the heat of the night, wondering if she had been quick enough. The smell of dead bodies, hacked limbs and blood nauseated her. However, she kept looking at the entrance to the Valley of Illusions, worrying about Ashwatthama. He had given strict instructions that no one should follow him, no matter how long he took to emerge.

The Kimpurushas were swift and had ably tackled the asuras, who by now had lost all hope of winning the battle.

Their morale had gone down with the exit of their leaders and they were running helter-skelter to save their lives.

Druma looked over the battlefield, even as his son Shifa came up to him.

'Will take time, Father, but will get them. They are scared, lack leadership.'

Druma nodded.

'What next, Father? We go back to Mandara?' Shifa asked.

Druma shook his head. 'Many kingdoms attacked by asuras. We go and kill them. Yeti kingdom, Avanti, Surparaka. All my life, I escape war. No more, Shifa. We are warriors, born to kill evil, not just drink and make merry.'

Shifa nodded, happy that their tribe had finally found its spine.

~

The warriors stood near the entrance of the Valley of Illusions, unsure of what had transpired in there. Rana wanted to go in but Shreya held her hand out and stopped him.

'Ashwatthama dau said that none of us must go in, come what may.'

Rana looked uncomfortable and shook his head. 'What if he needs help?' he asked. 'How can we be sure that a part of Dandak will not escape again this time?'

Shreya looked calmly at the entrance. 'The Smoke Warriors. They will not allow Dandak to escape.'

Rana looked at her in amazement. 'But why would they help us?'

Shreya shook her head. 'Not sure about it but dau mentioned that he had to fulfill the promise made when he met the warriors again while coming back from Himavant after the battle at Rakshastal Lake.'

Rana sighed, recalling the promise Ashwatthama had made a few months ago, to save their lives when they had gone inside the Valley for the first time. He wondered if the beings of white fog could be trusted.

Urmila, standing near Rana, searched for her father but he was nowhere to be seen. She wondered if he was fighting the Kimpurushas. He wouldn't survive the attack. Suddenly, her gaze fell on a fallen man, far away on the battlefield, who looked familiar to her. She motioned to Janamejaya and they all galloped towards the fallen king. Urmila jumped down from the horse as soon as they reached Ahilsena, who was writhing with pain. An asura's blade was stuck in his back.

'Father,' Urmila sobbed as she held his head in her lap.

Ahilsena winced, unable to bear the pain.

'You...were right, daughter...I...I could not fight the Hastinapur army... So, Kaal... Kaalnemi stabbed me.'

Urmila wept as Ahilsena seemed to be taking his last breath. 'Don't...don't leave me, Father, I will be alone,' she cried.

Ahilsena smiled feebly. He pointed towards Janamejaya, Rana, Shreya and Manvita who stood a few steps away. 'No... You will not be...' With those words, Ahilsena's breath left his body, even as Urmila's tears washed his face.

Rana walked up to him and closed Ahilsena's half-open eyes. He then put his arm around Urmila as she burst into tears, mourning the death of her only parent. Like Rana, the war had made her an orphan. However, despite losing her old family, she had found a new one.

49

A Different God

Dawn broke softly, the deep orange hue of the sun complementing the steel blue of the sky. Ashwatthama opened his eyes slowly, feeling as vulnerable as a day-old infant. His head was bursting with pain. He looked at the sky and moved his hand slowly to wipe the blood off his eyes. Every part of his body hurt as he tried to get up. It was then he realised that he was not alone. With intense effort, he pulled himself upright and crawled to a rock by the side of the valley wall, resting his back against it. He saw a blue figure sitting at a distance on a rock, looking at him intently. The figure was not clear though, because the warrior's vision was still blurred.

'Have the juice. It will help with your headache,' the figure said.

Ashwatthama picked up the cup that appeared by his side. With some effort, he took a few sips of the warm lime juice. In minutes, his headache disappeared, although his body still hurt as much as before. As his vision cleared, he looked again at the stranger who sat observing him from afar.

This was no stranger!

'Krish...naa...aahh!' Ashwatthama slurred, pain reverberating in his voice.

'You did well,' Krishna smiled and spoke with an alluring calm, appearing before Ashwatthama as a young man.

'Did I?' Ashwatthama tried to laugh, sitting motionless in his place, looking blankly at the space ahead where a few moments ago, Dandak had been towering.

'Is he killed...destroyed?'

'All of him,' Krishna said.

Ashwatthama sighed. His ribs hurt when he took a breath. He tried to regain his strength and speak, for he knew that Krishna wouldn't stay for long.

'Why...why did I not die? The gem...it was supposed to bring back my...mortality.'

'You cannot supersede the curse. Had you died now, you would have been trapped forever in the loop of life and death. I do not want that. Nothing else on this earth, other than that gem of yours, could have taken the impact of the Brahmastra. So, I used this to divert the Brahmastra from your gem,' said Krishna, waving his flute, now cracked on one side.

'It was my favourite, I will need a new one,' he said with a sigh.

Ashwatthama looked at the Lord. He felt as if he could look at Krishna's face forever. It gave him great solace to meet someone who had been part of the old yuga.

'Why me, Krishna?' he asked.

'This had to go another way, Ashwatthama. Someone else had to do this. Sometimes evil has a life of its own, beyond our control. So, we too need to make sure we improvise. Your karma on the final day of the Kurukshetra War changed your destiny. You were one of my favourites, Ashwatthama but a deed like that could not have gone unpunished. You had to suffer for your actions.'

Ashwatthama chuckled wryly. 'A punishment this...this big, Krishna, for eternity?' He closed his eyes to let the pain pass through him. 'Some have committed much bigger sins and they go free.'

'They will pay, Ashwatthama. They will suffer in one birth or the other. Even the Pandavas and Kauravas have not ascended Vaikuntha, and are not free from the birth-death cycle. For some, it's a smaller cycle, for others, longer. Some of us have to sacrifice ourselves for the good of others. I chose you for one such sacrifice.'

'Will it…will it ever…end?'

'Kaliyuga will end one day. You are going to lead the new yuga yourself. You will be the one to write the scriptures of the new yuga. Before that, you will help me to bring an end to this yuga, when I appear in my tenth avatar.'

'And what will that be?' Ashwatthama asked with his eyes still closed.

'You will know in time. You don't worry about that. I will guide you when the time comes.'

Ashwatthama felt blood oozing from his forehead, at the spot where his gem had been. He opened his eyes and felt the blood with his hands.

'I got my gem and lost it again.'

'You were not destined to have it, anyway. But there are reasons behind everything that has happened so far. You have seen what would have become of Aryavarta if Dandak had won.'

'Would you…have let him win, Krishna?' Ashwatthama asked.

'Depends,' Krishna said. 'There have been Dark Ages before. The good forces in the world try to protect the world and make it better but the evil ones try their best to control it. The ones with more power win. And sometimes, it's just a name that gets you to victory. The more faith one puts in me, the more their life is made simpler. As long as enough people believe in goodness over evil, this world is going to be a better place.'

Krishna smiled, even as Ashwatthama recalled the ice-bridge on Himavant.

Rama.

'Hanuman? Did you send him, too?'

'You were curious to know about Rama, so I asked Hanuman to go meet you. He is happy to go wherever there is devotion to Rama, for he loves hearing Rama's name and telling his stories. He was also eager to meet you, anyway. Also, you would have needed the Kodanda eventually.'

Ashwatthama shook his head. He was not sure whether he should be thankful or angry at Krishna at this turn of events.

'Too much for one life,' Ashwatthama mumbled.

Krishna shook his head in turn. 'Ashwatthama, a parent is never happy to see his child suffer. But a parent also must ensure that the child treads the right path, even at the cost of suffering.'

'So, you...you have forgiven me?'

Krishna looked at him calmly, with a faint smile. 'You have suffered a lot more than you had to. There is no question of forgiveness.'

Ashwatthama coughed, spitting out blood, letting out a chuckle even as tears rolled down his cheeks. He shook his head in disbelief. 'I...I never cared for you, I despised you, when you walked among us. And you are blessing me?'

Krishna nodded. 'A God never leaves his devotee alone. I will be with you, Ashwatthama, whichever path you choose to tread. I believe Dronacharya has told you what you need to know.

'Your path is going to be a long one, Ashwatthama. But let me give you a boon that only a handful of blessed ones in

Kaliyuga will have. May you always have peace in your life, Ashwatthama, even when you are in the darkest of alleys.'

Ashwatthama sighed deeply.

The blue-skinned God got up from the rock he was sitting on. He looked at the bow in his hand.

'I need to go now,' Krishna said. 'I have taken the Kodanda and will give it to Rama. That might cheer him up. Do you have any wishes to make before I leave?'

Ashwatthama lay back on the rock, injured and bleeding. He craned his neck to see Krishna as the God stood vibrant in front of him. His divine presence made Ashwatthama feel comforted. For the first time in his life, he wanted Krishna to stay on but he knew it was not possible.

'Will...you fulfill the promise?'

'I give you my word.'

'Free her.'

Krishna looked at the demigod, his eyes widening a little. Smiling, he nodded, and then disappeared.

50

Farewell

The girl walked in the clouds. She was free again and seemed like she was flying. As she looked back, her eyes were happy and full of gratitude. Back to her old self, she smiled lovingly, beckoning to him with her hands. Ashwatthama knew that face. But even as he moved towards her, Rati started disappearing.

He woke up, realising it was a dream. But it was a dream he had needed to dream. Krishna had kept his word.

He got out of bed and walked towards the window of his chamber inside the Hastinapur palace. It was still a couple of hours to dawn but he had decided to leave early. Ashwatthama's mind had become calmer after Krishna had bestowed his blessing. All the turmoil in his mind, collected over the last hundred years, had come to a standstill. He felt he was above the happenings of the world. The pain did not touch him anymore; he saw that as a passing event. For the first time in ages, he felt at peace, like he had never felt before.

Eternal peace—this was the best gift Krishna could have given him.

~

Ashwatthama walked out of the palace with a small cloth bundle. Shreya, Janamejaya and Manvita followed him, along with Rana and Urmila who were holding hands. All of them walked towards the gates of Hastinapur palace where Arya stood waiting for his master. Ashwatthama put the bundle on the back of the horse and patted him. He then turned and looked at the group, and all of them gazed back at him. For the last two weeks, they had tried to get things back in order together, taking care of the ones who had lost their loved ones and tending to the injured. It had been exhausting and yet they all felt better for it.

Exhausted by the war, they had decided not to talk about it for a few days, until the dust had settled. They had recovered from their injuries; the army had taken care of the wounded and performed the last rites of those who had died.

Rana updated everyone about the status of the other kingdoms. 'The Yeti kingdom has been retaken. The remaining Yetis have returned and are settling down again. Guru Agnishringa has agreed to mentor them, although I don't know how long he will be doing that. The asuras were decimated by the Kimpurushas who, along with the Hastinapur army, are now helping many kingdoms resettle the destroyed villages and cities.'

Ashwatthama felt elated on hearing that. He knew that Yetiraj would be happy that the safety of his endangered tribe was assured.

Rana went on. 'The work of rebuilding the homes of people is being given the highest priority in all the affected territories. Refugee camps are being set up, food and medical supplies are being sent to those affected. Temporary sanitation facilities are being arranged for all, and we also have set up temporary gurukuls for the children so that they do not miss out on their education. Everything was destroyed in the cities the asuras raided, and the rebuilding has to be done from scratch. We have contacted all allied kingdoms to help everyone in this crisis, and they have readily joined hands in providing resources and labour to rebuild the kingdoms.'

'You are learning fast, Rana,' Janamejaya smiled.

Rana acknowledged the compliment and continued. 'We are hoping things will go smoothly for all. There is much corruption in this Kaliyuga but change has to be embraced. It will be our duty to ensure justice prevails, to ensure that the society we set up is fair and provides enough opportunities for all to live their lives well.'

'I am sure you will make a good king, Rana,' Ashwatthama said, placing his hand on the prince's shoulder.

'Are you sure you do not wish to stay a bit longer?' Janamejaya held Ashwatthama's arm, with a bitter-sweet feeling of seeing his ancestor and friend leave.

Ashwatthama answered politely, 'It's time, Janamejaya.'

Shreya moved forward and embraced Ashwatthama. 'Thank you for everything, dau,' she smiled. 'I could not have found a better mentor who placed all his confidence in me. I know what I want to be now.'

Ashwatthama beamed at her and said, 'You will do well, Shreya.'

He looked towards the horizon, the rising sun dazzling his eyes as in the olden days. He did not feel any pain or burning in his forehead. The wound had started to heal. His injuries bore marks but they did not hurt anymore.

'Do you need something to read on the journey?' Rana asked.

Ashwatthama shook his head uncomfortably; he knew what Rana was going to offer.

Urmila rolled her eyes. 'For Vishnu's sake, I have burnt that diary. Your poetry is pure torture.'

Rana looked horrified as Shreya giggled.

'She's joking, dau,' she said. 'You write well; keep writing.'

Ashwatthama turned towards Manvita. Her face was sorrowful but she was holding up well, holding little Shrutika in her arms. Ashwatthama picked up Shrutika, looked into Manvita's eyes and spoke in an even tone, 'I am very sorry about Vikram. I could not say it before but I should not have taken him with me.'

Manvita nodded, tears filling her eyes. 'It was never your fault, dau,' she said. 'Without you, even we would not be here. Vikram always told me that if any of us survived, it would be due to your efforts. You had no reasons to get involved in this, yet, because of your friendship with him, you accompanied him. Vikram died a martyr, a king's death, and I am proud and happy to be his wife.'

Ashwatthama nodded, feeling lighter. 'Where do you plan to go next, Manvita?' he asked.

'I have received word from Kaustubha, the general of our army, that Surparaka is safe; the Kimpurushas threatened the mercenaries, told them to either leave or die, and they have left. He said they are waiting for their queen. So, I believe I have some work to do.'

Ashwatthama smiled. He felt happy for Manvita and Shrutika as they would be able to return to their home.

'Meanwhile, Shrutika has a gift for you,' Manvita said. 'Why don't you give it to him, Shrutika?'

Vikram's daughter handed over a cloth to Ashwatthama.

'I made this,' the little girl said.

It had a drawing of Ashwatthama and Vikram riding out together on their horses. Ashwatthama's eyes filled with tears. He felt overwhelmed, unable to speak, he choked up. He simply nodded his head as tears fell onto the cloth. He hugged the child warmly as he had hugged Vikram at Rakshastal Lake, and held her for a while. Then Ashwatthama kissed the little girl on the forehead and silently blessed her, handing her back to Manvita.

'We pulled you onto this journey, to where you did not want to go, and then you pulled us through. Did you find what you were looking for?' Rana asked.

Rati's face flashed before Ashwatthama's eyes and then it turned into Krishna's face. Ashwatthama smiled. 'A lot more, my friend,' he said.

Rana came forward and hugged him tightly, and so did Urmila. He hugged them back and felt warmth pervade his heart again.

As Ashwatthama mounted Arya, he looked at his friends one last time.

'Will we ever see you again?' Urmila asked as Rana and she held each other for comfort.

Ashwatthama looked at the road going north towards Himavant, still fresh and damp from the drizzle of the previous night and carrying the scent of wet earth.

'I don't know,' Ashwatthama said as he felt the cold breeze from Himavant brushing against his face.

He sighed.

'I don't know.'

Acknowledgements

Ashwatthama's Redemption: The Bow of Rama, the sequel to *Ashwatthama's Redemption: The Rise of Dandak*, is the final part of the duology. The entire story was initially supposed to be in a single book but as destiny would have it, the story became bigger and so the sequel saw the light of day.

I am grateful to many people who have helped me on this journey. First of all, thanks to my family members who suffered my long phases of writing at night, understanding my need to finish this manuscript.

Thanks to my brother, Saurabh Porwal, for reading the first draft and encouraging me to go ahead. Thanks to my cousin Priti Jayanthi and brother-in-law Aditya Jayanthi for reading it and giving their detailed feedback. The comments from Aditya helped me fine-tune the book at an early stage. I'm thankful to my friend Ashutosh Gore, who read the draft and suggested improvements. It delighted me when his daughter Mriganka asked for a sequel to the first book when she finished it, and I was happy to provide this one as the draft was almost done.

Many thanks to my friend Arun Dhavali for creating one of the key sketches in the book. I truly await the day he opens his own studio.

A book is course-corrected the most by its editors. I am glad to have worked with Sheila Kumar, who has impeccable command over the language and an instinctive understanding of the essence of the story. Thanks also to Vineetha Mokkil for preparing the final version of the book. If the work shines, it is due to Sheila's and Vineetha's efforts.

Thanks to the team at Om Books International—Ajay Mago and Dipa Chaudhuri—for bringing this story to the readers. Thank you, Karan Mago, for bringing out the digital edition.

Finally, thank you readers for appreciating this story. I hope my portrayal of Ashwatthama's character helped you to get to know him better. May he be at peace wherever he is.